THE BEAT OF YOUR OWN DRUM

the history, science and contemporary use of drumming as a path for women's wisdom, health and transformation

Sophie Messager PhD

WOMANCRAFT PUBLISHING

Copyright © 2025 Sophie Messager.

All rights reserved. No part of this publication may be reproduced, distributed, or transmitted in any form or by any means, including photocopying, recording, or other electronic or mechanical methods, without the prior written permission of the publisher, except in the case of brief quotations embodied in critical reviews and certain other non-commercial uses permitted by copyright law.

Published by Womancraft Publishing, 2025
www.womancraftpublishing.com

ISBN 978-1-916672-06-2

The Beat of your Own Drum is also available in ebook format: ISBN 978-1-916672-07-9

Cover photo © Ali Dover

Womancraft Publishing is committed to sharing powerful new women's voices, through a collaborative publishing process. We are proud to midwife this work, however the story, the experiences and the words are the authors' alone. A percentage of Womancraft Publishing profits are invested back into the environment reforesting the tropics (via TreeSisters) and forward into the community.

No part of this book may be used or reproduced in any manner for the purpose of training artificial intelligence technologies or systems.

PRAISE

This is the book that many of us drummers have been waiting for!

Sophie manages to hold perspectives from the science and the woo-woo, she supports us in having a deeper "inner-standing" of the drum as a healing tool.

Backed up with scientific papers, quotes and resources, Sophie leads us through drumming for healing, for birth, death, circles, mental health, physical health and so much more. She talks about drumming for stilling the mind, for going into an altered state, for empowerment: empowering women, empowering women's circles and drumming circles.

She helps us to remember the drum in ancient culture and where the drum has its place in future culture building community and connection.

This book encapsulates everything you need to know about sacred drumming, in fact this book should come as standard issue with every drum – bought and birthed.

Rachael Crow, mother, medicine drum maker and teacher, women's circle facilitator, Moon lodge/Red Tent/ Women's Mystery holder and author

Watching Sophie research this book has been nothing short of inspirational! She has delved deeply into the world of drumming and created an amazing handbook for those who hear the call of the drums. It has so much to give someone on the path to drumming or as a seasoned drummer.

This book is a handbook for the drumming woman – giving the benefits, the scientific shifts that occur, guidance on drumming throughout the phases of womanhood and so much more – it is a blueprint for contemporary drummers.

Her words echo my experience of reading Layne Redmond's When the Drummers Were Women *– for me too it was like I was reading something I already was part of, I already knew but at the same time reading something completely new to me. I have a feeling that Sophie's book is going to be doing the same for its readers, a modern and timely anchor for those drumming and bringing drumming to women.*

This book will be recommended reading for my Sacred Women's Drum Circle Facilitator students.

Melonie Syrett, thedrumwoman: master drum maker, sacred drum circle teacher and Earth Grid worker

Sophie Messager brings a message for our time, for all who hear the call of the drum. Bridging the science with the spiritual, she understands that rhythm is truly our Mother Tongue and literally returns the beat to the belly – its origin – as a drumming birth doula.

With a clear voice she shares her personal drum story, one that speaks to the collective yearning for the sacred in general, and rhythm specifically. She comprehensively gives nod to women's drum herstory, offers tools for today's healing and transformation through the drum, and envisions a future of women drumming in circle as an everyday, restorative practice.

Whether you're just stepping onto your drumming path anew, or have been on a lifelong drummer's journey, you'll find plenty of information and inspiration here.

The Beat of Your Own Drum *is an accessible and enjoyable read. Don't hesitate, get this book, you'll be glad you did.*

Barbara Gail, founder of 'The Rhythm Inlet', 'DrumRise! The Art of Women's Drumming' and 'The Tambourine Path'

The Beat of Your Own Drum *bridges the neurological and practical power of rhythm as a means to forge a deeper connection with one's self and the greater fields of consciousness. Sophie Messager's knowledge and skill in using drumming for healing are evident: read this book and you will see the power that drumming has on its players and listeners. Heed the message from this book and your life will transform with every beat of the drum.*

Jeff Strong, director of the Strong Institute, co-founder and music creator (drummer) of BrainStimAudio.com, and author of eight books including *Different Drummer: One Man's Music and Its Impact on ADD, Anxiety, and Autism*

From the shamanic to the scientific, this book informs, reminds and guides. From a forgotten history of women as drummers, to the science of drumming, neurodivergence, stress and drumming through rites of passage. This book invites you to experience the ways drumming can be your sail, your anchor and the beat you march to. Unlocking your emotions, regulating your systems and connecting you into the pulse of life.

As women across the world seek a more spiritual life reflecting what they feel and reaching beyond the guilt-ridden oppression of man-centred religions, Sophie leads us to a spiritual connection with the beat of a drum. The rhythm resonating with our hearts, a wisdom we recognise in our bones. Women have had the ancient rituals around life transitions forbidden, stripped, sanitised or repackaged by patriarchal systems. Sophie reminds us of the power of women in circle, the healing power of rituals and the primeval response of our body and mind to this universal sound.

From observing how the sacred can be brought of everyday life, the science of the brain and the journey of a woman through the life stages. Sophie weaves science, and a remembering of an ancient knowledge. This book is a journey of self-discovery, a lesson in women's history and a guidebook of how to use the drum as a profound tool for the transformations of life.

Bridget Supple, author of *The Birthkeeper of Bethlehem*

CONTENTS

Our mother
whose waters broke on that first day
and made song possible,
We sing now for you,
Drumming to your heartbeat
with nothing left to give but our bones and flesh as an offering,
so that we too can drink in life from the shores of your veins
for another million moons
and another million cycles around the sun.

Christy Belcourt

FOREWORD

Listen... the drum beats rhythmically, calling us home –
a stillness, a calm, a pulse, a quickening, a rising energy.
The drum beats, and our bodies respond – almost involuntarily.
The drummer is drummed, and the rhythm restores balance for all.

Imagine a practice that calms the nervous system, soothes body and mind, deepens connection and empowerment – that's drumming. That's what Sophie helps us to remember through this book.

When I made my first drum thirty-five years ago, I had no idea how central the drum would become in my life and work.

In my role as a midwife and facilitator I've drummed for ceremonies and births for over three decades. My own most empowering and transcendental birth experience was to the beat of a drum, and my deepest personal healing has come through drumming for myself. The drum became my teacher, guiding me into altered states of consciousness and the shamanic dimensions of healing.

At the School of Shamanic Womancraft, we use the drum for clearing energy, healing, singing, dancing and journeying to other realms. We drum for hours, forging deep connections with ourselves, each other, the drum and the Land.

When I teach about the drum during the drum-making process, I share this quote from Layne Redmond's *When the Drummers Were Women*, where she traces the drum's origins to ancient goddess traditions:

"Priestesses of the Goddess were skilled technicians in its (the frame drum) uses. They knew which rhythms quickened the life in freshly planted seeds,

which facilitated childbirth, and which induced the ecstatic trance of spiritual transcendence. Guided by drumbeats, these sacred drummers could alter their consciousness at will, traveling through the three worlds of the Goddess: the heavens, the earth, and the underworld."

Hearing this unlocks a deep remembering for many women, and when they experience the neurological, physical and transcendental effects of drumming, new paradigms are born.

The drum teaches us about our Birth Imprint – how our own experience of being born shapes how we birth anything, including our drums. This insight turns drum-making into a profound healing process.

I'll never forget the first time I witnessed this. In 2008, at the school's first gathering, fifteen women made drums. With my midwife eyes I watched as the women moved, spoke, and expressed themselves just like women do in labour. It became clear: their drum-making journey mirrored their birth experiences. From that moment, I knew drum-making was far more than crafting an instrument – it was a path to healing.

The drum also taught me that the energetic medicine of the wood, the animal hide, and the woman's personal journey through making the drum – all infused together to be the specific healing energy of the drum.

Today, women are reclaiming their power especially at their transformational rites of passage. The drum can support women with this reclamation. The drum can calm the body and mind during the menstrual cycle, create better conditions for childbirth and soothe the nervous system through menopause, offering a reset without side effects or cost. And at death, the drum can create a powerful container to hold the process.

The drum can create a supportive environment, its soundscape offering vibrational medicine, for everyone. I often suggest women in labour wear an eye mask and listen to live or recorded drumming through headphones, creating a private cocoon where birth can unfold naturally. I deeply believe that the drum can help in the global birth crisis, where less than 50% of women give birth vaginally each year and one in three women experience birth trauma.

We need to hear the drum – at births and deaths, during ceremonies and rites of passage, in homes, hospitals, woods and even offices. The drum is calling us back to ourselves.

Welcome to a journey of reclamation!

Sophie's book arrives at the perfect moment: as women reclaim autonomy in a patriarchal world. With her help, the drum emerges as a potent tool of empowerment. With her rare gift for bridging science and spirituality, Sophie illuminates the ancient practice of drumming, making it an accessible, relevant and obvious tool for our time.

Thank you, Sophie, for sharing this ancient treasure with us through your superb book. We are blessed by your wisdom.

Jane Hardwicke Collings, 2025

INTRODUCTION: THE FIRST BEAT

"The drum is sacred; it carries the heartbeat of Mother Earth."

Mickey Hart

It's early morning in a woodland. The air feels like it's been washed clean overnight. It's got that special lightness that only exists at dawn, before the day's heat settles in. The sunlight dapples through the trees, making beautiful patterns on the mossy ground. Birds are singing their dawn choruses.

In the middle of a clearing, a woman stands, ready to drum. She holds the drum's handle in one hand. On its circular wooden frame, a taut supple skin is stretched. The beater sits in her other hand, ready. As she pauses, the air seems to hold its breath in anticipation.

With a flick of her wrist, the beater connects with the drum's skin. A "BOOM" pierces the silence, sharp and clear. The drum's skin ripples from the impact, sending out invisible waves and suddenly the air is alive. The deep "BOOM" rolls through the space, through her body. She feels it in her chest, in her belly and hips, in the soles of her feet. It's not just a sound – it's a force, a presence.

She finds her rhythm. BOOM-Boom-Boom. BOOM-Boom-Boom. The beater dances across the drum's surface, sometimes striking the edge, sometimes the centre, creating different tones. Each beat resonates through the skin, the frame and into her body, as if the drum was speaking directly to her bones.

The tempo increases. Her arm moves faster, the beater a blur. Boom-Boom-Boom-BOOM, Boom-Boom-Boom-BOOM. The rhythm becomes a pulsing energy, flowing from the drum and into the space around her.

Her eyes are closed, and she is lost in the rhythm. Her body sways gently. The beater seems to move of its own accord, as if guided by an unseen force. She can no longer hear the birds or see the forest around her. She is no longer playing the drum – she is the drum, the beater, the rhythm. Past and future melt away, leaving only the now of the beat.

The beat shifts, slows. Now it's a gentle pulse. Boom…Boom, like a heartbeat… Each strike is deliberate, mindful. She feels her breathing deepen; her muscles relax. The world outside disappears, leaving only this moment, this connection between her, the frame, the skin and the beater.

As the final beat fades, its echo seems to linger in the air. The silence that follows is rich and full, vibrating with otherworldly energy. The nature around her is grateful for this honouring and even the birds are quietly listening. She is left with a profound sense of peace, of presence, of connection to something ancient and powerful that continues to resonate within her long after the drum has gone quiet.

This is what I have been doing weekly for the last four years: drumming at dawn in a woodland with two other women. This practice has given me more gifts than I can count: a deeper connection to nature, to myself, a sense of sisterhood and belonging. It has fulfilled my longing for more connection to the sacred. But perhaps most importantly, it has given me a growing sense of peace and spaciousness in my heart, something to hold on to in the midst of life's busyness and challenges. What my ever-busy mind could not achieve with meditation, the drum gives to me without my even having to try.

FRAME DRUMS

I feel it important to explain here at the beginning that this book will focus almost exclusively on frame drums, as all the drums I own and play are of this type. However, the majority of the research I share on the effects of drumming is applicable to any type of drumming.

One of the oldest known musical instruments, frame drums are found in various forms across many cultures worldwide and play significant roles in spiritual or ceremonial contexts. They are sometimes referred to as shamanic drums.

A frame drum is a simple percussion instrument, typically circular in shape, consisting of a round wooden frame 2-4 inches deep, with a single drumhead stretched over one side. It can be played with the hand, or with a beater. The drumhead is traditionally made from animal skin, but synthetic materials are also used in modern versions. The skin is usually secured to the frame with lacing. Frame drums produce a warm, resonant tone and are capable of a wide range of sounds, from deep booms to crisp, high-pitched tones.

Known for their portability, expressiveness and the intimate connection they allow between player and instrument, frame drums' simple design allow a complexity of sound and techniques that has made them a staple in music traditions globally.

A global cultural phenomenon

"The drum is one of the most ancient instruments, dating back tens of thousands of years. It has been used for festivals, celebrations, healings and rituals in the most diverse cultural areas. The sound of the drum and its simple, strong rhythms allow humans to experience a connection with the earth and its natural flow. Drumming awakens a noticeable energy, a vitality in us, which lets us know intuitively that rhythm is good medicine. The beating of the drum is an intimate dialogue that shifts us into another world, where spirit, bodies, soul and nature can dance together as one."

William Two Feathers

Why women and drumming?

In many cultures, women have been silenced, discouraged from taking up space, and burdened by the weight of expectations, leaving them stressed, overwhelmed and disconnected from their true power. Drumming offers a profound way to reclaim that power. This book is aimed at women because, through rhythm and sound, drumming provides a path to healing, empowerment and growth. It encourages us to break free from silence, reconnect with our bodies, and create space for our voices. By empowering women's growth, we unlock the potential to heal not only ourselves but also the earth, as we are deeply connected to its rhythms. This book is a journey to reclaim that connection, and to inspire women to rise into their full power through the heartbeat of the drum.

Drumming exists, or used to exist, in almost every culture on the planet. The drum is one of the oldest musical instruments there is. Contrary to popular belief, it is not drumming which is not normal.

From the Sámi to the Siberian shaman, the Irish bodhrán to the Indian dhol, the Native Americans to the Australian Aborigines, the drumbeat has led us into song, dance and into journeys through the worlds.

Jonathan Weekes

Even if the practice of drumming has been erased from much of contemporary Western culture, its echoes still resonate deep within our daily language, and our collective unconscious.

Many European languages still contain everyday expressions that reference the drum, pointing to its previous centrality in these cultures. In English we have:

- Drumming up support/business/interest.
- Drum roll, please!
- The beat of your own drum.
- Marching to the beat of a different drum.

In French, my mother tongue, there are also these expressions:

- *Battre le tambour* (beat the drum) – To promote or advocate for something.
- *Tambour battant* (with beating drums) – Quickly, energetically.

In Spanish there is:

- *Dar la vuelta al tambor* (turn the drum around) – To change one's mind or opinion.

And in Italian:

- *Fare il tamburo* (to make the drum) – To create a lot of noise or fuss.

Every culture has music (including drumming), dancing and singing. However, in the modern world we have an unconscious belief that only 'special' people, as in people who have formally trained, or exceptionally gifted, can do this.

As trauma researcher Dr Bruce Perry explains: "One of the most powerful sets of associations created in utero is the association between patterned repetitive rhythmic activity from maternal heart rate, and all the neural patterns of activity associated with not being hungry, not been thirsty, and feeling 'safe' (in the womb). Patterned, repetitive, rhythmic somatosensory activity… elicits a sensation of safety. Rhythm is regulating. All cultures have some form of patterned, repetitive rhythmic activity as part of their healing and mourning rituals – dancing, drumming, and swaying" (Perry, 2013).

Many people in our culture hesitate to use their voices to sing in public, or even to speak, paralysed by the fear of doing it 'wrong' or sounding 'bad'. This hesitation is a stark reminder of how deeply ingrained these limiting beliefs have become. It's crucial to remember that for most of human history, music-making, dancing and singing were communal activities, integral parts of daily life rather than specialised skills reserved for the few.

The discomfort we see today is a relatively recent phenomenon, the result of a society that has professionalised creative expression. We've moved from a culture of participation to one of performance and perfectionism, where the fear of judgement often overshadows the joy of creation.

In traditional societies, music-making was often a communal activity, integral to daily life and special occasions alike. From African drum circles to Native American powwows, from European folk dances to Asian temple chants, music was created by and for the community. It wasn't viewed as a specialised skill but as a birthright of every individual.

By viewing music as the domain of the gifted or trained few, we deny ourselves the joy, emotional release, and community-building aspects of active music participation. By doing this, we have lost touch with a fundamental aspect of our humanity.

The universal nature of music, song and dance in human cultures suggests that we all have an innate capacity for musical expression. Neuroscience research supports this, showing that music processing is a fundamental function of the human brain, not a specialised skill.

Breaking down our cultural barriers requires a conscious effort to reclaim our capacity for creative expression. It involves creating safe spaces where people can rediscover the simple joy of making sound, moving their bodies and connecting with others through these practices.

By encouraging everyone to drum, sing and dance, we can begin to heal this disconnect and tap into the potential of communal creative expression. When we do this, we not only enrich our individual lives but also strengthen the bonds of our communities.

Reclaiming the drum

The many women I have drummed for during pregnancies, birth and post-partum, during difficult life transitions, loss, trauma, grief, illness, accidents, changes of circumstances, end of relationships and more, have told me that the drum spoke to something deep within them, something they recognised: a remembering. They spoke of feeling like they were inside of a temple, of feeling their ancestors around them, of being reminded of their strength, of receiving powerful messages of guidance from within, including messages from goddesses and the divine feminine.

At home, I felt in my own space but in the hospital, I felt at the mercy of the system, a lot of vulnerability. The drumming stirred up the empowerment and standing up for myself. It felt like it was saying open up, relax, trust your body, have faith in the journey. It made me feel more confident in my abilities.

Leigh

For the last few years, I have noticed a shift around me, where the yin, feminine energy is rising and people are actively seeking activities that reconnect them with themselves.

So when I read about this prophecy, in the book, *The Soul of Money* by Lynne Twist, it gave me goosebumps:

"Among the Achuar Indigenous people there is a long-told legend and prophecy that says that in the beginning all the people were united at one, but that many

years ago they divided into two groups, each group following a different path.

"One group, known as the Eagle, were highly scientific and intellectual. The other group, the Condors, were highly attuned to nature and the intuitive realm. These two groups continued along their own paths becoming further evolved in their own ways. It was prophesied that both groups would eventually come to a point where their very existence was threatened.

"Thus, the Eagle people – those of the intellect and the mind – will have reached a point in their development of their scientific knowledge and technology and their ability to build and construct so well that it would bring tremendous material wealth, but at the same time they would be so spiritually impoverished that their very existence would be at risk.

"At the same time the people of the Condor – people of the heart, the spirit, who are deeply connected to the natural world – would become highly developed in their intuitive skills and in their understanding of the spiritual realm. At the same time, they would be hungry and impoverished for knowledge that would enable them to be successful in the material world.

"The prophecy continues by saying that now is the time for the Eagle people and the Condor people to reunite, to remember that they are actually one people with a common origin. It is time for the eagle and the condor to fly together in the spirit of partnership and collaboration. Neither the eagles nor the condors will survive without this collaboration and from this new partnership will emerge a new consciousness that will result in a sustainable future for all."

Drumming can be a conduit to support this process: to help rebuild a bridge between the scientific and the intuitive, spiritual knowledge that we need to create a new paradigm for women and for the world to come.

Drums: gateways to the heart and soul

– Melonie Syrett, aka The Drum Woman

There can be no doubt that the drum supports and brings about great change. I have spent the last twelve years drumming and watched countless women come into circles or ceremony with shoulders up round their ears, closed body language and tension speaking volumes of their current sense of wellbeing.

I've watched over and over that as they begin to drum, tears flow and/or they soften. It is like the body is able to speak its truth, through the beat of the drum, for the first time.

Gently, as women gather again and again, you can watch the peace move across their faces and bodies as they step into the drumming space. I regularly hear 'I needed this today' as a woman flops into their chair or 'I am so glad to be with you' as they look around the circle. This is a space where life's challenges can be met, expressed, acknowledged and witnessed without judgement or competition.

When drumming, the drum becomes an extension of your body. Each beat, when we drop into it, tells the story of how we are feeling, what we are going through and what we need without words.

As we drum, particularly with other women in a safe space, that freedom of expression seems to spread into the body itself, creating movement, shaking, dancing, stamping – somatically allowing emotion, trauma and tension to move, be seen and perhaps released. Then that beat and safe space spreads to the voice. It opens up the throat, our space of authentic truth. It allows us to let out that which is held within – in roars, tears, tones, words and song.

The drum gives us permission to feel that which perhaps we have pushed down or don't want to admit: the next step in our lives, the unrest in our bones, the discontent with our current lot. The drum seems to shake it all up and bring it to the forefront. And if women are in drum circles, held as a safe space, there is the opportunity to be held in these realisations. To share fears of 'what next?', realisations of 'who am I now?' and to be held over and over as the new you emerges.

And with this comes the opportunity to hold the space for every transition in a woman's life. Whether it is creating ceremony where the drums are used by avenue of sisters that the woman walks through, every beat infusing her with welcome and celebration as she crosses over a transition point such as menopause or menarche, or whether it is in the holding as she lies on the floor and her sisters drum for her as she grieves the old life and releases that which stops her moving into the new, the drum can be used for all of this and more.

Perhaps, these were the rituals and ceremonies of the ancient drummers. Perhaps, the Priestesses who held temple space knew the power of the drum for holding and great change and perhaps, that is why it was taken away from them.

Why drumming matters

Like the majority of us in Western culture, I did not grow up with drumming. It was not a part of my family or community's rituals or ceremonies. Coming, as I did, from a scientific background, there was a time when I viewed drumming as something that belonged exclusively to other cultures or alternative lifestyles. In my mind, it was a practice far removed from my own background and daily life. I saw it as the domain of Indigenous ceremonies, New Age retreats, or counterculture gatherings – interesting, perhaps, but not something that could be relevant to my personal growth or wellbeing. This perspective isn't uncommon, especially for those of us raised in Western societies where drumming isn't typically integrated into mainstream culture. It is certainly true that many of our contemporary Western practices have borrowed in recent times from Indigenous cultures, because, as I share in Chapter 2, our own native practices were extinguished. There is a deep hunger for other forms of spirituality and ways of creating a more meaningful life to what modern Western culture offers. This is a tricky subject for sure, with no easy answers, but one that I and so many others are deeply aware of.

The healing power of the drum

– Hollie Hope

I was invited to a drum circle by Native Americans. They were holding the event as a fundraiser and to raise awareness. These beautiful men brought out a massive powwow drum and began playing rhythms I had never experienced before.

At the time, I didn't know how to drum and felt it wasn't something allowed for me as a non-Native woman. When the Elders kindly invited me to join, I refused, saying, "No, no, that's not for me." Having experienced abuse and violence from men in my past, I was incredibly cautious about overstepping any boundaries that could make someone uncomfortable.

However, another woman encouraged me to simply try drumming. As uncomfortable as I felt to even attempt it, I knew refusing would be worse. So, with trepidation, I grabbed a drumstick, took a deep breath and struck the centre of the huge drum.

In that moment, it was like an electric jolt shot through me. The vibrations seemed to travel from the drum into the earth, up through my bare feet, zinging through my entire body until reaching my heart. Suddenly, it felt like something deep inside me cracked wide open. A torrent of emotions flooded out – I cried, I laughed, I screamed and released everything I had bottled up. The sensations were inexplicable yet deeply profound. For those moments, I was absolutely present despite having no concept of what was happening.

After that experience, I was hooked. I sought out a drum circle facilitated by a woman, who helped me make my own elk skin drum. As I worked with it, original thoughts and expressions began arising that didn't feel like my own. I started a solitary drumming practice, not realising at the time all the healing it provided.

Soon after, I spiralled into a suicidal depression when my husband left me for another woman after thirteen years of marriage. Questioning everything about myself and my faith, I could barely eat and spent whole days hiding in my closet, wanting to no longer exist.

Then one morning, I recalled I had commissioned someone to paint a drum for me with a lion's image. Feeling like that wasn't me at all, I decided that day I needed to choose to live. So, I grabbed that drum, held it to my heart and drummed until I could finally breathe again. Each morning after, I would drum until catching that one breath.

Over time, the drumming became a huge part of my healing journey. It allowed me to process emotions I lacked words for. The drum became a profound partner in my life. People started asking me to drum for them and I began incorporating sound healing. Now, I get to teach others how to let the drum into their lives, harnessing its transformative power.

In our modern, hyper-rational culture, science holds an almost religious authority. Many are sceptical or dismissive of anything perceived as 'woo' or as lacking in scientific grounding. The sad truth is that many of us have been conditioned to see drumming as 'exotic' or 'foreign', rather than a universal human practice with potential benefits for everyone.

It was not until I first experienced shamanic drumming, during my first year working as a doula, that I really got how powerful it was, and its very real potential for healing and transformation. The experience was so vivid and powerful that I was hooked instantly. I acquired my first drum shortly after that and it soon took an ever-increasing presence in my work with women and birth, with ceremonies and with healing work.

I am passionate about sharing the power of drumming with people. And I feel like I am well-placed, as a former sceptic who has dedicated her life to it. Over my lifetime, my work has bridged the scientific and spiritual realms, and so my approach to understanding and sharing why drumming matters and how it impacts us involves both scientific research and women's personal stories.

Empowering women's voices and healing the earth

For centuries, women's voices have often been silenced, their power diminished, and their spirits constrained by societal norms and expectations. Drumming emerges as a powerful tool for women to reclaim their voice, reconnect with their inner strength, and contribute to global healing.

Reflecting on my journey, I now realise that introducing drumming into my work – first during pregnancy and postnatal rituals and later during labour and birth – was guided by an intuitive understanding of its necessity. It emerged as a powerful antidote to the patriarchal system's continuous attempts to undermine women's power and agency.

The drum serves multiple profound purposes:

- It brings a sense of reverence and connection to the divine.
- It acknowledges the enormity of the rite of passage women undergo.
- It helps women calm their mental chatter and access their inner wisdom.
- It empowers women to trust their intuition and stand up against systemic pressures
- It fosters connection and community.

Drumming re-introduces a raw, instinctual element that contrasts sharply with the clinical and detached approach common in modern birthing environments. Drumming creates a sacred space that honours the transformative nature of birth and the inherent strength of women.

For me, the drum became a tool of reclamation – of power, of tradition and of the profound spiritual nature of bringing new life into the world. It's a call to remember and embrace the wisdom that resides within each woman, a wisdom often drowned out by the noise of modern medical practices and societal expectations.

Since stepping away from doula work a couple of years ago, I've come to the stark realisation that not only is the current maternity care system beyond repair, but that the thread of disempowerment weaves through every stage of a woman's life. Its pervasive narrative that begins in infancy, winds its way through our experiences of parenting, education and careers. This insidious message – that we are somehow ignorant of our own needs and should defer to those who 'know better' – isn't confined to any one sphere. It permeates politics, the medical and education world and is woven into the very fabric of our society. From the moment we're born, we're subtly (and sometimes not so subtly) taught to doubt our own instincts, to question our inner wisdom. It's as if society has conspired to whisper in our ears, "You don't know what's best for you." This message echoes in the halls of schools, reverberates in workplaces and finds its way into the most intimate moments of our lives.

The result? A deep-seated, often unconscious belief that our own knowledge – especially when it comes to our bodies, our choices, our lives – is somehow inferior to the 'experts'. This belief chips away at our autonomy, erodes our confidence in our own experiences and intuition. And it's a belief that I've come to recognise as not just false, but deeply harmful to the wellbeing and empowerment of women everywhere.

The most pervasive aspect of this disempowerment is how invisible it is to us. Like fish unaware of the water they swim in, we are oblivious to the very nature of these disempowering narratives. This cultural water we swim in is so omnipresent, so all-encompassing, that we rarely pause to question its existence or its impact on our lives. It's not until we step out of this familiar environment – whether through personal experiences that challenge our assumptions, exposure to different cultures, or conscious efforts to critically examine our beliefs – that we begin to see the water for what it is: toxic, polluted and harmful.

This awakening can be jarring, as we realise how deeply these narratives have influenced our sense of self and our place in the world. It can also cause turbulence in our relationships, and our sense of belonging, as people close to us who are still submerged in the familiar currents may view our awakening as unnecessary waves in their calm sea. Yet it's precisely this awareness that opens the door to change, allowing us to challenge these ingrained beliefs and reclaim our power and wisdom.

Beside the paternalistic approach of our world, the lack of community holding we experience as women when we go through major life transition is also hurting us deeply. I have always felt a deep longing for more meaningful acknowledgements of such transitions, which led me to craft my own.

I started offering mother blessings for my doula clients as an alternative to the spiritually impoverished, commercial, baby-orientated 'baby showers'. This is also what led me to write my first book, *Why Postnatal Recovery Matters,* a call to arms for a return to a period of rest and nurture after birth.

The same nurturing needs are present throughout every single one of our lives' big endings and beginnings: menarche, motherhood, menopause and countless other moments in our lives where we need to be surrounded by a community of experienced, wise and compassionate women to navigate them with grace. We were meant to be supported, seen, held, understood, witnessed and celebrated. We were never meant to do this alone.

The very system that confines us cannot be the key to our liberation. We cannot outsmart or out-think a structure designed to keep us doubting ourselves. This is where drumming enters: as a transformative force. Its power lies in its ability to shift our consciousness. The beat of the drum helps us bypass our logical minds, tapping into something far more ancient and wise within us.

As we drum, we don't just think differently – we experience the world differently. This altered state of being opens doorways to new perspectives, allowing us to imagine and embody alternatives to the limiting narratives that have been unconsciously programmed into us. In essence, drumming doesn't just challenge the system – it transports us beyond it, offering an experience of what true autonomy and connection feel like.

Drumming and women

Drumming, because of its ability to modify our state of consciousness, can help us get out of a rational, masculine-centric way of thinking and re-learn how to access a more intuitive, more feminine way of knowing. Drumming can provide an antidote, not only to the ever-increasing speed and busyness of our world, but also to the systematic destruction of women's power and autonomy. It can help re-teach us how to access the resources and wisdom within a culture that seems to only value knowledge that comes from outside, from 'experts'. It can provide a trusted tool and companion to guide us. And whilst this feels particularly important for momentous life transitions, such as giving birth, it feels equally important for us as we navigate life's challenges from a place of autonomy, presence and power.

As I sifted through the historical research, it came as a surprise to learn that drumming used to be done exclusively by women and that it was purposefully taken away from us along with our spiritual authority and leadership roles in our communities. I strongly believe that it is time that we reclaim the drum's power and wisdom for all people, but especially for women.

Remembering and reconnecting with ancient rhythmic practices associated with the frame drum recovers the power of personal creativity; returning their use to our daily lives in the modern era, we invoke the divine in our homes, in our lives and into our communities to create harmonising healing pathways for the upliftment of ourselves and humanity at large.

Tahya

There are many women around the world who are actively working to reintroduce the power of the drum to women. I have interviewed several of these women in my podcast, The Wisdom Messenger, who do such work in the UK, the US and Australia – Jane Hardwicke Collings, Barbara Gail, Melonie Syrett, Hollie Hope and Rachael Crow. You will find their stories and quotes dotted around this book, as well as those of many women who have experienced the power of drumming in their own lives.

Reclaiming our power

Drumming is powerful. At the heart of what the drum can do for us is the transformative power of finding our own answers. We need to stop asking other people to tell us what to do. Our entire life experience is often based on this: we are expected to do what our parents tell us, without questioning their authority. When we go to school, we are expected to absorb what is being taught, again without question. Then when we become someone's employee, the same is true. This is not experienced consciously and this process, little by little, chips away at our inner trust.

Every one of us is unique, with a unique history, unique life experiences and circumstances and unique bodies and spirit. Whilst more experienced people may help us look at options we may not even know exist, what we really need is help to access our own knowledge and our own wisdom.

There are many ways to access our own wisdom and power: self-reflection, creative expression, meditation, journalling, body awareness practices, mindfulness, mindful movement practices, being in nature, the list goes on and on. These methods all share common elements in how they facilitate accessing inner knowing. They encourage us to be fully present to the here and now, rather than getting caught up in thoughts about the past or future. They involve stilling the mental busyness, allowing intuitive feelings to be perceived more clearly. They engage the right-brain's artistic modes of perception and knowing – such as dreams, visions and metaphors. This facilitates access to subconscious wisdom. Practices of body awareness also help increase the physical senses and somatic intuitions within the body, not just the intellectual mind.

Being an eternal seeker of knowledge and personal growth and a lover of new modalities, I have tried countless versions of the practices listed above. In fact, I practice several of them on a regular basis, in particular walking in nature daily, year-round wild swimming (even in near freezing water), 5Rhythms dancing and doodle journalling. But the drum consistently provides something deeper for me: a unique, more profound and transformative experience.

Drumming might be easier than other methods of accessing inner knowing for several reasons:

- **Ease:** Drumming can induce altered states of consciousness more quickly and reliably than some other methods, due to its ability to entrain brainwaves. The presence in the moment that comes with practising or listening to the drum requires very little effort on the person's part, because of it. It is easier to do than quieting the mind whilst meditating.
- **Direct physical engagement:** Drumming involves a tangible, physical action that engages the body more actively than many other practices. This physical aspect can help ground a person in the present moment more effectively.
- **Non-verbal expression:** Drumming doesn't require verbal processing, which can bypass the limitations of language that might hinder other practices.

- **Primal connection:** The drum's rhythm mimics the heartbeat, connecting practitioners to a primal, instinctual part of themselves that predates language and conscious thought.
- **Communal aspect:** While drumming can be done alone, it's often practiced in groups, adding a communal element that can amplify the experience and provide support.
- **Cultural and historical significance:** Drumming has been used for spiritual and healing purposes across many cultures for thousands of years, tapping into a deep well of collective human experience.
- **Accessibility:** Drumming, especially if using a frame drum and beater, requires less training or intellectual understanding than some other practices, making it more accessible to a wide range of people.
- **Emotional release:** The physical act of drumming can facilitate emotional release more directly than some other practices, allowing for catharsis and healing.
- **Play:** The only effort required is to pick up a drum and this can feel easier and more playful than trying to meditate or journal.

While drumming offers these unique benefits, I feel it is also important to acknowledge that different methods may work better for different individuals and a combination of practices often yields the best results for accessing inner knowledge.

The reason why I find drumming so powerful and unique, amongst these many ways of changing our consciousness, is because with practice, it can also become incredibly quick, allowing us to enter trance states at will. It works a lot faster than with meditation. When I'm feeling low, off balance or overwhelmed, when I procrastinate, I feel much less resistance to picking up my drum than when trying to write or meditate, because drumming, with its sound and movement, feels a lot more playful and fun than writing or sitting still.

The drum, in this context, becomes a powerful tool for women to reclaim their inner authority. It serves as a bridge between the physical and the spiritual, allowing women to tap into ancestral knowledge and personal power.

As more women embrace this approach, we're witnessing a collective awakening. Women are supporting each other in trusting their intuition, honouring their unique experiences and recognising the wisdom that resides within.

This shift is not just about individual healing; it's about reimagining our approach to knowledge, power and community. By empowering women to trust their inner guidance and share their gifts freely, we're fostering a new paradigm of healing and growth that has the potential to transform our communities and society at large.

The irresistible pull of rhythm

– Barbara Gail

From my earliest memories, I've felt the irresistible pull of rhythm and movement. I remember being just three years old, sitting in a restaurant with my parents, when suddenly I leapt from my seat and started dancing to the music playing in the background. That moment was the first hint of the path my life would take.

In my late twenties, my journey took a remarkable turn when I met Gabrielle Roth, creator of the 5Rhythms dance practice. This formless form of dance, rooted in shamanism, opened my eyes to the profound teachings embedded in rhythm and movement. I realised dance wasn't just about expression or creativity; it was a gateway to personal growth and evolution.

Two years later, another pivotal moment arrived when I encountered Layne Redmond, author of When the Drummers Were Women: A Spiritual History of Rhythm. *Through her, I discovered women's ancient herstory of rhythm and the forgotten legacy of women as keepers of the drum. I was already playing the djembe (West African drum), and the frame drum expanded my rhythmic repertoire.*

These experiences merged into a life-changing realisation. I began to see drum and dance not just as art forms, but as powerful tools for personal and social transformation. This insight became the driving force behind my life's work.

For nearly three decades, I've immersed myself fully in this world of rhythm and movement. I founded and developed The Rhythm Inlet retail store and The Space, a teaching studio, both dedicated to exploring folkloric percussion and hand drums from around the world. My mission became clear: to share the transformational power of rhythm with people of all ages, abilities and challenges.

Throughout my journey, I've had the privilege of touching thousands of lives, from preschoolers to elderly in memory care. I've worked with diverse populations, including groups of at-risk youth and autistic children. My drum circles and workshops have become spaces of healing, connection and empowerment.

Now, at sixty-two, I find myself in a new chapter of life, still driven by the same passion that first moved me as a child. I continue to evolve, grow and share my wisdom, firmly believing in the innate human capacity for rhythm and movement. Through my work, I invite others to reconnect with this fundamental aspect of human expression, empowering them to find their own voice and rhythm in the process.

The drum is just one of those things that can transcend everything and bring people to a place of unification and harmony.

1

RHYTHMS OF AWAKENING: MY JOURNEY WITH THE DRUM

"Drumming gets people out of their heads and into their hearts; out of the past or future and into the present moment."

Christine Stevens

For context I think it is important to explain how I came to drumming and to writing this book.

I was born in Brittany in 1970. I grew up in the countryside and I loved being surrounded by nature. From an early age I expressed unusual sensitivity to subtle things around me: I often felt the energy of the future before events happened, and I knew of important shifts before people told me. For example, I spoke of my great-grandmother's death at age two, despite not being told about it. Aged eleven, I knew that my grandmother had died, again before her death was announced. I always felt other people's emotions, although I wasn't consciously aware of it.

From an early age, I felt a fascination with animals and understanding how the body worked. I knew I wanted to be a research scientist, and so I studied biology, gaining a PhD in Physiology of Reproduction, before moving to Scotland in the late 90s to pursue postdoctoral research. There I met my Hong Kong-born husband. I carried on working in research and after two postdocs, worked for a biotechnology startup in Cambridge.

I was always instinctively spiritual. Being raised Catholic does not bring back good memories. My formal experience of the sacred took the form of weekly mass service at my local church and catechism classes with the local priest, both of which I found terribly boring and tedious. God was portrayed as a judgemental father figure, and I always thought that he was somewhat displeased with me because I did not pray daily like the priest told me. Not a good way to connect with spirit! I rejected the church in my teens. But there was still something in me which longed for a deep connection to something greater than myself. In the early 2000s I came across Reiki and did my Level 1 training, but I did not do much with it at that time.

My first child was born in 2006 – a very positive experience, at home, supported by a doula, it completely shifted my work focus. For the first half of my pregnancy, I was a product of the system – utterly convinced that birth was a terrifying, painful and horrible ordeal. I wanted every form of pain relief available, seeing it in the same way as getting anaesthesia when going to the dentist. Then I hired a doula, and everything changed.

This decision opened a door to a world I never knew existed. Gradually, my beliefs began to shift. It was a journey of unlearning and rediscovery, culminating in a decision that my former self would have thought impossible: I chose to give birth at home, supported by my husband, my doula and a compassionate community midwife.

The experience was nothing short of transformative. To this day, when asked to recall a positive moment in my life during meditation, my mind invariably returns to this first birth. It wasn't just positive: it was utterly beautiful and profoundly empowering. I was on a high for weeks afterwards.

The impact of this birth went far beyond the event itself. I emerged from the experience feeling fundamentally altered – as if the cocktail of birth hormones had rewired my brain. In those first few weeks postpartum, I floated on a natural high that I can only compare to the transformative effect of a psychedelic journey. Colours seemed brighter, sensations more vivid and I felt a connection to something deeper that I hadn't known existed within me.

It wasn't until much later that I understood the true significance of what I'd experienced. I had tapped into the state that nature intends for birth – one of the biggest rites of passage in a woman's life – a state of power, of rebirth, of profound transformation. Those initial days of euphoria were more than just post-birth bliss: they were a glimpse into the incredible potential that lies within every woman's birth experience as a tool for deep personal growth and spiritual awakening. The altered state of consciousness that is meant to happen when birth is undisturbed, achieved naturally through the intense physical journey of birth and its accompanying cocktail of endorphins and oxytocin, can serve as a gateway to self-discovery, empowerment and a renewed sense of purpose in life.

My journey from fear to empowerment, from doubt to trust in my body's wisdom, became the foundation for my future work. I felt on a mission to help other women understand how they had been sold a lie and how different it could be from what was portrayed by our media and culture. It ignited a passion to reclaim birth as the transformative rite of passage it's meant to be. My experience stands as a testament to the life changing potential of a positive birth experience.

I spent a couple of years soul-searching, before retraining as a doula, an antenatal teacher and a baby-wearing instructor. I started teaching during evenings and weekends and offering consultations on my days off. I gave birth to my second child, also at home, in similar conditions as my first birth.

In the summer of 2012, I attended a birth as a last-minute backup for another doula. I loved every minute of supporting this birth. It felt like I was meant to be there. I was on a high from it.

I started this new work the first year that I also started experiencing my first perimenopausal symptoms, aged forty-two. After ten years working as a doula, I felt a deep knowing inside that I had outgrown this role and that I would not be able to make room for the next step unless I stopped doing this work which took so much time and energy. I left doula work behind in 2022, to make space in my life for the new calling.

Now, twelve years later, at the cusp of the menopause, I feel guided to offer myself as a journey guide for women through life transitions, helping them access their inner knowing and bring themselves more peace in their hearts using reconnection with nature, with the support of the drum.

The drum's first appearance

The first time I heard someone mention that they did drum healing all I felt was judgemental. When I look back, given my scientific background, it is perhaps not surprising that I reacted this way. Funnily, we all accept that sounds can be used in a scientific and medical context (for example with ultrasounds), but because drumming looks and feels so esoteric, it elicits suspicion, and we automatically dismiss it as 'woo' or pseudoscience.

My journey into the world of drumming began unexpectedly. Fresh-faced and wide-eyed in my new role as a doula, I signed up for a doula retreat. My primary motivation was simple: to connect with fellow doulas, buzzing with the excitement of my new-found calling.

Among the workshops offered was one intriguingly entitled 'Shamanic work for doulas', led by Kay Gillard. I approached it with a large dose of scepticism, particularly when the teacher announced we'd be doing a drum journey. "This isn't going to work," I thought to myself, settling in with more than a little doubt.

As the beat of the drum filled the room, I found myself reluctantly relaxing. What happened next defied all my expectations. Vivid visions of past lives flooded my mind's eye, as clear and tangible as my present reality. I saw myself as a Native American woman, a shaman, working inside a cave of rich, red earth. The details were incredibly specific – I could see a fire nearby, smell the earthy aroma of the cave and feel the cool, damp clay in my hands as I moulded it into a perfect sphere.

The experience was so profound, so unexpected, so real, that it stayed with me long after the drumming stopped. Compelled by an inexplicable urge, I sought out a local stream in the days following the retreat. There, I recreated the ball of clay from my vision. As I worked the earth between my palms, I felt a deep connection to that other self I had glimpsed and to new aspects of my being.

SHAMANIC DRUMMING

A note on terminology: throughout this book, I use the term 'shamanic drumming' with careful consideration. While the terms 'shaman' and 'shamanism' originated with the Tungusic peoples of Siberia, it has evolved into a widely-used academic framework for studying ceremonial drumming practices across cultures. I acknowledge the complex implications of applying this terminology globally, yet choose to use it as it best describes the remarkable parallel practices found worldwide – where drums serve as bridges between ordinary and non-ordinary states of consciousness, facilitate healing work and spiritual journeying. This choice allows us to engage with established scholarship while maintaining deep respect for the unique context, history and significance of each culture's distinct traditions.

Shamanic drumming is an ancient spiritual practice found in many cultures around the world that uses rhythmic percussion to induce altered states of consciousness, facilitate healing and connect with the spirit world. It's an ancient practice that's as old as humanity itself, yet as relevant today as it ever was.

At its core, shamanic drumming is about altering our state of consciousness. When we drum at a steady beat, typically around 4 beats per second, our brains start to sync up with this rhythm, through a phenomenon known as auditory entrainment (more on that in the science chapter).

This synchronisation can lead our brains into what's known as a theta state – a slower brainwave pattern, a dreamlike state of being, where the barriers between our conscious and subconscious minds become more permeable. It's in this state that shamans believe we can access deeper wisdom, whether that's from our own inner knowing or from what some traditions call the spirit world.

Michael Harner, a renowned anthropologist and shamanic practitioner, describes the power of shamanic drumming: "The shaman's drum is a vehicle. Its sound is what the shaman rides, like a horse, to reach the spirit world."

Now, you may be thinking. "Spirit world? Really?" But here's the thing: whether you believe in spirits or not, the effects of shamanic drumming are very real. Participants often report profound insights, emotional release, and a sense of connection to something larger than themselves. From a scientific perspective, we might explain this as accessing parts of our brain that we don't usually use in our day-to-day lives.

Sandra Ingerman, another well-known shamanic teacher, emphasises the healing potential of this practice: "The drum is also a tool for healing, as the vibrations of the drum can break up energy blocks in the body and restore harmony."

Shamanic drumming isn't about performing or showing off. It's about intention, about using the drum as a tool for exploration and healing. The steady, repetitive beat serves as a focus point, allowing our usually chatty minds to quiet down. It's a bit like meditation, but for those of us who find sitting still a challenge (hello, fellow ADHD folks!), it can be a more engaging way to achieve a similar state.

In our modern world, where we're constantly bombarded with stimuli and rarely get a moment's peace, shamanic drumming offers a way to tune out the noise and tune into ourselves. It's a practice that bridges the gap between ancient wisdom and modern needs, offering a path to self-discovery and healing that doesn't require you to abandon your rational mind.

While rooted in ancient traditions, shamanic drumming has found its way into contemporary healing practices. It is now used in various contexts, including:

- Sound therapy sessions.
- Meditation and mindfulness practices.
- Stress management programs.
- Spiritual retreats.
- Community drum circles.

Shamanic drumming continues to evolve, adapting to modern needs while maintaining its core principles of inducing altered states of consciousness for healing and spiritual growth.

So next time you hear about a shamanic drumming circle, consider giving it a try. You might be surprised at what you discover when you let yourself be carried by the beat.

This unexpected foray into the world of shamanic drumming left me craving more. I left the retreat with a desire to own a drum, to explore further what this powerful tool had unlocked within me. The universe, it seemed, was listening. Just a few weeks later, whilst on holidays in France, I shared my desire with my mother. She gifted me a traditional Irish drum, a bodhrán*, which she had bought on a trip to Ireland from a famous drum maker called Malachy Kearns.

* Pronounced *bow-rawn*

It felt like a sign, an invitation to continue this journey of discovery.

That first drum journey, still etched in my memory even now, was more than just an interesting experience. It was the beginning of a new path, one that would weave itself into my work as a doula and my understanding of the deeper, unseen connections that bind us all.

Overcoming impostor syndrome

The bodhrán came home with me. But as eager as I was to play it, I felt out of my depth. My brother, a professional musician, shared videos demonstrating how to play it with the tipper, the small wooden stick it came with. But I couldn't master the swift wrist movements required. I felt deflated and frustrated.

Enter my friend Peter Voshol, an unusual blend of scientist, shamanic practitioner and drum maker. When I shared my struggles with him, his response was simple yet profound: "What do you want to do with this drum, Sophie? Do you want to play in an Irish band?"

"No," I replied, "I want to do some shamanic drumming."

"Then you don't need to use the stick," he said, proceeding to show me how to make a felt beater.

This was a pivotal moment. Peter's encouragement to explore drumming beyond its traditional confines ignited a new confidence in me. More importantly, it made me realise that, despite my best intentions, I had fallen into the trap of believing there was only one "right" way – a very Western, prescriptive mindset.

My experience with Peter and the bodhrán became a cornerstone of my approach. This shift in perspective rippled through all aspects of my life and work. It taught me the value of experimentation, of finding my own path rather than adhering strictly to established norms. Now, when I guide others, I encourage them to play, to have fun and to develop ways of exploring without relying on anybody else telling them what to do.

The lesson went beyond drumming. It taught me about breaking free from the constraints of 'should' and trusting my innate wisdom, allowing myself to connect with ancient practices in ways that felt authentic. In the end, my bodhrán taught me far more than just a new skill. It opened a door to a more intuitive, playful and personally meaningful way of engaging with the world.

The concept of a 'right way' to engage in creative expression has permeated our culture, creating barriers that separate us from our innate abilities to play and express ourselves.

Going deeper

A year after I first encountered shamanic drumming, I attended the same retreat again. There was another drumming workshop, this time with Carolyn Hillyer. We spent the day drumming inside a thatched roundhouse. It no longer felt odd, and it resonated with something even deeper in me. I vowed to make drumming a more regular practice.

During that retreat, I gave someone a closing the bones massage, a healing postpartum massage ritual I had also learnt the previous year. A woman healer, Rebecca Wright, drummed in the background whilst we rocked, massaged and wrapped the women receiving the ritual. This accompaniment of the ritual by the drum felt very powerful. It made me want to add drumming to my own closing the bones treatments, as well as part of the ceremony I held when I taught it to birth professionals.

CLOSING THE BONES

Closing the bones is a traditional postpartum massage ritual, mostly known from its Mexican and South American cultural roots. However, similar practices exist, or have existed, across all continents, including in Europe. This ritual serves as a powerful tool for healing and honouring various life transitions in a woman's journey.

A closing the bones ceremony typically involves:

- A sequence of rocking the body using scarves.
- An abdominal massage (sometimes full-body).
- A sequence of tightening scarves around the whole body.
- In some traditions, a steam bath or sweat lodge is added.
- Drumming and/or singing (as incorporated by some practitioners).

A closing the bones ritual supports healing on multiple levels:

- **Physical:** it promotes movement in joints, muscles, tissues and fluids, aiding in physical recovery and realignment.
- **Emotional:** it provides a safe space for rest, witnessing and emotional release, allowing for processing and honouring of feelings.
- **Spiritual:** it facilitates closure, creates space for letting go of the past, and helps redirect energy back to the woman.

While traditionally associated with postpartum care, the closing the bones ritual holds profound significance for various transitions and rites of passage in a woman's life. The ceremony can be particularly powerful during times of loss and trauma – whether that's the physical loss of pregnancy or birth, the loss of a baby, the emotional landscape of relationship endings, or the invisible yet deeply felt losses that come with life changes.

In our modern culture, where significant milestones are often overlooked, this ritual offers a much-needed opportunity to pause, reflect and honour the depth of transformative moments.

Rituals play a vital role in personal growth and healing by:

- Creating a sacred, intentional space for processing and integrating profound experiences.
- Calming the nervous system and facilitating grounding and connection.
- Tapping into the collective subconscious through symbolic elements and practices.
- Providing a structured framework for processing trauma or shock.
- Fostering a sense of community and shared understanding.

By embracing rituals like closing the bones we:

- Honour the profound transformations occurring within the body, mind and spirit.
- Bridge the physical and spiritual realms.
- Create space for healing, integration and celebration.

- Recognise the intrinsic value of life's transitions.
- Acknowledge the potential for growth emerging from these experiences.

In a world where women often feel isolated during significant life changes, a closing the bones ritual offers a powerful way to reconnect with oneself, one's community and the sacred nature of life's transitions.

Although I started offering drumming as an option to clients who booked the ritual, I wasn't yet confident enough to offer it to everyone. I still had impostor syndrome and worried about women being put off by something so 'woo'. I had the same worries about owning my new expanded Reiki training, because people hiring me as a doula kept saying that they'd picked me because of my scientific background. Cambridge is full of scientists and medical professionals, so it's not surprising that my background felt reassuring to them. They would often say that they'd chosen me because I wasn't a hippy. I would cringe inside upon hearing this.

I grappled with this internal conflict between my scientific background and my emerging spiritual practices. I worried that revealing my spiritual side might put potential clients off or damage my professional credibility. I even considered creating a separate website for my healing work, effectively compartmentalising these two aspects of myself.

This cognitive dissonance led to a subtle but persistent sense of shame about my spiritual interests. I found myself struggling with the notion that it wasn't possible to be both a scientist and a person with spiritual beliefs. This false dichotomy created tension within me, as if I had to choose one identity over the other.

My struggle reflected a broader cultural bias that often opposes science against spirituality, treating them as mutually exclusive. My journey towards integrating these contradictory aspects of myself is not just a personal challenge, but a reflection of a larger need for society at large to embrace more nuanced, authentic, multifaceted identities.

Eventually, I 'came out' in a blog post I wrote entitled, "Confessions of a Hippy Scientist". Sharing this was very vulnerable and I worried about being criticised. However, the responses I got were incredible, the exact opposite of the backlash I had expected to receive. Many people expressed gratitude for my writing. They said they felt the same and that my sharing had helped them identify this and understand themselves better. My article gave them permission to embrace their multidimensional selves.

Today, I've overcome my perceived divide between the rational and the esoteric. This personal experience has become a cornerstone of my work, enabling me to guide others through their own struggles with impostor syndrome and the integration of their authentic selves. My journey has evolved into a unique approach that bridges scientific understanding and spiritual wisdom.

This isn't just a personal philosophy; it's become my professional signature, allowing me to offer a more nuanced perspective to those I work with. By modelling this integration, I demonstrate that embracing both scientific and spiritual knowledge isn't just possible – it's utterly transformative, opening up new dimensions of personal growth.

Making drums and medicine

Three years after my first drumming experience, I felt a deep desire to make my own drum. In the summer of 2016, I attended a drum making workshop with Jo Gray. Under Jo and her partner's gentle guidance, I spent the day in sacred craft in their garden on a beautiful summer's day. I made a deer hide drum and the most gorgeous drum beater, complete with wood burning decorations and amethyst crystals embedded in the beater's handle.

What I remember most about the creation of my drum was the state of deep flow and peace that this sacred crafting gave me. Looking back, it feels very significant that I experienced this, because this was at a time in my life where I felt overworked and overwhelmed, busy with a growing self-employed business, juggling the demands of being on-call for births as a doula and raising two young children.

This day gave me something I longed for: a sense of deep calm and peace, where time stood still and nothing else mattered, other than being immersed in crafting work, as well as the production of a magical and beautiful tool. It made my soul sing.

I didn't know at the time that this kind of crafting causes the brain to slow down into alpha waves, a more focused, slower state of consciousness. I really craved being in this 'time out of time' space, because my life was too busy, and I always felt that I didn't have enough time to do everything I needed to do. I didn't know then that I could create space like this in my life. It felt that this only happened in specially designed containers like retreats and wasn't possible in everyday life.

When I look back, making this drum marked a pivotal moment in my life. It was the start of a new phase where I began to prioritise self-care without guilt. Instead of constantly pushing myself to work harder and complete every task on my to-do list, I learned to embrace moments of rest and relaxation.

Creating this drum made me realise that, to create more spaciousness in my life, I needed to make this a priority. Recently I sat with this drum, holding her on my lap and asked her what her medicine was. Unsurprisingly, she replied that her medicine was time out of time, spaciousness and presence.

I birthed another drum at a doula retreat. We spent two days making deer drums and beaters with Carolyn Hillyer. There were thirteen doulas there, all making their drums together, and little did I know then that this would lead to my drumming during births later on. I had only intended to use this drum for healing women at the time, but not specifically for birth. Carolyn explained which deer the hides had come from (culled deer, due to overpopulation, and skins which would have otherwise been wasted). I loved the gentle yet deep process she led us through to connect and honour the hide and the animals our drum skins had come from. I loved this process, which hadn't been part of my previous drum birthing. It felt right and deeply spiritual to do this, and to express reverence and gratitude to the animals. I have come to learn since that it is an essential part of the process of drum making, to know and honour the fact that some animal has died in order for the drum to be made. For the process to have integrity, this needs to be acknowledged (more on this in the chapter about choosing a drum). Shamanic drums, especially the ones you make yourself, are powerful medicine. They usually carry the energy of the intentions and the process that happens whilst making them. This is not necessarily the ones you want, but the ones you need. I intended to use this drum for healing others, but it healed me first.

Immediately after finishing the drum and beater, I started feeling like I was coming down with a stomach bug and then I went to bed and slept for eighteen hours. When I woke up, I felt completely fine. I had experienced a healing crisis, powered by my drum and the sacred crafting process.

This drum became my favourite. I do not let other people play her as I want to keep her energy mine alone. I have anointed her with my menstrual blood. This drum has helped me become more confident in offering drumming to my clients. She has been instrumental in my journey towards drumming becoming more normal and central in my life.

A few months after making this drum, I decided to attend a Reiki Drum training. I had already taken my Reiki journey further, after witnessing the enormity of the energy in the room in the moment after a baby had just been born. I had trained as a Reiki Master and I was teaching Reiki to birth professionals.

REIKI AND REIKI DRUM

Reiki is a Japanese energy healing technique where the practitioner uses gentle touch or hovering hands to channel universal life force energy to promote physical, emotional and spiritual healing and balance.

Reiki Drum is like a power duo of healing practices. By using the drum to channel the Reiki energy, it combines the gentle energy healing of Reiki with the rhythmic, consciousness-altering effects of drumming, and the power of vibration.

Reiki Drum was developed by the shamanic practitioner and teacher Michael Arthur Baird and was brought to the UK in the 1990s by his student Sarah Gregg, whom I trained with.

In a Reiki Drum session, the practitioner uses a frame drum over and around your body, creating vibrations & energy that penetrate deep into your tissues. These vibrations, much like sound therapy, can help release tension, move stuck energy and promote relaxation. Meanwhile, the steady beat of the drum helps shift your brainwaves into a more receptive state – similar to what happens in meditation. At the same time, the practitioner channels Reiki through the drum, directing it with intention to support the body's natural healing processes. The drum acts as a tool to amplify and direct this energy, much like an antenna boosting a signal.

Whether you approach it from a spiritual perspective or a scientific one, Reiki Drum offers a unique, multi-sensory experience. It's a bit like getting a sound bath and an energy tune-up all at once.

The course facilitator, Sarah Gregg, told me the course was full, but I knew somehow that I would attend the course anyway. A space opened for me at the last minute. During the training Sarah mentioned that I was a master manifestor as I had created a space for myself despite the course being full. Once again at this course, I thought I was mostly going to learn something to heal others, but of course I experienced some deep heart healing for myself over the course of the weekend.

Having become a Reiki Drum practitioner not only added a new string to my bow, it meant that I also got to attend Sarah's spring equinox gatherings, where Reiki Drum healers gather for a day of Reiki Drum healing shares, drumming and singing. Drumming together in a large room with sixty other drum practitioners is a powerful experience I will never forget.

After I learnt Reiki Drum, I changed the way I taught Reiki to birth workers, adding drumming to the attunement parts of my training. I didn't realise how much this would impact people and it's only now, years down the line, that I hear back from students how much this experience ignited their desire to drum. The same is true for having introduced drumming during other workshops I teach, such as closing the bones. I love that it helps other women start their drum journey too.

That year marked a turning point. Drumming became something normal, something that no longer felt weird to do. I incorporated drumming as standard as part of my closing the bones treatments and perinatal rituals. I also used it in women circles and mother blessings and of course as part of Reiki and healing treatments. It felt very good to be able to do this so easily, like something I was really meant to be doing.

I carried on acquiring new drums slowly, not knowing quite why and built up quite a collection, which stands at over twenty-five at the time I write this (I share more on this in the chapter on how to choose a drum). As it turned out, these drums needed to come to my drum circles and my training, to help more women experience their power and start their own journeys.

Drumming during births

Whilst I already offered drumming during pregnancy and during the postpartum to women I supported as a doula, I also dreamed of drumming during births. I hadn't heard or read anything about it, it was just a deep longing. In 2019, I ticked off this 'bucket list' wish. I got to drum during two births that year. The first time was a home birth, with fellow doula and friend Malwina.

I joined Malwina at her home during her labour. Knowing that drumming appealed to her, I brought a drum with me. I did not know if I would end up using it. Malwina laboured beautifully and instinctively and for most of her labour, I did not feel like she needed any help apart from my quiet, supportive presence. However, I found myself intuitively picking up my drum as she started to push her baby out, because it felt like she needed more support then. I sat in the corner and gently drummed, as she squatted in the birth pool, supported by her partner. I could feel that it was right to do this. Malwina would later tell me how wonderfully supportive the drumming had felt for her (I share more on Malwina's story in the chapter about drumming and birth).

The same year, I also drummed for the first time during a birth in the hospital during Ailsa's birth. I was hired by Ailsa specifically to drum at her birth. I remember being incredibly excited when I received her enquiry. She had specifically sought me out because she wanted a doula who could drum to support her during her second birth. When I received her message, I remember thinking: this would have never happened if I had continued to shy away from offering this side of myself to the world!

Ailsa's birth took place in the birth centre in my local hospital, which is staffed by midwives who are usually more on board with natural birth than in the obstetric unit. Still, I was acutely aware that our drumming would probably raise some eyebrows.

I worked in a team with another doula, and I was glad I had the support of my doula colleague whilst we drummed together, as it felt less vulnerable to share the drum work together rather than doing it alone. My colleague did confirm that the midwife had a very odd look on her face when we started drumming. Her lack of curiosity fascinated me. I would have loved to explain the spiritual and scientific reasons why drumming was beautifully suited to support birthing. I was delighted with the experience. Ailsa had the most beautiful healing birth, and I remember crying tears of joy as I walked out of the hospital (there is more on her story in the chapter about drumming and birth).

Drumming takes centre place

In late 2019, I felt a pull to take my drum work even deeper and I decided to train to become a Reiki Drum teacher. I did twenty-four Reiki Drum sessions as case studies in the space of a couple of months. It was a deeply affirming experience for me. Some of my case studies experienced almost unbelievable healing from our work together, way beyond my expectations. It gave me a lot of confidence.

One woman in particular had pain and tension for years in her shoulder, which had proven resistant to any bodywork manipulation, from massage to osteopathy. The first time I drummed over her shoulder, the sound of my drum was completely muffled, as if it was being absorbed by her body. I concentrated my drum over this part of her body for over twenty minutes before the drum sound started showing a shift and resonated normally. After the first treatment her body relaxed, and she said that she felt like she'd just been to see an osteopath. The tension completely dissipated over the course of her four treatments, especially when spirit guided me to ask questions about the origin of the tension.

This experience only strengthened my desire to carry on with my drumming practice and offerings. I attended the training in early 2020. I didn't have the opportunity to teach this modality as I intended, due to the lockdowns that occurred shortly afterwards. I found that the universe had other plans for me. Sometimes what we intend and what we get are completely different things and I have found this to be often true in my work and life journey.

In February 2020, I started running a drum circle in Cambridge. I did this because I wanted to be in one but there wasn't one near me, so I thought, "why not create one myself?" It had been on my mind for quite some time and the Reiki Drum teacher training and case studies experiences gave me the confidence to finally get started.

I spent a long time preparing a teaching plan, complete with a spreadsheet of activities and timings, I read books on running drum circles and I spoke to several people I knew who ran drum circles, asking for their wisdom and support. Once again, I noticed the impostor syndrome feeling creeping in, because this was completely new to me. I even worried that people would think that it wasn't worth the money, even though I only charged £10 per person for it!

What I had envisaged was that a small group of like-minded friends who already had drums would attend. Instead, fourteen people turned up right from the first session, many of whom I did not know and who had never done any drumming before, nor owned a drum. Luckily, I had quite a few drums by then and they all got used during this drum circle, in fact there was just enough for everyone. I needed not to have worried about people not enjoying it because everyone was delighted with the experience.

When the country went into lockdown, after only two live sessions, I ran my drum circle on Zoom for several weeks, then in the local nature reserve and finally in a friend's garden. I am still running these circles four years on.

Over the last eighteen months, my drum circle has finally found a steady home, inside a geodome in a private woodland near Cambridge. I am also considering starting a women-only circle and would love it to be welcoming to pregnant women and new mothers. Interestingly, my circle keeps attracting complete beginners, who do not own a drum, the majority of whom are women. I am delighted when they start attending regularly and acquire a drum of their own.

Let me share with you some of the feedback I have received from people who have attended my drumming circle:

After the circles I feel that I have fully expressed myself and been seen, not by other people so much as by myself.

SJ

In a world where it's difficult to access spaces with integrity, your circle has masses of it. It left me able to be myself and able to enjoy myself. In other spaces, am I often triggered by the lack of authenticity. I found your circle a breath of fresh air.

Sophie

I loved it. It's so easy and accessible yet sounds so incredible. I was wowed! I'm a big live music fan, from a young age live music has been very important and spiritual for me. So powerful to actually be making rhythm and music with others.

Anon

The theme of surprises, unexpected gifts and personal growth carried on. In May 2020, I turned fifty. Due to lockdown restrictions, I couldn't organise the big party I had planned. My family could not join me from France.

Instead, I shared my intention with the group of people who had been part of my drum circle to start the day drumming in the woods with me. Two women joined me. This was four years ago, and we have been drumming together on a weekly basis in the same place ever since.

This has probably been the most supportive and transformative part of my drumming practice. It ticks all my boxes of wellbeing needs: connection to myself, to nature and to women I love.

For my fiftieth birthday I also got three new drums as presents, one of which has a carving representing the opening of the energy field during birth on the back of it, based on a tattoo I have on my arm.

When in-person activities fully reopened later that year, I was amazed by how much confidence and progress my small private practice had brought me. When I started in 2020, I needed my printed teaching plan to run my circle. Now that I had been drumming so regularly and for so long, running a drum circle – from opening sacred space to leading the drumming – felt like the most natural thing in the world and I could just run it from experience alone, without the need for a written guide.

My private drumming practice

Once a week I get up at 6 am and drive to a local woodland to drum with two other women. We have done it throughout all seasons, in the warmth and light of summer, in the dark of winter, in the rain, in the sunshine, in the snow even.

Each time we start by co-creating an altar, using objects we bring and some we find in nature. Each of these altars is beautiful and unique and it also changes with the seasons. We set intentions for our drumming and then we drum.

The beat of our drums resonates through the trees, muting the natural sounds of the woodland. Each drum has its own unique voice and together, we create a complex tapestry of sound. The rhythm often starts slow. Gradually, it builds in intensity, sometimes becoming fast and powerful. Other times, it's as gentle as a heartbeat.

It's as if our drums are speaking an ancient language, one that communicates directly with the spirits of the forest and our deeper selves. The boundary between us and nature seems to dissolve, leaving only rhythm and connection.

There is a connection to something larger than ourselves that quiets the busyness of our minds. Our drums transport us into an altered state of consciousness. When the drumming finishes, there is a palpable sense of calmness, presence and grounding that comes from it. It gives us connection beyond words.

After the drumming, we sit down on logs with our flasks of warm drinks, and we share what's going on in our lives. Our social time takes on a deeper quality. Conversation flows more freely. There is a deep respect and understanding between us, especially as we have been sharing this practice for so long.

Over the last four years, the three of us have all experienced deep personal challenges. Our practice supports us, and we always feel clearer and more positive afterwards.

One of the reasons this feels so important to me, is because for many years I longed to attend such gatherings. I used to believe that deep spiritual experiences were reserved for special retreats or sacred spaces, removed from the routines of everyday life. But this practice has shattered that notion. It is a part of my life, because I made it happen. It is deeply sacred and yet feels completely normal. I have noticed that when things become "normal" in this way, in a "chop the wood, fetch the water" way, this is when true magic happens.

I look forward to our drumming gatherings. They meet so many of my needs: my needs for belonging and sisterhood, for doing something sacred, ancient and magical yet deeply grounded and for connection to myself, to nature and to my drum sisters. It is the mix of the deep sense of reverence and more informal sharing afterwards that makes it so special.

One recent morning, after our drumming, my eyes were drawn to a stone on our altar. Created by artist Jaine Rose, it's a small black pebble, one that fits in the palm of the hand, with a drawing of a woman holding a drum, with gold accents. On the front, it says *"she drums."* On the back it says *"She drums forgotten magic in wild and hidden spaces."*

When I first acquired this stone, I felt a bit like a fraud owning it. Back then, drumming was a sporadic practice for me, something I dabbled in but couldn't fully claim as part of my identity. The image and words seemed to represent an aspiration rather than a reality. I felt like I could not quite call myself a drum woman. And yet, I know I bought this pebble because I wanted to call more of this magic into my life.

Yet here I was, five years later, standing with my drum sisters in the forest. I marvelled at the journey that had brought me to this moment. The stone's message had evolved from a mere aspiration into a living truth, manifesting in ways I'd only dared to hope for when I first held it. Its power had unfolded beyond my dreams, transforming my life in profound and unexpected ways. As I stood there, I felt the full weight of that transformation and the magical path it had carved for me.

This stone has become a powerful talisman, marking not just the passage of time, but the profound evolution of my relationship with the drum. It is a testament to the power of dreams and intention, reminding me that we can grow into the identities we once only dreamed of embodying.

In that moment, with those two women I love and our drums, standing in this beautiful place in nature, I felt a deep sense of gratitude. The woman holding the drum was no longer just a drawing on a stone – she was me, she was my sisters around me, each of us living the truth of "she drums" in our own unique way.

I want to share what the two women I drum with – Samantha and Amanda – have to say about it here with you.

What drumming means to me

– Samantha

My drum journey started about eight years ago, at a retreat workshop held by two wise and powerful women. I felt I had lost myself in work and the essence of the workshop was to return to nature, to connect with self. There was a workshop drum, which we were encouraged to use. I was drawn to it, and found somewhere private where I wouldn't disturb anyone and started to play a rhythm. Words came, snippets of a song, I found myself moving, connecting with something deep inside me, through the drum. It was a magical experience, one of many as I returned again and again for further retreats. I wanted to create my own drum, but it took me a long time to make it happen. When I finally took part in a drum-birthing workshop, I was really moved by the process and was unprepared for the love I would feel for my skin-drum.

I would get up extremely early before people were about and take my drum out to some trees to play, connecting with her and with nature. It felt like a prayer. At first, I was nervous to be seen – would people think I was insane, or even dangerous? Gradually, I became more confident about revealing this side of myself, mirroring my own journey of personal development and joined a local drum circle.

Now I have a regular drumming practice. Starting early before work, with two women who have become dear friends. It is a spiritual practice, an anchor point in my week, however busy I am. I've also now got a synthetic drum, for when the weather is too damp for a skin-drum. Being outside in nature is calming and connecting. My drum sounds, she adds her rhythms to the mix, sometimes echoing the others' drums, sometimes choosing her own beat. I connect deep within myself and also connect to the trio. A meditative prayer or a rousing uplift, the drumming helps me access parts of myself that I often forget in life's busyness and helps me feel calm and grounded and whole. I am enormously grateful to my drums, to my fellow drummers and to this regular practice.

Drumming for me

– Amanda

Drumming invites me to connect deeper underneath my skin. To be more aware of my blood, my heart beating in my chest, the firelight inside. It brings me deeper to my bones. More steadiness opens out, a deep sort of wildness is more present, more accessible and I like it. I feel more alive, more whole.

An invitation to drum in the woods to celebrate a birthday four years ago has also turned two almost strangers into very valuable friendships. But it has also brought me to a deeper friendship with myself.

We have each continually said yes to arriving early morning to drum in a woodland nearby. It's so beautiful to give this to myself and to these lovely women. Sometimes just five or ten minutes at home can be so strengthening, easing the too-fast button inside just enough to reconnect with the inside again.

I have a fabulous strong skin drum and a man-made drum, a gift, which is perfect for rainy or damp mornings. They have both become a part of my life now and are in my living room.

I love the combination of drumming and being in nature best of all. Having the elements around me so close. The seasonal changes, the sounds of so much around me, the leaves dancing and reflecting light around and above us. The bird song, the smell of the outside allowing me to feel more and be in a fuller picture of all this beauty, all this wonder and sacredness of Life. The good fortune to be here as a human on Earth.

Drumming helps me to honour myself and to feel myself as part of the bigger Life: that is priceless.

Personal growth

I don't think it is a coincidence that I discovered drumming the year I entered my perimenopause. It is often only when you look back that you can see your own growth and progress. When I look back over the last eleven years, the drum is woven deeply within my journey of self-discovery and healing, as well as in that of the many women I have supported.

When I look back, I see that the drum played a role in my growing what I call my 'true self,' growing into my power and embracing the whole of me. These days I no longer carry any discomfort around what is often perceived as a paradox by people. I often get asked, "How come you were a scientist and now you do all this weird shit?" and now I no longer even feel the need to justify myself, especially if the question is coming from a place of judgement instead of one of curiosity. I often simply reply: "because I can!"

I can see how many of my drumming experiences helped me grow out of the boxed-in, patriarchal pigeon-holing that is so prevalent in our culture. You can only be this and not that.

For instance, remember how my friend Peter helped me embrace the fact that I did not have to play my bodhrán using the wooden beater that came with it? Well, ten years on, I got an adufe drum as a Christmas present. This is a traditional square, double-skinned drum from Portugal, which is mostly played by women.

An adufe is played in a complex and technical manner, either by striking it with the hand or simultaneously hitting it with the hand and a stick.* This drum also has jingles inside and is often shaken up and down. Ten years ago, when my brother shared his knowledge about proper bodhrán technique, I took this guidance to heart. When he later suggested mastering the traditional adufe technique, I had an enlightening moment: while I deeply respect and am curious about traditional playing methods, I also realised that I could explore multiple approaches – from classical techniques to experimental styles with beaters or my hands. This reflected my growing confidence in finding my own style and power as a drummer.

This shift in perspective exemplifies my evolving relationship with drumming, one that embraces personal exploration and intuition, a more liberated approach to musical expression. And here lies the beauty of the simple tool that is a frame drum. When you beat the drum with a beater, it requires almost no skill. This makes it accessible to everyone, including those who have never played a drum before in their lives.

My experience with the drum has also helped me to see the patriarchal mindset at play for what it is: a state of mind where people are squeezed into tiny little boxes and where we are made to feel incompetent and not good enough and that we cannot possibly do anything unless we are masters at it. Such disempowering bullshit!

Yes, there are people who are experts and artists in their craft, and it is wonderful. But it doesn't mean that those of us who are enjoying something for its own pleasure do not have our place within the landscape of a practice or an art. Restricting something to only professionals or masters is akin to saying that only Michelin-starred chefs should be allowed to cook, or that the cooking you do in your own kitchen to feed your family isn't cooking at all.

We all have to start somewhere and some of us will practice something as a hobby and some will go on to become professionals, experts, or may even reach the top of their craft. But to dismiss or devalue the former group is a manifestation of the elitist, gatekeeping mentality perpetuated by patriarchal systems.

In a world with more feminine values, the emphasis should be on the process itself – the personal growth, creativity and fulfilment it provides – rather than adhering to narrow, arbitrary standards of 'elite' mastery. Such an approach not only empowers a wider range of people to explore their interests

* For an example of this type of playing, see youtube.com/watch?v=Bf9LFZtSnEc

but also enriches the cultural landscape by welcoming a multitude of voices and expressions.

Because of the experiences I had in overcoming impostor syndrome with my drum, I feel on a mission to help women see that they can drum. In my drum circles, a lot of women come who have never drummed before nor taken part in a drum circle. I have started encouraging members who need to receive healing to raise their hands and lie down and then suggest that people who feel guided to do so get close and drum for them. Every time I do this, the ones who seem to benefit from it the most aren't the ones lying down but the ones giving the drum healing, because they didn't realise that they could do that. People often mention how good it feels.

I trained to become a Reiki practitioner, then a Reiki Master teacher and then did the same with Reiki Drum. Whilst I love the techniques and taught Reiki for several years, there has always been something somewhat prescriptive and masculine in the way they were taught that didn't sit quite right with me. That niggling discomfort grew stronger with time. I also did not like that to become a Reiki Drum practitioner you needed to train at two levels of Reiki beforehand.

There seems to be a paradoxical dynamic where spiritual and therapeutic disciplines get entangled with patriarchal dogma – the opposite of the openness and equality they should embody. Controlling who can access knowledge and engage in a practice based on credentialism rather than learning and experience perpetuates systems of inequality.

In 2024, I taught an intuitive drum healing course. I had trepidations because I wasn't sure it would work. But when I handed drums over to my students, most of whom were new to drumming and simply instructed them to drum for one another, magic happened. It was so inspiring to witness how tenderly and beautifully they held the space for each other. I did not need to speak or explain anything further because the process was enough. It had taught them that they could, that they knew what to do. No amount of theory could do this.

I find it helpful to view the tension between theory and practice through the lens of the masculine and feminine principles, as well as the dynamics between rational and creative modes of thinking. In mainstream knowledge systems, theory has been associated with the masculine, the realm of logic, rules and universal truths. It aligns with the analytical left-brain mode of cognition that categorises and seeks rigid patterns. In contrast, exploration and practice are aligned with a more feminine principle, of intuitive experience, more fluid and context-specific wisdom. It resonates with the creative right-brain thinking that thrives on emotional intelligence and an adaptability to unique situations.

The most powerful expressions of knowledge come from a dance between theory and practice, rationality and creativity, masculine and feminine modes of thinking, embracing both the universal and the particular, the systematic and the organic.

Riding the phoenix

The couple of years from 2021 to 2023 were extremely challenging for me emotionally and mental health-wise. My youngest child struggled with severe anxiety. I battled tirelessly with the local authorities, both on the education and the mental health front, to gain the support we needed. Despite the underfunded, understaffed systems throwing up constant roadblocks, and mental health challenges of my own triggered by this situation, I persevered. Finally, after eighteen gruelling months, we won the fight and got the funding for the small specialist school we knew would be instrumental in her recovery. As relieved as I was, I felt utterly weary and drained from being a warrior for so long.

Just when I thought I could catch my breath and celebrate with a family holiday, I landed in hospital with a kidney stone. The excruciating pain caused me to faint and concuss myself. Instead of our planned trip, I spent the week bedridden, feeling very sorry for myself.

When my child started at their new nurturing specialist school, it proved to be everything I had hoped for and more. Three months in, my once completely housebound child was happily going on overnight school trips. Small wins like this gave me strength during a period where my own health crashed from chronic stress.

Around the same time, I received an ADHD diagnosis which shed light on my struggles with boring tasks but ability to hyper-focus on exciting projects, as well as helped me start being less harsh on myself. I started tapping into resources like coaching and decluttering help through an access to work grant. With this extra support system, I knew my life and business were going to improve tremendously.

When I finally had more space for my work again, as my child settled into their new school, it had been two years since I stopped working as a doula. I felt restless and impatient for the next calling to emerge. A wonderful neurodivergent coach I was working with, Kanan Tekchandani, helped me get unstuck by asking: "What would really excite you right now?" Without hesitation, I replied, "Teaching a course on how to use drumming to support birth."

I booked myself into Melonie Syrrett's Sacred Women's Drum Circle facilitator training. I booked this for me, as a personal retreat, knowing that I needed a deep immersion in nature to reset. Over four days camping at the Clophill Shamanic Centre, I spent hours in the roundhouse and the woods, in the company of like-minded women, drumming, creating ceremonies, and crafting my own drum with an intention to lead circles and other women to the drum. This was just what the doctor ordered, it was as if my entire soul finally breathed and expanded after so long in a dysregulated state.

Working with the horse hide I had chosen for my drum was very challenging. I fell behind the others, eventually finishing late into the night, several hours behind everyone else. But I wouldn't give up until it was complete, my tenacity echoing the fight for my child's needs. When I finally played my new drum, he told me its name was Mountain Rider and that his medicine was overcoming obstacles.

A year later, I went on to make yet another drum at Melonie's drum birthing pilgrimage in Glastonbury. I had never been to Glastonbury before, and I loved the energy there. I also loved how steeped in grounded spirituality the whole experience was: from bathing with our hides during a private ceremony in the White Spring, to crafting our drums in the Avalon room near the goddess temple, to taking our newly made drums to the Chalice Well Gardens and crafting our beaters there. We then walked to the top of the Tor to present our drums to the four directions and carry out a drumming ceremony to welcome and bless them.

This new drum is made from an oak hoop and stag hide. Its energy is much gentler than the horse drum I made the year prior. It was also incredibly easy to make. This was the first time I made a drum for my own healing, instead of making it to heal others and this feels deeply significant of my own healing journey.

Going mainstream

The medicine of my new horse drum kicked my creativity into a new stratosphere. I offered a free webinar on drumming for birth and around a hundred people joined. Despite my initial fears that this new topic was too niche, I decided to launch an online course. Ten women joined me from several different countries, and we all had powerful, transformative experiences guided by the drum over the summer whilst I ran the course. Within months, I had cascading opportunities – publishing articles, starting to write this book, starting a podcast, being invited to several conferences, giving talks and workshops, all about drumming.

Around the same time, much to my surprise, I was invited to write an article about drumming and birth for the *International Journal of Birth and Parenting Education*.* This felt unexpected and really cutting edge on the part of the journal. I was deeply grateful to the editor of the journal for taking such a leap of faith. I was also delighted because I knew that, in our science loving culture, the existence of this article would help validate the power of the drum and help open the minds of sceptics.

In spring 2024, I was invited to speak about drumming and birth at two midwifery conferences. Rather than delivering a traditional lecture, I chose a more experiential approach. After a brief introduction, sharing some of the cutting-edge science that demonstrate the effects of the drum on our physiology, I guided the audience through a drum journey. The power of the drum cannot be fully conveyed through words alone – it must be experienced. As far as I know this was a first in a midwifery conference!

Aware of the potential scepticism towards drumming, I opened both talks with a thought-provoking question. Pointing to my drum, I asked the audience if they rolled their eyes when I suggested it could help with the pain of birth. I then explained that, twenty years ago, waterbirth was met with similar scepticism, yet today, birthing pools were standard in every UK hospital.

The feedback I received was overwhelmingly positive. Many attendees expressed surprise at the profound impact of the drum journey. This gives me hope for the future, because only a few years ago, the world wasn't ready for this.

Through this drumming work, I tapped into the pioneering spirit that has allowed me to forge new paths my whole life – from childhood dreams of

* You can download this article from IJBPE.com

science, through my PhD days, all the way to integrating spiritual traditions in my work supporting families. The drum awakened that trailblazer energy within me again when I needed it the most.

I realised that worrying about winning over the sceptics and laggards was fruitless. My role is to connect with the curious early adopters, people energetically aligned with my offerings. When I share authentically from that space, no justification is needed – my offerings resonate with the right people.

Healing with drums

I ran an intuitive drum healing training early in 2024 as I was in the middle of writing this book. It felt so right and so beautiful to encourage my students to work in pairs and drum for each other. As I watched them drum, I saw that not only was it beautiful, healing and nurturing, but that, most importantly, each of the students drumming for another woman looked completely natural and delighted that they were able to do this. I did not need to explain or theorise about it.

This shift towards inner-centred wisdom is not unique to my journey; it reflects a growing trend among women across various fields and cultures. Many are recognising the limitations of solely relying on external authorities and are instead turning inward, trusting their intuition and innate knowledge. This movement is particularly significant for women, who have historically been discouraged from trusting their own instincts and bodily wisdom.

Recently I gave a drum healing session to a friend. She wanted to explore the causes behind an ailment she was experiencing. In the past I would have been tempted to read about it in books, but this time, rather than simply using my drum and my intuition, rather than doing a classic healing session, I was guided to offer her a drum journey, to connect with the spirit of her ailment. I was slightly nervous offering her healing because she told me she had been disappointed by several healers she'd worked with.

This approach really suited her, and she was delighted with her session, finding it more powerful than what she had experienced so far. I was the space-holder, and this felt good and more true and real than what I'd done in the past, which was trying too hard to 'heal' and 'fix' the person, fearing that I wouldn't give my clients their money's worth if all their problems didn't go away at once…

Where I am now

Today, drumming feels as normal as breathing to me. It has become such a regular practice, that I can now get myself into the modified state of consciousness that drumming elicits by just thinking about it. I use drumming in most of the rituals, in-person and online teachings, mentoring and healing work I do. I attend drumming circles and events. I drum weekly with my sisters and every six weeks at wheel of the year ceremonies.

I love to introduce others to the power of the drum and to see the delight in people when they realise how easy it is. It is very heartening to see and hear how delightful it is for people who have never done drumming with others, that they can.

I make a commitment to drum almost every day for at least a few minutes. When I'm stuck with finding the answer to a question I have, I drum on it. This commitment to daily drumming has given me access to something I have sought all my life but did not succeed in finding until now: a sense of growing inner peace and presence. I've reached a point where drumming feels like a completely normal part of my life. It is also an utterly supportive activity for me. The drum is my ally, my guide and a way to get my thinking brain out of the way and speak directly to my soul. This book could not have been written without the support of the drum.

Most importantly, my drum practice has supported me through the biggest transitions of all: perimenopause and the entry into the crone phase of my life. The discomfort of these recent years has stripped me down in preparation for a rebirth. While the time in the tunnel has been long and dark, I can feel the expansiveness, openness and tolerance this profound growth has brought me. Drumming gave me the courage to fully lean in and trust myself once again. Through its grounding, healing presence, I rediscovered the truth of who I am. It has sustained me, through deep personal and multiple challenges and crises and it has supported my shedding of outdated parts of myself and my rebirth. I have been on a deep healing journey and whilst it was not always comfortable, I feel so much happier, more present and peaceful and I know this is just the beginning.

One of the main reasons I decided to write this book is because I feel that humanity is going through a major shift and one of these shifts is that knowledge will no longer come through teachers or gurus but directly from source. We are shifting away from reliance on external authorities and towards direct access to our inner wisdom. I have felt and known this for several years. It came first in a meditation, in which I was shown that the main cause of our collective suffering is disconnection. Disconnection from ourselves, from each other and from the earth.

What we need most at this moment in time, to heal ourselves and to heal the earth, is to support women to stand in their true power. The power that resides within us, in our ability to trust ourselves and know what's right for us, rather than abdicating knowledge and power over to the system. What we need is to support a feminine way of accessing knowledge.

Modern culture tends to gatekeep knowledge, especially in the healing field by centralising and controlling access to these domains through established institutions, authorities and systems. This reflects a cultural belief that healing and knowledge must be strictly controlled and dispensed only through approved, centralised channels. It disempowers individuals from accessing their own inner wisdom and taking authority over their wellbeing.

Our culture conflates formal education with genuine competence. We place academic qualifications above practical experience, creating a culture where diplomas and certificates are prised more highly than the hard-won wisdom gained through years of hands-on practice.

While formal training certainly has its place, it's only one aspect of skill development. True mastery often emerges from a combination of theoretical knowledge and practical application, honed through trial and error in real-world scenarios.

Unfortunately, our current system tends to overemphasise standardised credentials, sometimes at the expense of recognising the depth of knowledge and skills that comes from direct experience. This leads to overlooking highly skilled individuals who may lack formal qualifications but possess deep, nuanced understanding of their craft.

This lack of self-trust is more pervasive in women, the drum feels particularly important because it offers a way to relearn how to access our own wisdom, one that is easy and fairly effortless. Drumming offers a way back in through the layers of parenting, education and societal conditioning that have eroded our self-knowing. Reclaiming this knowing is critically needed in a culture that conditions women from childhood to seek truth outside rather than within.

When I work with women and the drum, I see exactly this happen. The drum gives a voice to inner emotions and feelings and acts like an inner pilot light, putting women back in touch with their unique expression, voice and power.

I experienced this myself, with impostor syndrome feelings, having trained and learnt to offer many aspects of my work, especially the ritualistic aspects, through exploration and experience, rather than through formal training.

A shift from outer to inner centred wisdom

The shift I see happening at grassroot levels challenges the top-down model, a de-institutionalisation of knowledge and healing – enabling direct access to source wisdom within each person rather than relying on external authorities and systems as intermediaries.

For me, this shift has manifested itself in a reluctance to learn from others and explore things for myself, after several years of training obsessively with as many teachers as possible. I do still train but I only pick mentors who work in the same, empowering and unique way, offering not their own path, but encouraging others to carve their own.

Whilst I loved learning to offer and teach Reiki and Reiki Drum and still do, and whilst this was a big part of my personal growth journey, today I prefer to show a way which gives permission to people to offer drumming to one another straight away. I believe that we can all do it. I believe that healing and drumming are innate abilities present within all of us. When I offer the opportunity to women to do this, I always see that this is true.

In my evolving approach to healing, I've shifted away from relying on the idea that I, as the practitioner, am the source of healing. Instead, I'm drawn to use my drum as a space holder and a facilitator of self-discovery and inner wisdom. My role has transformed from that of a 'healer' to a guide. This approach honours women's unique journeys and empowers them to be active participants in their own healing process.

2

ECHOES THROUGH TIME: A SHORT HISTORY OF WOMEN AND DRUMMING

"Because drumming was recognised as an ancient source and symbol of the power of the technicians of the sacred, drumming was banned. Henceforth, divinity was to be exclusively masculine. The suppression of women was directly linked to the suppression of the goddess."

Layne Redmond

In the modern world, drumming is seen as a male activity, so much that it is estimated that there is only one woman drummer for every hundred men (Smith, 2014). The drum is also often perceived as something which evokes feelings of aggression, stereotypically connected to military activities. Therefore, it may come as a surprise to hear that historical evidence shows that, in pre-biblical times, women were the primary keepers of drumming traditions. But we were not taught this in our history lessons, we have no recollection of this innate wisdom, because women's cultural contributions, knowledge and authority have been systematically suppressed, devalued and marginalised over many generations.

"Women often feel that, along with a portion of their history, they're missing a part of their psyche. They have lost access to important regions of their

minds. Until they can reclaim those parts of themselves, they are not whole."

Layne Redmond, *When the Drummers were Women*

When I first read Redmond's book I was struck by a peculiar sensation – a blend of awe and recognition that I've encountered at pivotal moments in my life, such as when I first supported a birth. It was as if I was simultaneously discovering something new and remembering a long-forgotten truth. This feeling of déjà vu suggested a connection to experiences beyond my current lifetime.

I experienced the same sensation in my journey with drumming – when I first held a drum, joined a drum circle or united in drumbeats with other women. These moments created a paradoxical experience of the sacred within the mundane. It was as if I was straddling two realms: one foot in the everyday world, the other in a mystical dimension.

These experiences feel like threads connecting me to a tapestry of women's consciousness, when the veil between the ordinary and the extraordinary thins, where I find myself at the intersection of novelty and familiarity, wonder and recognition.

"Over the years, much of the balance of the masculine and feminine has been lost and we have existed in a patriarchal programming with male dominance for far too long. Most women have forgotten even how to connect and activate their natural intuitive gifts and connection to the divine spirit."

Hollie Hope, *The Healing Power of the Sacred Drum*

When the women were drummers

"The drum is a feminine form, which emulates Mother Earth and the woman's womb…the womb that renews all life and is also the continuing heartbeat at the centre of life."

Brooke Medicine Eagle

A SHORT TIMELINE OF WOMEN'S DRUM HISTORY:

Before 5000 BCE: Women as primary drummers.

- Archaeological evidence shows women as primary keepers of drumming traditions.
- Central roles in ceremonies, healing rituals, community gatherings, fertility rites and life-cycle ceremonies.

3000 BCE – 500 CE: Rise of patriarchal religious structures.

- Shift to male-dominated priesthoods in emerging civilisations.
- Women gradually removed from ceremonial roles and drumming.

500 – 1500 CE: Christian church's influence.

- Church actively suppresses women's ritual music.
- Drumming labelled as "pagan" and dangerous.

1500 – 1800: Age of suppression.

- Colonial expansion destroys Indigenous traditions.
- Witch hunts target women who maintained old practices.

Nineteenth to early twentieth century: institutional exclusion.

- Professional music becomes male-dominated field.
- Women excluded from percussion.

Mid twentieth century to present: Reclamation and revival.

- Women's movement sparks renewed interest.
- Active challenging of gender barriers in drumming.

Layne Redmond's groundbreaking book, *When the Drummers Were Women* (1997), provides a new perspective on the origins of drumming as a predominantly female practice in many parts of the ancient world. Redmond's work explores the history of women as ritual leaders in ancient cultures around the world, with a focus on drumming. It challenges the common misconception that drumming is a predominantly male activity by highlighting archaeological evidence of women as drummers in ancient societies.

"The rituals of the earliest known religions evolved around the beat of frame drums. These regions were founded on the worship of female deities... Women became the first technicians of the sacred, performing religious functions we would today associate with the clergy. [...] Sacred drumming was one of their primary skills."

Redmond explains that in many agrarian cultures, rhythmic percussion music played by women was associated with events like birth, agriculture and the seasons. Drums held sacred powers and were played by priestesses of the goddess to induce trance states during spiritual rituals.

"Priestesses of the Goddess were skilled technicians in its [the frame drum's] uses. They knew which rhythms quickened the life in freshly planted seeds; which facilitated childbirth; and which induced the ecstatic trance of spiritual transcendence. Guided by drumbeats, these sacred drummers could alter their consciousness at will, travelling through the three worlds of the Goddess: the heavens, the earth and the underworld."

Redmond examines drumming traditions in cultures like ancient Egypt, Mesopotamia, Africa, ancient Crete, Ireland and more to demonstrate the central role women once held as ceremonial drummers. The book contains countless archaeological findings and illustrations, cave drawings, goddess figures, carvings and other works of art from ancient times which depict women holding frame drums.

The oldest depiction of a woman drummer was found in Çatalhöyükin Turkey, dating from 7500 BC to 6400 BC. (Redmond, 1997, Smith, 2014). The first named drummer in history was the Mesopotamian drumming priestess Lipushiau, who served as intermediary between divine and human realms. She was the head of the temple for the moon god in the city of Ur in 2380 BC. There is a terracotta figure, found in the City of Ur, representing her playing a balag-di, a small frame drum used in liturgical chanting. (Redmond, 1997; Smith, 2014).

"Drums in those early civilizations were used solely to accompany singing

and dancing or in rituals related to fertility or the growing of crops. No evidence has been found that they were ever used for military marches or for any military purpose."

Angela Smith (2014)

Both Redmond and Smith suggest that the position of women as sacred drummers was eroded over time as patriarchal attitudes spread. Drumming was still used during pagan rituals, but in the 6th century, Pope John III banned playing of the tambourine. Church leaders felt that singing and drumming were connected to heathenism (Smith, 2014) and percussive music was banned as "mischievous" and "licentious" (Hart, 1990).

Alongside the removal of drums as objects of spiritual power, modern cultures fear trance, something the drum is known to induce. Josh Schrei, author of The Emerald podcast, argues that the distrust of trance states in modern Western culture stems largely from issues of control and power. This distrust led to bans on drumming in religious contexts as Christianity spread, both in European populations and colonised countries (Schrei 2021).

"Far from being a 'primitive' instrument, the drum is advanced technology – more often than not, it is the essential instrument that opens up the doorway to states of rapture. This long-known power has led to the development of intricate cultures of trance drumming from West Africa to Cuba to Tibet to Scandinavia. This power has also led the drum to be vilified, even banned. Seventeenth century European witch trials banned ritual drumming, even, in some cases, executing drummers."

Josh Schrei

The fear of trance also relates to the dualist worldview in Western culture that cannot reconcile being both rational and civilised while also experiencing 'out of control' states (Schrei, 2021). According to Schrei, distrust of trance is entangled with power dynamics. Schrei suggests that both institutionalised religion and science have pathologised trance states, effectively delegitimising these experiences and exerting control over how people perceive and engage with altered states of consciousness. Unsurprisingly, drumming was also banned among enslaved populations in eighteenth-century South Carolina, with the code stating that, *"All due care be taken to restrain…the using or keeping of drums, horns, or other loud instruments, which may call together or give sign or notice to one another of their wicked designs and purposes."* (Sullivan 2019.)

A population that regularly enters trance states is much harder to control. Altered states of consciousness foster independent thinking, spiritual experiences, and a deeper connection to one's intuition and inner wisdom, making individuals less susceptible to external manipulation and more likely to question authority or societal norms. Is it therefore not surprising that totalitarian regimes often ban music and dance. A recent example of this is the the Taliban implemented a new morality law in September 2024, that includes severe restrictions on women's rights, including a ban on singing. Afghan women have taken to the internet to protest by posting videos of themselves singing.

"It is no exaggeration to say that all popular modern music is based on what were once African ritual trance rhythms. In this way, the recent history of drumming has a lot to teach us about how the postmodern mind – in a culture that outwardly marginalizes trance states – still longs for trance, and what it looks like when trance rituals are taken out of their traditional context and become more of a free-for-all."

Josh Schrei

The erasure of shamanism

The practice of shamanism has existed in various forms across cultures worldwide for thousands of years. Shamans, serving as intermediaries between the physical and spiritual worlds, have been integral to many Indigenous societies in Asia, Africa, the Americas and Oceania. Shamanic practitioners typically use altered states of consciousness to interact with the spirit world, often employing tools such as drums, rattles, or psychoactive plants to facilitate their journeys. Shamanic practices commonly involve healing, divination and maintaining harmony between humans and nature.

The history of shamanism in Europe is also rich and varied, spanning back thousands of years. Various European cultures, including the Celtic, Viking, Germanic and Sámi people, practiced shamanism, which involved connecting with the spiritual realms through drumming, chanting and other rituals. Shamans, known by different names in different cultures (e.g., druids, seidhr), also used drums as a tool for trance induction and journeying to commune with spirits, seek guidance and perform healing ceremonies to accompany life and death.

We need to remember that the Roman conquest of Europe led to a profound erasure of Indigenous cultures and spiritual practices, leaving modern Europeans disconnected from their ancestral wisdom and traditions.

"We know about the land that has been stolen and all that this implies; the destruction of culture and language and ceremonies, of food systems; the attempt to annihilate a vast diversity of ways of life."

Rachelle Seliga (2024)

With the spread of Christianity across Europe, shamanic traditions and practices were suppressed and demonised as pagan or heretical. Shamanic drumming, along with other shamanic rituals, faced persecution and was actively discouraged by religious authorities. Many Indigenous cultures had their spiritual practices banned and knowledge of shamanic drumming was lost or went underground. The same happened worldwide during colonisation.

The drumming traditions that survived into modern times tend to come from cultures living in remote areas that were difficult for religious evangelists or colonialists to access. For instance, the Sámi people of northern Scandinavia and the Mongolian shamans maintained their long-standing drumming practices. These groups, inhabiting lands distant from centres of colonial control, managed to preserve some of their cultural drumming heritage, despite suffering the same attempts to destroy their culture as the rest of the world.

Corinne Sombrun is a French ethnomusicologist, writer and shaman who spent nine years training with a Tsataan woman shaman, Enkhetuya, in the grasslands of outer Mongolia. In her book, *Les Esprits de la Steppe* (The Spirits of the Steppe), Sombrun explains that around the mid-twentieth century, the Soviet regime sought to suppress traditional and religious practices, including shamanism, which was seen as backward and counter-revolutionary. The government made practising shamanism illegal, confiscating or destroying drums and putting shamans in jail. During Enkhetuya's childhood, her parents carried on practising rituals in secret, which allowed her to be identified and trained as a shaman (Sombrun, 2012).

In Europe too, remnants of shamanic traditions persisted in some regions, particularly in remote areas. In the northern parts of Europe, such as Lapland and Siberia, the Sámi continued their shamanic practices, including drumming, despite suffering the same fate as their Mongolian counterparts.

In the twentieth century, there was a resurgence of interest in shamanic practices and spirituality. Influenced by a growing recognition of the value of Indigenous knowledge, shamanic drumming began to experience a revival.

Layne Redmond was instrumental in this revival for women, through her performances, teachings and her book *When the Drummers Were Women.* She helped spark a revival of women's frame drumming. This revival highlighted drumming's ancient roots in goddess-based civilisations and female spiritual leadership, inspiring many modern women drummers.

More recently, some people in Europe have started reviving ancient drumming traditions:

Peter Ananin, at the Woodland Tannery in Scotland, is the only person today making traditional Scottish Wecht Drums. The Wecht drum, a large shallow frame drum, has a unique history and purpose. Named after a farm implement used for winnowing grain due to its similar shape and size, its primary use was not musical but practical, serving a role in Scottish agricultural communities for processing corn and wool.

Finnish drum artist Juha Jarvinen realised that there were only about seventy traditional northern drums remaining in existence, most were kept in museums. Nobody was making such drums anymore, nor playing them. He decided to make one hundred drums to reclaim this tradition. He has met this goal, and he now aims to make one thousand (Jarvinen, 2022). I am the lucky owner of two of his beautiful drums, one of which he custom made at my request, to be used to support birth, with a carving of a birthing woman's opening energy field built into the handle.

There are also examples of governments trying to repair the harm that was done to shamanic cultures during colonisation. A Sámi drum which was confiscated during a witch trial in Denmark in the seventeenth century was recently returned to the Sámi people (Russell 2021). Norwegian Sámi singer Mari Boine has reclaimed traditional Sámi music and drumming. Boine adapts the distinctive Sámi vocal style – *joik* – and incorporates traditional Sámi drums alongside other contemporary instrumentation. This is a beautiful example of modern revival by contemporary artists connecting back to their cultural roots.

It's important to note that the relationship with drums in Sámi culture remains complex and, in some regions, deeply painful. While there are examples of revival and reclamation, in many Sámi communities the drum continues to be a sensitive symbol of cultural loss and historical trauma. Some areas still maintain cultural protocols and taboos around drumming that stem from the period of drum destruction. Similar challenges are likely to exist across many other regions in the world where drumming was banned and where the impacts of governmental suppression of drumming practices continue to reverberate today, even as communities work to reconnect with these traditions.

As women, we carry a double burden of historical trauma around drumming – in the general suppression of Indigenous spiritual practices (including European ones) and the specific targeting of people who dared to maintain these traditions, and in the systematic subjugation of women since the inception of patriarchy, and the removal of objects of power that accompanied it. Throughout history, men and women have been persecuted, and in some cases killed, for keeping their Indigenous spiritual practices alive. The ancestral memory of persecution lives in our collective consciousness, which helps explain why many women today might feel an inexplicable fear or resistance when first approaching the drum. Understanding this historical context helps us understand that the fear unworthiness we may feel when called to use a drum maybe due to a natural response to a complex cultural legacy, rather than just personal limitations.

There's also a resurgence of shamanic drumming in modern music. A prime example is Heilung, an experimental folk band that incorporates ancient Germanic, Iron Age and Viking traditions into their music, drawing inspiration from historical texts and runic inscriptions. They describe their music as amplified history from early medieval northern Europe and state on their YouTube channel that they *"try to connect the listener to the time before Christianity and its political offsprings raped and burned itself into the northern European mentality."* Heilung considers the drum the most important instrument. They aim to alter the conscious state of mind of their audience and use knowledge about how certain rhythms can alter brainwaves in their performances.

This modern resurgence of drumming means that drumming circles and workshops can be found in many countries around the world, providing people with a means to explore altered states of consciousness, connect with their inner selves and each other, and tap into spiritual dimensions. This revival, which is gaining in popularity, often draws inspiration from both Indigenous traditions and shamanic practices worldwide.

In 2024, Dutch drummer Dennis Wessier organised the global drum gathering, which included several hundred drum circles taking place across over forty different countries on the same day, aiming to create a wave of healing energy across the world. On that day I led a drum circle, where over twenty of us, mostly women, walked to the top of a hill overlooking Cambridge, to join in the worldwide drumming event and drum. We drummed with the intention to send an energy of grounding, healing and connection to the city and the world. It was both touching and powerful.

Drums played by women today

Today there are still a few remaining traditions of drums that are played mostly by women around Europe. These include the Portuguese adufe and the Middle Eastern daf.

The adufe (also known as pandeiro quadrado in Portuguese) is a double-skinned square frame drum originating from the Iberian Peninsula, specifically Portugal and Spain. Traditionally, the adufe is played almost exclusively by women. These female players are known as adufeiras. The instrument has ancient roots, with origins traced back to North Africa. It has been documented in medieval Iberian literature, architecture and iconography. The adufe serves as an artistic outlet and has historical associations with religion, ritual, agriculture, fertility and sexual symbolism. The adufe's frequent association with springtime and Easter continues its old link with fertility, as does the long association between frame drums and winnowing sieves (Cohen, 2008).

There is a Kurdish version of the daf, called the erbane, which is played mostly by women. While it was the ancient instrument for weddings, funerals and laments, it also served as a spiritual sound that was thought to cure fear and diseases. Drum teacher Jiyan Tekçe says the erbane drum is a woman's rebellion against patriarchal society and a cry for peace:

"It is a woman's cry, her voice, her sadness, her happiness. A woman expresses her own feelings with the erbane. […] The woman created the erbane because it best reflects her feelings. There is an accumulation of thousands of years in every rhythm. In these lands where pain is always present, women's voices echo with the erbane. The erbane is the woman's cry for peace. Therefore, it has a special value for Kurdish society. As long as the woman exists, the erbane will also exist." (Tekçe 2022.)

Reclaiming the systrum
– Tahya

For fifty years I have dedicated myself to the study, practice and sharing of drumming and dance practices deeply steeped in millennia-old traditions – all leading to my amassing an extensive vocabulary of rhythm and dance practices we can use to arise and revive our confidence and grace These practices have helped me build community, develop deeper states of awareness, elevate my joyful self and enliven the creative spirit within.

Drumming and dance have always proven for me to be a (necessary and) beautiful balance to life's challenges, while also facilitating the full expression of the complexity and fullness of Being in this body for this lifetime's journey. These practices buoy me along what I call the River of Life. They help me navigate rough waters, attune to inner guidance and intuition, celebrate momentous occasions and connect me with an ever-expanding circle of kindred spirits!

From an early age I was referred to as a 'chubby' child which resulted in my being a timid insecure girl with low self-esteem. Thankfully, in my late teens, I was introduced to the circular and spiral movements of belly dance, a celebration of women's bodies and femininity – every age, every body (type). Simultaneously I was taught to play hypnotic rhythms on the frame drum and finger cymbals, while also learning these practices dated back thousands of years to matrilineal goddess-worshipping cultures in which women gathered in support of one another during the phases of the moon moving ceremonially with drums in hand; and I blossomed into a confident woman with drumming and dance as the cornerstones of a rich and meaningful life.

Furthermore, the practice of drumming and its ability to calm the mind has awakened in me the ability to fully attune to my 'soul whisperings'. For example, following travels to Egypt in 2007, I found myself experiencing what I can only describe as being "beckoned" by the Egyptian Goddess Hathor 'commissioning' me to re-emerge the systrum in the twenty-first century (and at the time, I knew very little about this ancient Egyptian deity). I began a journey of deep research that ultimately led to the design and manufacture of a beautiful instrument deeply embedded in ancient Egyptian tradition, learning more about one of the most beloved deities of the ancient Egyptian pantheon the Goddess Hathor – and about musician (percussion) priestesses and chantresses, who used the frame drum and the sacred percussion instrument known as the sistrum/systrum!

Remembering and reconnecting with ancient rhythmic practices associated with the frame drum and sistrum/systrum recovers the power of personal creativity; returning their use to our daily lives in the modern era, we invoke the divine in our homes, in our lives and into our communities to create harmonising healing pathways for the upliftment of ourselves and humanity at large.

Women and drum circles today

"Traditions that once honored the feminine became focused on controlling and silencing the wisdoms of mysteries of women. This applies to many areas of our lives, especially at home, in religions and in the workforce. Women originally were the wisdom keepers of primal civilizations over the globe, dispersing power, love and healing in matriarchal societies. Sexualizing and socializing may have once robbed us of our intuitive leadership rights, but we are reclaiming them more and more every day."

Hollie Hope

Since I started running my drum circle in 2020, one thing has been clear: despite my drum circle being open to everyone, it is mostly attended by women. This was true right from the first circle, where I had about fifteen attendees and only one man. And it is still true four years later. I usually have between fifteen and twenty-five people attending and it is almost always 80% women.

I know the same to be true for several of my friends who run drum circles and when I attended a mixed gender UK Drum Convention in the spring of 2024, with over 150 attendees, once again, about 80% or more of them were women.

From my experience of facilitating drum circles, of witnessing women's transformative experiences in drum healing rituals, of supporting them through the birth journey and through other life transitions, it is clear that there is a deep visceral longing within women, to re-establish a sense of connection to the sacred. The drum, with its primal rhythms, provides a powerful conduit to access this realm.

In our modern world, so driven by productivity, rationality and a disconnection from natural cycles and the divine, women often find themselves adrift and this is even more true when experiencing periods of deep growth and transformation (puberty, becoming a mother, menopause and other times of deep transformation during a woman's life). Drumming offers a pathway to step away from the mundane and reunite with our sacred essence.

As the drum's vibrations move through their bodies, women remember the creative well within. The drum serves as a symbolic re-integration of the sacred feminine, so often subjugated throughout patriarchal history. Whether consciously or unconsciously, this profound calling draws women to the drum – a deep remembering that, by immersing themselves in its rhythm, they can find belonging, community, healing and spiritual wholeness.

Carolyn Brandy articulates this extremely well in her article, "Global Movement of Women Playing Drums":

"I believe that there is a Global Movement of Women playing drums on the planet at this time. There are thousands and thousands of women playing drums all over the world. This would not seem so incredible, except for the fact that in the majority of cultures of the world, drums have been strictly forbidden for women to play for eons. This taboo is part of the psychological and spiritual acculturation that claims that the female and that nature is inferior. Women have been so brainwashed and tortured that we actually have believed this ourselves for centuries.

"Why are we waking up now? Because the planet's very existence as we know it is threatened because we are so out of balance. The force of technology, destruction, greed and constriction has become so strong that the creative, nurturing, expansive power of the planet, a complete and conscious living

organism, has to come into balance in order to survive. I believe that this movement of women drummers is a manifestation of this waking up and process of evolving consciousness."

Brandy (2008)

I asked women why they attend drum circles and this is what they said:

Although drumming alone is wonderful and brings me peace, clarity and provides a sanctuary from my busy home life, drumming in a group is a different experience and brings me deep joy and a feeling of bone deep rightness that I cannot always replicate by myself. The experience of community intention is something that I miss profoundly when I don't have access to a circle. It brings community, shared intentions and a lasting feeling of being grounded in the now.

Jo

For me, it was like I was doing something I've already done before.

Datura

The communal spiritual nature of the activity, the ancient connection to the mother goddess.

Beverley

It's just a moving experience. It's carnal and emotional. It goes deep within. It's kind of hard to explain.

Irene

The feeling of unity, togetherness, feeling the ancestors around us, connection to past lives and to true self /soul.

Asia

It teaches me to accept whatever happens. Drumming and singing can take me to the NOW. I love the ecstatic vibe and the connection with other drummers and manifesting something magical through the unified sounds vibrations. It is a healing space, beyond words and everyone adds to the magic.

Era

It is pure energy in the present moment, without the mask of the ego.

Shash

I become one with the drumbeat and I don't think about anything else. To share the rhythm and sense of connection is very special. In a world where being alone and disconnected is the norm, to have shared purpose and rhythm is very enriching.

Jan

One of the most powerful and magical experiences of my life was at a women's gathering in the US, where a group of experienced women drummers drummed for hours as a massive bonfire was lit, ceremony was done and then we danced whooping and cheering round and around, shedding our clothes as we went. Over a hundred women, most naked, fire reflecting off our skins – all different shapes and sizes and ages and colours – the rhythm weaving through our bodies. It was a primal experience, one that I know our very first ancestors would also have experienced: ecstatic elemental embodied unity of humans, fire and drums. How I wish this were a part of contemporary culture, that more people could experience it, I can't help thinking what a different world we would inhabit if this was how we partied…and worshipped.

Lucy H. Pearce

I think that today, we are returning to rhythm. So more and more there's an idea of "maybe I can learn to drum". I have a woman in my djembe class right now, a West African style of drumming. She's a woman of a certain age, who told us this is the first musical instrument she has ever learned to play! And that's the beauty of it, I think. You know, we can all move, we can all sing. If you can walk, you can dance. If you can talk, you can sing. And we can all drum, as long as we get out of our own way. I once had a student who said 'The only thing I ever learned to play was the radio.' But the drum is just such a natural thing. We can bring together a circle of people and in one hour, we're making music together.

Barbara Gail

3

VIBRATIONS OF WELLBEING: THE SCIENCE OF DRUMMING AND PHYSICAL HEALTH

"It has been said that the drums are one of the few instruments that access the entire brain, stimulating all the main sectors. Active engagement of practically playing rhythms aid in syncing the left and right hemispheres of the brain; leaving us feeling more connected with ourselves."

Lee Havenga

In this chapter, I will provide an overview of the research I have found on how drumming affects the brain, body, mind and spirit. I will be referencing published, peer-reviewed studies about the tremendous positive effects of drumming that have been substantiated by contemporary scientific research, which corroborates what humans have intuitively known since time immemorial.

Although research on drumming goes as far back as the 1940s, the first-ever paper studying the effect of shamanic trance on the brain was only published in 2017! I believe we are going to see a lot more research in this area in the near future, in the same way that we have seen an acceleration of research on psychedelics and mental health, since 2015.

To the best of my knowledge at the time I am writing this, no such broad review of the scientific literature, stories and books is yet available. I used classical research tools such as PubMed and Google Scholar to find papers.

I also researched the subject with new academic AI tools such as Semantics Scholar, Elicit and Consensus. I read many books and articles. I cannot claim to have covered every single paper, article or book that exists on the subject of drumming and wellbeing, but I hope to have covered the topic in enough depth to make a clear case about drumming's solid, scientifically proven benefits.

I feel that it is important to provide, because not only is the research truly mind-blowing, but if we are to overcome scepticism, the approach that works best in our world is to use published research to act as a bridge which helps open people's minds. In offering science as a bridge, we can guide people safely to access their own personal experience of what drumming does.

Facing bias and scepticism

Despite the fact that the scientific evidence is mounting on the impact of drumming, and that some of the recent research uses cutting-edge technology such as 3D neuroimaging brain scans, the inherent biases in our culture mean that we can still tend to dismiss it as pseudoscience. When I interviewed drummer and drum researcher Jeff Strong for my podcast, I asked him why this was so little-known despite the evidenced healing effects and the fact that he had himself been doing this kind of research since the 1990s. Jeff explained that drumming is still perceived as too esoteric for our modern world and that he even actively avoids using the term "drumming" because of this, preferring to use the term "rhythmic entrainment" instead.

I have faced such disbelief and dismissal myself. In 2023, I published the first ever article about drumming and birth in a scientific journal. When I started to share my findings on social media (including references to research that shows that drumming increases the release of endorphins, the body's natural painkiller), someone replied: "Drumming to alleviate the pain of childbirth? How ridiculous. What's next, bagpipes?". Ignorant comments like this one illustrate what we are up against when we want to bring forth something that appears to fly in the face of the current paradigm.

If drumbeats were produced by a modern, high-tech device with a sleek interface and digital displays, rather than a traditional instrument like a frame drum, they would likely be more readily accepted. Imagine a state-of-the-art computerised digital drum pad or even a smartphone app – such a setup would probably be perceived as more legitimate and scientifically valid and applauded for its technical prowess…

This shift in perception highlights our cultural bias towards technology and 'progress'. A digital drum machine or an AI-powered rhythm generator might be seen as more credible or effective simply because it aligns with our contemporary tech-loving landscape.

This preference for modern, digital solutions over traditional, analogue methods reflects a tendency to equate novelty with efficacy, often at the expense of simpler, time-tested practices. It is the product of a colonialist mindset which is still, albeit in a mostly unconscious and covert way, very much alive.

A colonialist mindset unconsciously biases our thinking, making us believe that shiny new gadgets must be better than ancient wisdom. It blinds us to the power of traditional practices. Just as colonisers dismissed Indigenous people as 'uneducated savages', we often write off traditional knowledge as 'unscientific nonsense', blindly choosing the latest 'advanced' tech over practices that have nourished cultures for millennia.

This colonialist perspective also manifests in the subtle devaluation of Indigenous and traditional practices, viewing them as primitive compared to Western technological innovations. It shows a hierarchy of knowledge where Western scientific methods and technologies are placed at the top, while ancient wisdom and practices are relegated to the realm of superstition. This bias not only limits our understanding and appreciation of diverse cultural practices but potentially deprives us of valuable insights and effective methods that have been refined over centuries. It reflects a larger pattern of cultural erasure and the homogenisation of global practices towards a Western model.

By recognising this bias, we can begin to challenge these assumptions and work towards a more inclusive and holistic approach that values both traditional wisdom and modern innovations. Progress doesn't always mean discarding the old for the new.

This bias also overlooks the unique qualities and benefits of traditional drumming – the connection, the ever-changing vibration and the direct human involvement that contribute so significantly to its effects. Presentation and cultural context can strongly influence our acceptance of practices, even when their core function remains the same.

Despite being a drum convert, I've noticed in myself a tendency to dismiss how valid the research is. I can understand how a lot of people might feel when being told about drumming and what it can do. If this is you (though I doubt complete sceptics would actually be reading this book!), I hope that after reading this chapter you may look at drumming differently.

Another aspect to keep in mind is that research itself is fundamentally biased because we live in a WEIRD society. I am grateful to anthropologist and doula Elle Fleming, who introduced me to this acronym, which stands for Western, Educated, Industrialised, Rich Democratic Societies. It was coined by anthropologist Joseph Henrich in the paper "The weirdest people in the world?" (Henrich 2010). The authors found that 96% of subjects from behavioural science were from Western industrialised countries. Yet these countries only represent 12% of the world's population.

This highlights a significant problem in how we understand what normal human behaviour is. The over-representation of WEIRD populations in scientific studies leads to a narrow and potentially skewed view of human nature. What we consider 'universal' human traits may, in fact, be specific to a small, unrepresentative subset of humanity. Moreover, this WEIRD-centric approach in research perpetuates a cycle where Western perspectives are overvalued, and other worldviews are marginalised. It leads to the dismissal of traditional practices, including those related to physical and mental health, simply because they don't align with WEIRD norms.

When I started supporting families as a doula twelve years ago, I witnessed regular examples of misguided and sometimes harmful advice given by maternity care professionals to new parents. I soon realised that, if we wanted to know what was normal for our species, we should turn to anthropologists instead of medical professionals. Recognising this bias is crucial for developing a more inclusive and accurate understanding of human diversity. It calls for a re-evaluation of research methodologies, increased cross-cultural studies and a more humble approach to generalising findings.

However, and this gives me immense hope, the times are changing. People and the world are more open and eager to understand things beyond just the flesh. One person who illustrates this beautifully is French ethnomusicologist Corine Sombrun. Sombrun was identified as having unique shamanic abilities by Mongolian shamans. After training with them over a period of nine years, she became the first Western woman fully trained in the Mongolian shamanic tradition. She came back to Paris with her new-found knowledge and spent a decade banging her head against the medical and scientific community, trying to convince them to study what happened to her brain during trance. They were all dismissive at first, telling her that her brain behaved like someone with a psychiatric illness and told her to stop her trance work immediately.

Fortunately, Sombrun ignored them. Intent on making research advance in this field, she eventually forged collaborations with researchers who shared her vision to understand the mechanisms associated with trance states. These pioneering research efforts culminated in the first ever scientific publication on Mongolian shamanic trance (Flor-Henry et al., 2017), marking a significant milestone in the field.

Sombrun went on to co-found the Trance Science Research Institute, an organisation that unites an international network of researchers devoted to exploring the mechanisms and therapeutic applications of self-induced trance. Currently, the institute is spearheading several ongoing research projects, investigating the impact of trance on diverse areas such as creativity, self-awareness, psychotherapy, post-traumatic states, functional motor rehabilitation and psychiatry. In 2023, a new university diploma course was started at University Paris 8, called *"Etude des transes et des états de conscience modifiés"* (the study of trances and altered states of consciousness).

Holism

Before I share my findings, I want to offer a caveat: drumming is a multisensory experience which affects all aspects of ourselves. This isn't reflected in the way Western research is constructed, because our research likes to look at small, isolated aspects as if they were independent from one another.

When I started reviewing the research, I wanted to understand how drumming works on all levels and how it affects different aspects of our bodies: the physiology and hormones, the nervous system, the auditory and vibration aspects…I wanted to put it all together and I was frustrated to discover that most pieces of work only focus on one tiny part of the whole.

Then I realised – of course it does, because this is the society we live in: one that likes to categorise and break things down into fragments, without being able to go back and understand how they all interact together. Research is conducted much in the way a child pulls a toy apart to understand how it works. The problem is that this approach only works if there are few parts and the interaction between them is simple. So, except maybe one or two review papers, most of the research I share focuses on small, set variables, separated from the whole. I wish it were different, because, despite being a scientist for twenty years, I have always been more of a 'bird's eye view' person than a 'fine details' one.

So, before I share the various categories of research, I want to re-emphasise how drumming affects the whole of us, mind, body and spirit. Beyond our physiology, drumming also often provides something that is also deeply lacking in our culture, which is a sense of connection to ourselves, to the world around us and to each other. It is not surprising that drumming groups have so many benefits.

What makes this topic even more complex is that the research has been done using many different kinds of drums, from drum kits to shamanic drums to djembes and more. But it doesn't matter, because the same benefits seem to appear regardless of what kind of drums are used.

Before I share the research, I want to give you a vivid reminder of what a drumming experience feels like to all of our senses:

As the drum is struck, it creates a complex ripple of sensations that resonate through the body and mind. The deep tones vibrate through the air and are not just heard by the ears but felt in the body, in particular in the chest and abdomen. This can create a physical sensation of being enveloped by sound, as if the rhythm is pulsing through your entire being.

The visual aspect of drumming adds another layer to the experience. The sight of hands or beaters striking the drum creates a visual rhythm that synchronises with the auditory experience. This visual-auditory connection can enhance the perception of the rhythm and contribute to the trance-like effect of drumming.

Touch-wise, the drummer feels the impact of each strike reverberating through their hands and arms. The tension of the drumhead, the resistance it offers and the subtle variations in texture all contribute to a sensory feedback loop that informs and guides the playing.

The olfactory sense might also be engaged, with the scent of wood, hide, or other materials used in the drum's construction, adding to the overall experience.

Emotionally and psychologically, drumming can evoke a range of responses. The repetitive beat can induce a sense of grounding and connection to the present moment. The act of drumming, whether alone or in a group, can foster a sense of expression, release or communion.

The multisensory, holistic experience of drumming transcends the sum of its parts, creating an experience that can be deeply moving, meditative or energising. It's this complexity and totality of experience that makes drumming such a powerful tool across various cultural and therapeutic contexts.

Effects caused by the vibrations of the drum

Modern science tends to examine biomarkers in isolation, without taking into consideration how they interact with each other. I want to paint a more holistic picture about how drumming affects every part of our body, mind and spirit. By exploring how drumming's vibrations impact various bodily systems, we can better understand the interconnected nature of its benefits.

We have all experienced the direct effects of vibrations on our bodies. If we have attended a concert, especially one where the music is being conveyed through deep bass speakers, we have all felt the vibration inside our abdomen. It is clear to me that drumming affects our bodies, minds and spirits through the vibrations it produces as well as the sound. Drumming is one of the few activities that integrate several brain functions all at once: body movement, decision making, musical awareness and emotional state. It also affects our state of consciousness, our nervous system and our physiology.

I haven't been able to find studies that specifically looked at this aspect using drums, and discussing this in person with Jeff Strong confirmed that the research on this appears non-existent.

There is some research available about sound healing in general, and what is true for sound healing applies to drumming too: sound healing works through the principle of vibration and its effects on the human body and mind. Here's an explanation of how sound healing works:

SOUND HEALING AND VIBRATIONAL ENERGY

Sound healing is based on the concept that everything in the universe, including our bodies, is in a state of vibration. This understanding draws from both physics – where we know that all matter consists of atoms in constant motion – and observations of how different frequencies of sound can influence our physical, mental and emotional states.

Sound healing is the therapeutic use of sound frequencies to transition patients to a state of harmony and well-being. It can be administered live using instruments (drums, rattles, Tibetan bowls, crystal bowls, gongs, tuning forks, voice and more) or through listening to recordings of the same instruments.

Research in this field examines how various sound frequencies interact with our bodies' natural rhythms and biological systems, potentially influencing everything from our brainwaves to our cellular activity. Nicholas Kerna and colleagues carried out a scientific review of the effects of sound therapy (Kerna 2022).

The review covered the historical context of sound healing, explaining that it has ancient roots (40,000+ years) across many cultures, that the first sound healers were Aboriginal Australians who used the didgeridoo for healing. Ancient Greeks, Egyptians, Indian, Chinese and Tibetan medicine traditions had sound healing practices. Modern sound therapy was pioneered by Sir Peter Guy Manners in the 1950s.

Kerna and colleagues explain that sound healing's effects are based on the following principles:

- **Resonance and entrainment:** Sound healing uses the principles of resonance and entrainment. Entrainment refers to how a dominant rhythm can synchronise with a weaker rhythm. It is relevant to how brainwave frequencies can align with sound frequencies to encourage relaxation or focus. Resonance often operates at the cellular level, where the body's own frequencies synchronise with external vibrations.
- **Effect on the nervous system:** The vibrations produced by sound

healing directly affect the nervous system. These vibrations can help shift the body from a state of stress (fight, flight or freeze response) to a state of relaxation, activating the parasympathetic nervous system.

- **Frequency range:** Every human organ has its own resonance frequency, with normal organ frequencies ranging from 3-17 Hz. Higher frequencies generally indicate better health. Sound healing instruments range from 4-1000 Hz +. Sound vibrations can affect the body at a cellular level, potentially influencing cellular processes and promoting healing.
- **Key applications and benefits:** Sound healing has been shown to reduce stress and anxiety, improve sleep quality, help with pain management, support emotional healing, be a useful complementary cancer treatment and assist with muscle recovery and rehabilitation.

In summary, sound healing works by using specific frequencies and vibrations to influence the body's physical state and nervous system, promoting relaxation, healing and overall well-being. While more research is needed to fully understand its mechanisms, existing studies and anecdotal evidence highlight its potential as a complementary therapy.

Drumming and hormonal health

Hormonal health is crucial for women's overall well-being. It influences not just reproductive functions, but also impacts mental health, energy levels, metabolism and even cognitive function. A balanced hormonal system contributes to emotional stability, physical vitality and resilience against stress.

The research I share in this chapter shows that incorporating rhythmic activities like drumming into a holistic health approach could be beneficial for women's hormonal health, offering a natural and enjoyable way to support endocrine balance.

As researchers delve deeper into the physiological and psychological impacts of drumming practice, they are uncovering a range of surprising benefits. From improvements in physical health to positive changes in hormone levels, the evidence supporting drumming as a holistic health intervention is mounting.

The review paper by Yap et al. referenced in the previous section also shows that:

"Six studies have shown that RMM has led to improvements in pain tolerance, balance, pulmonary function, blood pressure and immunological profiles of individuals. It has also been shown to improve parkinsonian tremors, finger dexterity, coordination and upper body stiffness."

Let's explore some of the key findings from recent studies, focusing on how drumming affects certain vital hormones in the body:

Oxytocin

Oxytocin is often referred to as the "love hormone" or "bonding hormone" due to its crucial role in social bonding, emotional attachment and intimacy. This neuropeptide is produced in the hypothalamus and released by the pituitary gland. It plays a vital role in various physiological and psychological processes. It's well-known for its involvement in childbirth and breastfeeding, where it facilitates uterine contractions and milk release.

Beyond these reproductive functions, oxytocin is instrumental in fostering social connections, promoting trust and reducing anxiety. It's released during positive social interactions, physical touch and activities that promote bonding, such as hugging or sharing a meal. Oxytocin has been shown to reduce stress responses, lower blood pressure and even improve wound healing. In the context of mental health, it's being studied for its potential role in treating conditions like depression, anxiety and autism, due to its ability to modulate social behaviour and emotional responses.

A study examined the effects of Taiko-Ensou, a Japanese group drumming practice, on emotionally disturbed children living in group homes due to separation from their primary caregivers. The research focused on changes in salivary oxytocin levels. Oxytocin levels were found to increase after drumming sessions, ranging from 112% to 165% of baseline levels (Yuki 2017).

Cortisol and DHEA

Cortisol, often referred to as the "stress hormone", plays a crucial role in the body's stress response and overall homeostasis. Produced by the adrenal glands, cortisol is released in response to stress, low blood glucose and other physiological triggers. It helps regulate metabolism, reduces inflammation and assists in controlling blood sugar levels.

Cortisol also influences memory formation, supports the immune system and affects blood pressure. While essential for survival, chronic elevation of cortisol due to prolonged stress can have negative health effects, including weight gain, impaired cognitive performance and weakened immune function.

Cortisol levels typically follow a diurnal rhythm, peaking in the morning to help us wake up and gradually decreasing throughout the day. Maintaining balanced cortisol levels is crucial for overall health and well-being, affecting everything from energy levels and mood to sleep patterns and immune function.

Another hormone that works together with cortisol is dehydroepiandrosterone (DHEA). This hormone is produced by our adrenal glands, which sit on top of our kidneys. DHEA is often called a "precursor hormone" because our bodies use it to make other hormones, including testosterone and oestrogen. DHEA is often considered an "anti-stress" hormone. It can help balance out the effects of cortisol, the primary stress hormone.

A study investigated the effects of group drumming on stress-related hormones and immune function. The research involved one hundred and eleven participants and compared various drumming protocols against control groups. The results showed that group drumming led to significant physiological changes, in particular, a reduction in stress. This was shown by an increased DHEA-to-cortisol ratio, indicating a decrease in the stress hormone cortisol relative to the "anti-stress" hormone DHEA. The researchers concluded that group drumming can counteract the typical stress response (Bittman, 2001).

Endorphins

Endorphins are naturally occurring chemicals produced by the body, often referred to as "feel-good" hormones. These neurotransmitters are released by the pituitary gland and the central nervous system in response to various stimuli, including pain, stress, exercise and certain foods.

Endorphins play a crucial role in pain management by binding to opioid receptors in the brain, reducing the perception of pain and producing a sense of euphoria or well-being. They are responsible for the "runner's high" experienced during intense physical activity. Beyond pain relief, endorphins help regulate mood, reduce stress and anxiety, boost self-esteem and may even enhance immune system function.

They also contribute to the feelings of pleasure associated with activities like eating, social bonding and sex. The release of endorphins is one of the body's natural ways of managing stress and promoting overall emotional and physical well-being.

A study demonstrated that active musical performance, including drumming, increases endorphin release. The endorphin increase was linked to the physical act of making music, not just the auditory experience of music. It was associated with an elevated mood. The researchers used pain threshold as an indicator of endorphin release, as endorphins are known to increase pain tolerance (Dunbar 2012).

Immune system and heart

Group drumming has been shown to cause a shift away from a pro-inflammatory immune profile and towards an anti-inflammatory one (Fancourt et al., 2016). It is now recognised that many mental health conditions are characterised by underlying inflammatory immune responses (Fancourt et al., 2016) and the Fancourt study also looked at mental health aspect (more on that in the part on drumming and mental health).

Another study on group drumming showed increased natural killer cell activity (our body's first line of defence against viruses and certain cancers – an increase in their activity means a more robust immune response) and increased lymphokine-activated killer cell activity (Bittman, 2001). Again, this makes sense because drumming relaxes us, therefore our immune system, which is known to be impaired by stress (think survival and preservation of resources) is positively impacted by the calming effect of drumming.

Heart health

Drumming literally heals your heart, not just in the spiritual sense (though I believe this is also an important reason why drumming is good for the heart), but in a direct physical way too. In a study involving djembe drumming, a forty-minute session was shown to improve cardiovascular health, as shown by a reduction in blood pressure post-drumming (Smith et al., 2014).

Drumming, the drum kit kind in particular, can provide significant cardiovascular benefits, similar to other forms of exercise. It can raise your heart rate, and burn between 400-600 calories per hour, comparable to going for a run. Regular drumming can therefore improve cardiovascular health and increase stamina (Whitherhall, 2024).

In a study where people were exposed to either relaxing music or shamanic drumming, with instructions of either using the music for relaxation or for shamanic journeying (guided instructions of finding an entrance point to a different world/space and then returning to it at the end), people in the drum journeying group experienced a decreased heart rate significantly more often than participants exposed to repetitive drumming or music with relaxation instructions alone (Gingras et al 2014).

4

PERCUSSION AND THE PSYCHE: DRUMMING'S RESONANCE IN BRAIN, NERVES AND HEALING

"One of the most powerful aspects of drumming and the reason people have done it since the beginning of being human is that it changes people's consciousness. Through rhythmic repetition of ritual sounds, the body, the brain and the nervous system are energised and transformed. When a group of people play a rhythm for an extended period of time, their brainwaves become entrained to the rhythm, and they have a shared brainwave state. The longer the drumming goes on, the more powerful the entrainment becomes. It's really the oldest holy communion."

Layne Redmond

How drumming supports wellbeing

Throughout human history, drums have played a significant role in various cultures, serving as instruments of communication, celebration and healing. In recent years, there has been a growing recognition of the therapeutic potential of drumming, extending far beyond its traditional musical applications. This shift in perspective is reshaping our understanding of drums as powerful tools for personal and communal well-being.

Remo Belli, founder and CEO of Remo Inc., a leading drum manufacturing company, says:

"It's time to stop thinking of the drum as just a musical instrument. Start thinking of it as a unifying tool for every family, a wellness tool for every retiree and an educational tool for every classroom. [...] The rhythm of life is a symphony and expression of our soul. When we drum, our inner voice resounds. Our energy rises, vitality improves, and our emotions are exhilarated. Group drumming opens the doors of communication and allows us to speak where words often do not pass. Music, rhythm and dance enhance self-esteem, ensure a healthy workout, stimulate our minds, boost our creative potential, make us laugh and connect us on many levels." (Remo, 2003.)

In a systematic review of research on drumming and percussion carried out in 2017, the authors reviewed eighteen published papers on drumming and wellbeing (Yap et al., 2017). They concluded that:

"Most studies have shown an improvement in psychological health of an individual, with lower stress levels, less anxiety, better mood, higher energy levels and feelings of empowerment. There were also studies which found effects of RMM [rhythm-centred music making] on physical health like the reduction in blood pressure, increases in pain threshold, improvement in symptoms of parkinsonism and improvements in immunological response as well as effects on social health with the empowerment of an individual to participate in group activities, facilitating social cohesion as well as group dynamics. This is consistent with studies that report music engaging areas of the brain involved in motivation, emotion, cognition, motor function and gait improvements in people with stroke.

"From the findings of the systematic review, we would like to recommend physicians to encourage patients to take up RMM as a form of activity with benefits that extend beyond the physical health of an individual."

The evolving perception of drums from mere musical instruments to multifaceted tools for health and well-being represents a significant shift in our understanding of the role of rhythm in our life. It is an emergent area of research, and one I expect to continue to unveil the wide-ranging benefits of drumming and highlight its potential as a holistic approach to enhancing individual and community health.

What drumming does to the brain

A lot of the effects of drumming on physiology derive from its effects on the brain. To put it simply, drumming, or at least the repetitive shamanic style drumming, at around four beats per second, calms the brain down, which in turn calms the physiology and influences the release of feel-good hormones.

Drumming literally changes our consciousness. One of the most powerful effects demonstrated by drumming research is how drumming changes brainwaves, recorded via electroencephalograms (EEG), which is when electrodes are applied to the scalp. You can find videos demonstrating this effect in real time on Jeff Strong's YouTube Channel.

Our brainwaves normally oscillate between five states:

- **Gamma waves** (above 40 Hz): these are linked to higher cognitive functions, such as learning, memory and perception.
- **Beta waves** (12-40 Hz): these are associated with conscious, focused awareness, problem-solving and active thinking.
- **Alpha waves** (8-12 Hz): these occur during relaxed wakefulness, light meditation and when the mind is calm but alert.
- **Theta waves** (4-8 Hz): these are associated with deep relaxation and meditation, light sleep and dreaming.
- **Delta waves** (0.5-4 Hz): these occur during deep, dreamless sleep and in deep meditative states.

Interestingly, whilst fast brainwaves are necessary to focus, they are also associated with stress and anxiety (Friedman, 2000). We may need to enter a 'fight or flight' state to survive, but our normal health state is the rest and relaxation one. High brainwaves are only supposed to be a state we enter for short amounts of time, returning to a lower, more peaceful state of relaxed awareness as our normal state of being.

In our modern world, we spend far too much time in a hyper alert state, which contributes to our feelings of stress, depression and anxiety and we have forgotten that our normal health state is one of relaxed awareness. Being in nature and drumming really helps to take this relaxed state one step further (more on this in the chapter on drumming and rituals).

Where the research on brainwaves and drumming gets even more fascinating is because of a phenomenon known as 'auditory entrainment', a process by which the human brain has a tendency to synchronise its frequency with periodic external auditory stimuli (Neher, 1961).

When we listen to a shamanic-style rhythm of repetitive drumming (about four beats per seconds, which is about 4Hz), our brainwaves synchronise with this rhythm and slow down, entering an alpha state, which is the slower brain state associated with relaxed awareness or meditative state. To put it simply, listening to, or drumming, a shamanic drumming rhythm, puts your brain in a relaxed state effortlessly. This can have a tremendous impact on healing and wellbeing.

Research shows that it only takes about ten to fifteen minutes of listening to drumming at about four beats per second (Konopacki & Madison, 2018; Maxfield, 1990) for the brain to shift gears and for the brainwaves to start to slow down and enter the alpha or theta state. However, my personal experience and that of others shows that, the more you drum or listen to drumming, the faster you enter this deeply relaxed state, in the same way people who meditate regularly become more adept at entering this state at will.

It is important to stress that you do not need to believe in the power of drumming for it to work in this way. Remember that I too was a sceptic before my first drumming experience and yet it was incredibly powerful right from the first experience. I have recorded myself drumming many times to share drumming tracks and journeys with others and as I was playing one of these tracks on my computer, my husband, who was sitting at another computer in the same room (and who doesn't believe in the effects of the drum), said, "Can you stop this thing? It's making my brain go funny." I laughed and said, "Exactly!".

Throughout my experience of guiding diverse groups in drumming experiences and journeys, I've consistently witnessed a remarkable phenomenon: participants, regardless of their experience in meditation, frequently express being amazed by the deep meditative states they achieve while listening to the drum. This ranges from complete novices to those who typically struggle with meditation and even extends to seasoned practitioners.

I listened to the drum meditation that you shared on the Imbolc group, and I was able to access insights that I had never before when sitting in silent meditation.

Josephine

In his online course, "Beyond Shamanism", and on his YouTube channel, drummer Jeff Strong shows live recordings of the electroencephalograms (EEG) of people who are listening to drumming tracks and/or meditating. When people are already meditating, their brainwaves are often in alpha. He then adds a shamanic drumming track, and you see their brainwaves almost instantly dropping down to theta, which is a much deeper meditative state.

In his book, *The Healing Power of the Drum*, Robert Friedman cites the work of clinical psychologist, Dr Barry Quinn, who works with stressed, hypervigilant people who do not appear to have alpha brainwaves:

"Until recently, I had never found anything that increased Alpha waves in people that needed most to have more of them, and I am speaking specifically of the hypervigilant population. I tried biofeedback, but it tends only to enhance the theta waves of relaxation and didn't really affect Alpha much at all. I even had some hypervigilant patients who were transcendental meditators, a group which typically has a higher amplitude of Alpha than the general population, but these hypervigilant meditators had low to non-existent Alpha.

"It was suggested to me that I do some research with drums and Alpha waves... Not expecting anything really, I went ahead and took four or five people and did an experiment wherein I got an Alpha wave baseline from them, which was, of course, typically low (below 10 MV) and had them drum for half an hour. The instructions I gave them were to drum a soft slow heartbeat type of rhythm. [...]

"I found that 50% of the ones I tested got a normal Alpha wave pattern after thirty minutes of drumming, which means that their Alpha waves doubled. One of the participants was a friend of mine. I had done 15 neurofeedback sessions with him and gotten him into theta waves but had never been able to get any Alpha waves from him. The drumming was the first and only thing that allowed him to produce Alpha waves. I was also impressed by the fact that the Alpha waves occurred in these hypervigilant, high stressed people after only 20-30 minutes. It wasn't after five sessions. It was immediately after the first drumming session."

The entrainment effect gets even more fascinating: whilst research has almost exclusively focused on the shamanic rhythm of drumming, which slows the brain down and therefore helps us enter an altered state of consciousness,

Jeff Strong has also shown that various complex drumming rhythms can also be used to modify other states of being (Strong, 2015).

For example, fast drum rhythms can be used to increase focus (up to ten beats per second, which is incredibly fast). It makes sense that, if you can slow the brain down with slow drumming rhythms, you can also speed it up, as the auditory entrainment process works in the same way. Different rhythms can be used to improve energy levels, mood, or to decrease anxiety. Some can be used to improve sleep. During the process of writing this book I discovered Jeff Strong's Brain Stim Audio website (brainstimaudio.com), which offers a range of drumming tracks based on seven different categories of needs (brain boosting, calm, energy, focus, meditate, sleep and mood lifting).

Beyond its ability to alter consciousness, drumming also stimulates the brain in many positive ways. In his thesis, "Cognitive Functioning of Drumming and Rhythm Therapy for Neurological Disorders", Logan Deyo explores the cognitive functioning of drumming and rhythm therapy for neurological disorders. He finds that:

- Drumming involves complex neural connections across multiple brain regions, including temporal, frontal, occipital and cerebellar lobes.
- Different rhythms activate different areas of the brain.
- Experienced drummers have faster reaction times and better rhythm-change detection abilities compared to non-musicians.
- Music-supported therapy (MST) offers an innovative approach to aiding brain function in various neurological conditions, including ADHD, Alzheimer's, Parkinson's disease and stroke recovery, in particular, this therapy can:
  - Improve concentration and behaviour in ADHD patients.
  - Enhance cognitive performance in elderly individuals.
  - Promote neuroplasticity in stroke patients.
  - Improve gait and motor control in Parkinson's disease patients.
- Drumming and rhythm therapy have the potential to rebuild neurological damage and improve quality of life for individuals with various neurological disorders.

Deyo concludes that drumming is not just a musical skill but also a powerful tool for cognitive enhancement and neurological therapy (Deyo, 2016).

There is a project called "Rhythm and the Brain" run by Grateful Dead percussionist Mikey Hart and neurologist Dr Adam Gazzaley using advanced technology to visualise brain activity during drumming which shows extensive neural communication:

"'This is about breaking the rhythm code, our genome project. Once we know what rhythm truly does, then we'll be able to control it and use it medicinally for diagnostics, for health reasons. To be able to reconnect the synapses, the connections that are broken in Parkinson's, Alzheimer's, that's where we are heading.' It's just the beginning, as far as Hart is concerned. 'I've been working in my field for many years and so has Adam, it's a handshake between science and art. Life is all about rhythm and the brain is Rhythm Central.'" (Hart and Gazzaley, 2012.)

How drumming supports nervous system regulation

Drumming can be a powerful tool for nervous system regulation because it supports many aspects of the re-regulation process:

- **Rhythmic stimulation:** The steady, repetitive rhythm of drumming can help entrain the nervous system, promoting a shift from sympathetic to parasympathetic activation.
- **Rhythmic entrainment:** The change in the brainwave state through auditory stimulation also facilitates a shift from stress to calm.
- **Sensory integration:** Drumming engages multiple senses simultaneously – touch, sound and sight. This can help ground individuals in the present moment, supporting nervous system regulation.
- **Social bonding:** Group drumming supports a sense of connection with others. This social engagement can activate the ventral vagal complex, promoting a state of safety and calm.
- **Emotional expression:** Drumming provides a non-verbal outlet for emotional expression, which can be beneficial for releasing stress or emotions that may be dysregulating the nervous system.

- **Mindfulness and focus:** Drumming requires focus and presence, which can serve as a form of mindfulness practice. This focused attention can help quiet the over-active mind and reduce stress and anxiety.
- **Physical movement:** The physical act of drumming involves movement, which can help release tension stored in the body.

In his article "Drumming, rhythm and regulation through a polyvagal lens", Simon Faulkner explains that, "This neuroceptive physiology is not able to be impacted directly through traditional 'talk-based' therapies, the dominant model for psychological support in current times [...] non-verbal, expressive therapies using rhythm, movement, entrainment and a focus on sensory integration are more often able to engage the senses and restore equilibrium." (Faulkner, 2023.)

He goes on to say, "the key neural pathway to calm and safety is through the ventral vagal system which is readily activated through sound and rhythm. [...] Many Indigenous rituals employ drumming to stimulate the vagal brake and help us connect positively to others and as such many drumming exercises serve as functional processes for ventral vagal development and activating our social-engagement system. Almost all studies of group drumming point to improvements in social connection and mood."

Faulkner goes on to explain that trauma often leads to sensory defensiveness, shutting down our ability to feel our internal states. Not being able to feel emotions makes it hard to name or process them. Drumming offers a safe way to identify and express feelings that may be trapped in the body. It bypasses the limitations of language. Faulkner uses drums for emotional check-ins, narrative expression and shared journeys. Mirroring exercises on drums also provides him with powerful insights into a person's emotional state. Music speaks the language of emotion, making drumming a tool for accessing and expressing sensations that contribute to both psychological and physical suffering.

Faulkner concludes by saying: "These exercises have their basis in a line of knowledge that extends through almost every Indigenous society on earth, across thousands of years – an evidence base beyond comparison. Linking this long history to current trends and understandings in therapeutic practice, polyvagal theory alerts us to the myriad of connections between the somatic nature of drumming and the biological determinants of health, as well as the central role of connection and belonging in restoring equilibrium and social healing. Drumming offers clinicians multiple ways of engaging and strengthening the vagal brake, regulating the defensive mechanisms of the SNS and enhancing positive social engagement, in a safe, fun and uplifting way."

Drumming through a polyvagal theory lens

In the process of becoming diagnosed with ADHD aged fifty-three, I hyperfocused on the subject of nervous system regulation, and learnt that neurodivergent people have a nervous system that gets very easily dysregulated, more so than the average person. This is certainly true for me.

A universal truth, applicable to everyone, regardless of neurotype, is that the key to resolving most life problems lies in developing awareness of our nervous system's state. Many of us experience irritability or exhaustion without recognising that our nervous system is dysregulated. Learning to identify these signs of dysregulation is crucial.

Equally important is prioritising methods to re-regulate our nervous system when it's out of balance. This is essential because when we are dysregulated, our ability to function is significantly impaired. By focusing on recognising and addressing nervous system dysregulation, we can improve our overall well-being and handle life's challenges more easily.

Before I share about how drumming helps with this, I want to explain what happens during nervous system dysregulation.

Stephen Porges' polyvagal theory (Porges, 2011) describes our nervous system's responses using a three-tiered model, similar to a traffic light, which explains how we navigate our world. Each colour represents a distinct branch of our autonomic nervous system:

The green light represents our ventral vagal state, a key part of the parasympathetic nervous system often referred to as the "rest and relaxation" mode. In this state, our body is at its optimal functioning for health, growth and restoration. This part of our nervous system also promotes a sense of safety and social connection, allowing us to engage openly with others and our environment. When we're in this green light state, our heart rate is regulated, our breathing is slow and deep and our digestive system functions efficiently. This is where we experience feelings of calm, contentment and social bonding. Nurturing this state is crucial for overall well-being, stress resilience and healthy relationships.

The orange light represents when perceived threats emerge: our sympathetic nervous system's "fight or flight" mode, priming us for action by increasing our heart rate and releasing stress hormones, preparing the body for quick action or defence. Physiological changes include increased heart rate, elevated blood pressure and the release of stress hormones like adrenaline and cortisol. While this response can save our lives in genuinely dangerous situations, chronic activation of this state can lead to stress-related health issues.

In the orange state, we may also exhibit a "fawn" response. This reaction involves attempting to please or appease the perceived threat. We may instinctively try to gain approval or avoid conflict by being overly accommodating, even at the cost of our own well-being. This can manifest as people-pleasing behaviours, difficulty setting boundaries, or a tendency to take on others' emotions.

The red light represents the dorsal vagal state. This state, often associated with "freeze" or "shutdown" responses, can be triggered by a range of experiences, from social discomfort to more severe stressors. When activated, it may cause a noticeable drop in energy, decreased heart rate and blood pressure and feelings of disconnection. In extreme situations, such as when escape is impossible, this freeze response can serve as a protective mechanism, potentially making us less detectable to predators or reducing physical pain if injury occurs.

Some people might experience the red state as feeling "spaced out," or having difficulty concentrating. In more intense activations, it can lead to a sense of emotional numbness or complete withdrawal or dissociation. While this state can be protective in certain situations, frequent or prolonged dorsal vagal activation may contribute to depression, chronic fatigue or difficulties with social engagement.

Recognising the subtle manifestations our nervous system states is crucial for understanding our body's responses to everyday stressors and for developing strategies to re-regulate our nervous system as needed.

Our normal state, the one we need to be in to thrive, is the green one. Since my diagnosis, I have embarked on a deep journey to notice when I become dysregulated (this happens often) and how to prioritise re-regulating my nervous system. I keep a drawing of the traffic light system on the wall near my desk, with an arrow moving up and down, to bring more mindfulness to my nervous system state and work to re-regulate when it's gone out of the green state. It is so much easier to go back from orange to green than from red to green. Drumming has been a big part of this process. I share more about this in the chapter on drumming and neurodivergence.

Psychological benefits

Mental health

Based on all the research I have shared thus far, it will probably come as little surprise that a growing body of evidence suggests that drumming can have profound impacts on the mental health, emotional well-being and social connection of individuals and groups. The review paper by Yap et al. confirms this:

"Fifteen studies have shown that RMM [rhythm-centred music making] has led to improvements in anxiety, depression, anger, stress, mood, self-esteem and motivation. It has also been shown to facilitate recovery in addiction and empowers the individual."

There have also been a wide range of studies and programmes aimed at understanding the social aspect of group drumming. A ten-week group drumming intervention demonstrated significant improvements across multiple mental health markers. Participants experienced a notable decrease in depression and an increase in social resilience by week six, both of which were maintained at the three-month follow-up. By week ten, significant reductions in anxiety and improvements in overall mental wellbeing were observed, also sustained at follow-up.

Ho and colleagues (2009) found that drumming not only increases oxytocin levels but also reduces depression, withdrawal and anxiety. This impact was further supported by Mungas and Silverman's clinical study (2014), which revealed that participants in group drumming sessions felt more awake, relaxed, cheerful, friendly and clear-headed.

The stress-reducing potential of drumming was also highlighted in Smith et al.'s (2014) research, where just forty minutes of group drumming significantly lowered stress and anxiety scores. Ascenso and colleagues (2018) explored the effects of djembe drumming on both patients and carers, noting improvements in various aspects of well-being, including happiness, agency, accomplishment, engagement, self-perception and social well-being.

Perhaps most strikingly, the DRUMBEAT program, which combined therapeutic drumming with group discussions, showed remarkable results in addressing the complex needs of disadvantaged adolescent boys (Martin and Wood, 2017). The authors reported significant improvements in mental well-being, reductions in post-traumatic stress symptoms and decreased antisocial behaviour among participants. These studies collectively paint a picture of drumming as a powerful, versatile tool for promoting mental health and fostering positive social connections.

There is even a study that shows that people who take part in a lab exercise where they drum in pairs whilst facing one another, have a higher activation of the right temporoparietal junction (TPJ) compared to when simply talking to each other. The right TPJ is a brain region involved in a variety of functions including attention, social cognition and emotional functions, including being associated with empathy and understanding the emotions held by others (Rojiani et al., 2018).

Healing from addiction

A review of drumming programs in the USA (Winkelman, 2003), revealed fascinating insights into how this practice supports addiction recovery. Participants reported entering states of deep relaxation and altered consciousness, providing a much-needed respite from the stress of recovery. Many found that the beats enhanced their self-awareness, facilitating emotional healing in ways traditional therapies could not achieve.

Perhaps most significantly, the communal aspect of group drumming proved invaluable. It fostered a strong sense of connectedness, effectively combating the isolation often experienced by those in recovery. The shared experience of creating music together helped individuals break free from self-centred thinking patterns, a common struggle in addiction.

Drumming also offered a bridge to spiritual experiences. For those uncomfortable with traditional religious approaches, drumming provided a secular pathway to access deeper states of being.

One story in the book *The Healing Power of the Drum* particularly touched me. Robert Friedman led a programme in a group of long-term drug addicts at a rehabilitation facility, which included several weeks of group drumming. The people there, being dopesick, were irritable and angry and constantly fighting with each other. One man confronted Friedman at the beginning of the first session, challenging why he was having to waste his time doing this. However, the man in question stayed and was elated after the session, saying it was the most amazing thing he'd done in his life. Not only did he come to every session after this, but he convinced several others to attend (Friedman, 2000).

Emotional regulation

People who are grieving, trying to recover from addiction, sufferers of trauma, people with PTSD and generally anybody in a deep state of emotional discomfort, often report the same thing when they experience drumming for the first time: they say that it allows them to bring up to the surface and express safely emotions they did not even know they had. Often the first emotion that comes is anger. Once the anger has been felt, expressed and released, then and only then, can the sadness, the grief, be safely felt and expressed and removed from where it was stuck in the body/mind. It's as if the anger needed to be washed away first. There is a popular saying that anger is just sadness's bodyguard.

The drum allows people to reconnect to themselves, each other and provides a path back towards a sense of inner peace and spaciousness inside. It also provides a sense of belonging to something bigger than ourselves.

Beside the science itself, in many of the books I've read and in the many stories I've gathered from women from my drumming work and for this book, people regularly mention how drumming helps them to express emotions without needing to use words, and they also mention a sense of shared humanity and belonging that transcends words.

When drumming, the drum becomes an extension of your body. Each beat, when we drop into it, tells the story of how we are feeling, what we are going through and what we need without words. As we drum, particularly with other women in a safe space, that freedom of expression seems to spread into the body itself, creating movement, shaking, dancing, stamping – somatically allowing emotion, trauma and tension to move, be seen and perhaps released. Then that beat and safe space spreads to the voice. It opens up the throat, our space of authentic truth. It allows us to let out that which is held within – in roars, tears, tones, words and song.

Melonie Syrett

Drumming, especially in a group, also provides each of the four healing principles mentioned by Gabor Maté in his book, *The Myth of Normal*: authenticity, agency, anger (as in, the ability to express it healthily) and acceptance (Maté 2024).

The alignment between drumming and Maté's principles is fascinating. It suggests that drumming, particularly in a group setting, can be a powerful tool for holistic healing. By providing a space for authentic expression, personal empowerment, emotional release and communal acceptance, drumming addresses core psychological needs that Maté identifies as crucial for healing.

This underscores the potential of drumming as a therapeutic practice. It's not just about making music or finding a rhythm; it's about creating an environment where individuals can reconnect with themselves and others in profound ways. The fact that drumming naturally incorporates these healing principles suggests that it might be an invaluable tool in addressing trauma, stress, and the disconnection that Maté sees as root causes of many modern health issues.

Social health benefits

In a world where isolation and disconnection are sadly the norm, drumming offers a unique pathway to rebuild community bonds and foster a sense of belonging. Drumming circles and structured programs are being used across various settings to address social isolation, improve group dynamics and support individuals facing diverse challenges.

The review paper on RMM explains that, *"Four studies have shown that RMM has led to a reduction in sense of isolation, alienation, self-centeredness, attention deficit or hyperactivity problems, oppositional defiant problems and post-traumatic stress problems. The participants were better able to connect to others, with improvements in group cohesion, cooperation and communication."*

Drumming provides more than a simple social gathering. The change of consciousness that it facilitates, the calming of the nervous system, the ability to express oneself freely, all of this provides a sense of shared humanity, a way to connect with others beyond politics, religious beliefs or social status.

I have been running a monthly drum circle for four years. Every month we have newcomers. In the most recent one, there were twenty-five of us, including about a third of people who had never come before, nor taken part in such a circle. There was a sense of discomfort at the beginning, of nervousness from the newcomers and also slight discomfort from the regulars. However, as is the case every time, by the end of our drumming, it felt like we were a group of old friends.

I have found more programmes than I can count, across many countries, such as Drums No Guns, in Richmond, USA, founded by Dr Ram Baghat in the early 1990s to honour his brother who died from gun violence. The organisation has since grown into a national non-profit, using drumming, dance and drama to empower youth and raise awareness about gun violence.

"Integrating practices such as drumming, mindfulness and peace-making circles, the foundation promotes non-violence in schools and communities, with a focus on supporting African American and Latinx youth. Drums No Guns offers drumming classes, community drum healing circles and workshops. Ram's work demonstrates how drumming and other creative practices can be powerful tools for social change and community healing." (Baghat, 2020.)

In Australia, the DRUMBEAT (Discovering Relationships Using Music – Beliefs, Emotions, Attitudes and Thoughts) programme is also used to support young teenage boys identified as at-risk of transitioning poorly to secondary school. Simon Faulkner, who developed the programme says:

"'We wanted to marry making young people feel interested and at ease with teaching them how to manage their thoughts and feelings… It works at a relational level, a cognitive level and a neuro-biological level,' said Faulkner, who designed the drum program intending to replicate the rhythmic patterns of early childhood that can be disturbed through trauma or neglect.

"Developing the initiative after becoming frustrated with existing, strictly

talk-based forms of therapy, Faulkner said DRUMBEAT's positive nature and its ability to return both observable and empirical results, restored his faith in youth work." (Croxford, 2017.)

In the book *The Healing Power of the Drum*, Arthur Hall, tells a story about doing a drum program with young gang members. A young man who attended his programme came back with a broken drum. He says that, before he had drummed that day, he felt so angry he wanted to shoot someone, anyone, and that he did not care who it was. He drummed so hard he broke the drum head instead.

Robert Friedman also shares this story by Jim Greiner, a drum teacher, who led a drum workshop in a women's prison:

"I had no illusions about turning their lives around in a two-hour drum session. There was nothing I could say to ease the anguish of the young woman there who cradled the battered rag doll as if it were the crack-addicted baby who had been taken from her by the court. I could not erase the hurt, fear and rage of the thirty-year-old who had been raped by her father until she ran away to a life of selling her body on the streets. I just wanted to bring respite from their daily lives and present a view of life different from the one they had been born into. I let them drum their anger, then their pain, until we finally got to a place where they could drum together, each adding their personal story to the rhythms. I started a simple chant that they took up and made their own in a full voiced gospel choir that spoke clearly of their power and pride. We drummed together and reached a common ground of cooperation and brief easing of their pain and distrust."

A study focusing on male Korean high school students examined the effects of a group drumming-based music therapy program on school violence prevention. The results indicated that group drumming may enhance self-esteem, assertiveness, emotional expression, anger management skills, cooperation, feelings of unity, empathy and active listening skills (Su, 2023).

Winkelman, in his article "Drumming out Drugs", explains that, "*Research reviews indicate that drumming enhances recovery through inducing relaxation and enhancing theta-wave production and brain-wave synchronisation. Drumming produces pleasurable experiences, enhanced awareness of preconscious dynamics, release of emotional trauma and reintegration of self. Drumming alleviates self-centeredness, isolation and alienation, creating a sense of connectedness with self and others. Drumming provides a secular approach to accessing a higher power and applying spiritual perspectives. Drumming circles have applications as complementary addiction therapy, particularly for repeated relapse and when other counselling modalities have failed.*" (Winkelman, 2003.)

How drumming supports healing from trauma

"According to both worldwide, tradition-hallowed human experience and modern research, drumming can be powerfully helpful and healing in times of stress, anxiety and physical pain."

Gabor Maté

Over the last few years, as I've supported one of my children through a mental health crisis, it has become crystal clear to me that the Western approach to mental health is woefully narrow and inadequate.

In the realm of social and emotional health, drumming has shown remarkable potential as a therapeutic tool. Everything that I've explained above, from its ability to foster self-expression, a sense of connection to oneself and others and its ability to calm the nervous system shows me that it might be more helpful and holistic than the Western 'top down', talking therapy/antidepressant drugs combined approach to mental health, which addresses the head/mind only, as if it is separate from the body and as if the body is just a vehicle for the brain. Our current approach is pretty useless at healing deep-seated trauma. Not only this, but only a minority of mental health professionals are trauma aware and talking about traumatic memories can re-traumatise people.

I was delighted to find research that proves what I already knew: that drumming can help us heal trauma:

"When drumming, the present time is all that is able to exist. The past and the future dissipates away, allowing the participant to release any stress and anxiety, relax the nervous system and release emotional trauma." (Hamme, 2017.)

Recent work that used drumming in clinical populations substantiates this hypothesis. Bensimon et al (2008) found drumming to be an effective intervention for PTSD patients by reducing symptoms, facilitating "non-intimidating access to traumatic memories" and allowing for a regained sense of self-control and for release of anger. In another study, the effectiveness of drumming for substance use disorder was heavily linked to its ability to induce relaxation and 'release' emotional trauma (Winkelman, 2003).

Interestingly, both of these studies highlighted the effect of drumming on increased sense of belonging, intimacy and connectedness. Rojiani and colleagues, who studied the right temporoparietal junction (TPJ) mentioned above, concluded that "Drumming may provide novel, effective clinical approaches for treating social – emotional psychopathology." (Rojiani et al., 2018.)

It is important to note here that many of us have a misguided view of what trauma is. We tend to think that only horrible events like wars, severe violence or neglect, or natural disasters are the cause of trauma. But much milder events can trigger deep trauma. As Gabor Maté explains in his book, *The Myth of Normal*, not having their need for emotional attunement met by their care-giving adult can be traumatising for sensitive children (Maté, 2024).

Many years ago, I read an article about how Western talking therapists were sent to support people in Rwanda after the genocide. The Rwandans felt that the aid workers were intrusive and re-traumatising people by dragging them back through their stories:

"Their practice did not involve being outside in the sun where you begin to feel better. There was no music or drumming to get your blood flowing again. There was no sense that everyone had taken the day off so that the entire community could come together to try to lift you up and bring you back to joy. Instead, they would take people one at a time into these dingy little rooms and have them sit around for an hour or so and talk about bad things that had happened to them. We had to ask them to leave." (Leach, 2015.)

Peter Levine, a trauma expert therapist also explains that: *"Traumatic events activate the sympathetic nervous system and dorsal vagus nerve as a defence reaction that leads to behavioural responses of fight, flight or immobilisation. These same neurological changes lead to the reasoning and language areas of the brain being shut down as well as a sensory defensiveness and a loss of sensory awareness that fractures an individual's sense of self and can lead to dysfunctional coping mechanisms and a lack of physical security within one's body."* (Levine, 2008.) (As I mentioned in the previous chapter, the vibrations of the drum activate the ventral vagus nerve, which creates the opposite response to trauma: one of safety, curiosity and social opening, as opposed to fight and flight.)

Levine's work highlights why the talking therapy approach fundamentally misunderstands trauma. Furthermore, by making healing an individual's sole responsibility, it ignores how trauma often originates from and is perpetuated by broader societal contexts. This individualistic medical model not only fragments our understanding of the body but also disconnects people from the very community support that could facilitate it.

Josh Schrei talks about this eloquently in his podcast episode "The Revolution will not be Psychologised." He explains that if a plant was wilting, nobody would declare that it had "wilting syndrome," but would ask whether it had enough soil, enough water, enough nutrients etc. The labelling of diseases, he explains, contributes to placing the blame for the illness solely on the individual. From this, the healing of said illness is also seen as the work of the individual alone, in isolation, as opposed to seeing it as a result of a society which is maladapted to even the most basic needs of human beings (Shrei, 2024).

Gabor Maté has similar views, expressing that the labelling of mental health issues as 'disorders' places the focus on the illness and distracts us away from the life experience and the conditions that led to the development of said disorder. He reflects that *"diagnoses reveal nothing about the underlying events and dynamics that animate the perceptions and experiences in question."* (Maté, 2024.)

Dr Bruce Perry, a leading trauma researcher, has done away with diagnoses completely, explaining that in the future we will look back with consternation that we thought about people in this way. Diagnoses, he says, aren't a valid way to think about the complexities of human beings (Maté, 2024).

The Human Givens Institute (Tyrell and Griffin) states that individuals whose emotional needs are met do not suffer from mental health problems. They list the emotional needs of humans as follow:

- **Security:** A safe environment which allows us to develop fully.
- **Attention** (to give and receive it): A form of nutrition.

- **Autonomy and control:** Having volition to make responsible choices.
- **Emotional intimacy:** Knowing that at least one other person accepts us totally for who we are, 'warts and all'.
- **Feeling part of a wider community.**
- **Privacy:** Opportunity to reflect and consolidate experience.
- **Sense of status within social groupings.**
- **Sense of competence and achievement.**
- **Meaning and purpose.**

How many of us in today's world can truly say that all of those needs are being met?

Drumming provides an **embodied, synchronous, and deeply rooted in community activity,** which closely mirrors the concepts Jonathan Haidt discusses about the needs for social engagement and human connection in his book, *The Anxious Generation* (Haidt 2024). Haidt highlights that humans are innately social, and meaningful experiences often arise when people are physically present and engaged together. This communal connection has decreased as society has shifted online, where interactions tend to be disembodied, asynchronous, and often involve shallow, one-to-many interactions.

Drumming, especially done in groups, counters this digital disconnection. Here's how it achieves that:

- **Embodied experience**: Drumming is profoundly physical; it engages muscle memory, rhythm and movement, allowing participants to be fully in their bodies and in the moment. This physical engagement can enhance self-awareness and the feeling of being grounded, which many report as calming and centring, particularly compared to the often-dissociative experiences of online scrolling or social media use.
- **Synchronous connection**: Haidt discusses how synchronicity – engaging in activities together, in time – creates a sense of unity and togetherness. Drum circles foster synchronicity as players sync their beats, creating an experience of 'entrainment', where individuals align with the group's collective rhythm. Rhythmic synchronisation builds social bonds and reinforces empathy, reducing stress and fostering a sense of belonging – qualities often missing in digital interactions.

- **Responsive interaction**: In a drum circle, participants respond to each other's rhythms, adjusting pace and intensity, which demands real-time attention to others' cues. This responsive interplay fosters deep listening, spontaneity and adaptability. These elements are missing from many digital interactions, where responses can be delayed, edited or misinterpreted. Drumming's live, unscripted interactions nurture interpersonal awareness, something Haidt argues is vital for healthy, resilient social connections.

By combining physical engagement, social synchronicity and responsive interaction, drumming serves as a powerful antidote to the isolation and stress that can result from a highly online lifestyle, fulfilling a basic human need for real, embodied community connection.

Can you also see how many of these needs can be so easily fulfilled when people introduce the drum into their lives? Especially if they blend a personal drum practice with a group one.

Beyond these basic needs, another aspect that is also an important part of drumming is the effect it has on moving energy in the body. While Western science has studied the physiological and psychological effects of drumming, there's a crucial aspect that often goes unacknowledged: the impact of drumming on body energetics. This concept is fundamental to many ancient healing traditions, but remains largely unexplored by conventional scientific methods.

The idea of energy in the body – often referred to as 'qi' or 'chi' in Traditional Chinese Medicine, 'prana' in Ayurveda, or 'ki' in Japanese healing – is a cornerstone of holistic health practices worldwide. These traditions recognise that balancing and moving this energy is essential for physical, emotional, and spiritual well-being.

Drumming appears to have a profound effect on this subtle energy system. Practitioners and participants often report:

- A noticeable shift in their energetic state.
- A feeling of blockages being cleared.
- A sense of energy moving or flowing through the body.
- An overall feeling of balance and harmony post-drumming.

These experiences, while subjective, are consistently reported across diverse cultures and contexts. In group settings, this energetic shift can be even more pronounced, suggesting a collective energetic resonance or entrainment.

The blind spot in Western science regarding body energetics is not just a gap in knowledge; it is a fundamental difference in how health and the human body are conceptualised. Where Western medicine focuses on measurable, physical phenomena, ancient healing systems integrate the concept of life force or vital energy as a key component of health.

As we continue to bridge the gap between ancient wisdom and modern science, it's crucial to remain open to perspectives that may not yet fit neatly into our current scientific paradigms. The consistent, cross-cultural experiences of energetic shifts through drumming suggest that there's more to explore in understanding the full spectrum of drumming's effects on human health and well-being.

My intuition tells me that the medicine and healing of the future will work from an integrative perspective that takes into account our uniqueness and also addresses us as a whole, body, mind and spirit and within a community perspective.

"Working early on in my career in Australian Indigenous communities, I became acutely aware of the limitations of my therapeutic training, which was entirely focused on cognitive therapies and relied heavily on the use of language as a medium for client engagement and behavioural change. Without a common language and with high levels of trauma impacting trust and engagement with individuals in these communities, I was in desperate need of a new medium and hesitantly turned to drums and music after witnessing the joy they evoked in local community gatherings. What started hesitantly, quickly turned to conviction as I witnessed the joy, connection, fun and sense of safety that emanated from my individual, family and group sessions and that led to positive changes in people's lives. These positive outcomes are consistent with findings from a diverse range of studies on drumming in therapeutic contexts." (Faulkner, 2021.)

Drumming to heal trauma

– Anna

The following story, shared by Anna, who came to my drum circle after her somatic therapist suggested that attending a drum circle may help her feel safer in her body, is a perfect example of this too:

*I first came to the drumming circle because I had read about the benefits of drumming for healing trauma and re-embodiment. I was working through some very deeply hidden trauma, intense fear and strong dissociation. I was already working with a somatic-based psychotherapist and using some elements of internal family systems.**

In the first round of drumming, I was flooded with a shame exile – although I'd become aware of it recently in therapy, I'd never experienced it so intensely before. I felt completely rejected, despairing and close to tears. I felt that I was unwanted in the circle, that I was ruining the experience for everyone and wanted to run away but I felt paralyzed by the emotion and couldn't. I was able to share with Sophie and the group how I felt and that I desperately wanted to leave but could they please encourage me to stay so I could work through the emotion.

In the next round of drumming, I then experienced the protector for that exile – numbness and dissociation. I spent the drumming round in a total daze, unable to feel my body or engage. I committed to continuing to drum – my only intention was to stay in the tent. This is a fairly normal pattern for me: emotional overwhelm and then shutdown after. However, for probably the first time ever, something different happened. The third round of drumming started, and I continued to drum in a daze until I felt something started to rise up in me. I raised my head, and I started to look around the room and believed that I deserved to be there. I took off my socks and stood up, feeling the carpet under my feet. The last round of drumming was strong and fierce in nature, and I felt or saw myself growing taller and taller. Everyone else in the circle was also standing up and I experienced us like huge flames, connected together. For a split second I 'saw' my dad in the distance, small in comparison to these huge flames and he was chased away by the power of the group. I banged my drum hard, in my head saying, "I'm here, I'm here, I'm here" – that I survived him, and he didn't defeat me.

This breakthrough has become permanent for me – when I feel overwhelmed, weak or numb, especially in therapy, I take off my socks, connect to the ground and stand up, remembering the feeling of rising power. My therapist says there has been a huge change in me within the few short months that I

*A therapy modality where you have different 'parts', including 'exiles' which are your inner wounded children and 'protectors', which are the defences or coping strategies for protecting those exiles.

have been drumming, which I feel too: more unity within myself, a sense of my own power, a sense of belonging with others and more capacity for joy.

With the knowledge that drumming supports healing from trauma, it makes sense that combining it with somatic bodywork can provide a powerful healing combination. Before I knew about how drumming supports healing, I intuitively added drumming to the closing the bones ritual I offered to new mothers (more about this in the chapter on birth). My intuition told me that it would deepen their relaxation and help them get out of their thoughts. Over the many years I have offered this ritual, gathering the threads of many stories shared by women who received the ritual, I have woven a tapestry of healing that shows that this ritual is particularly helpful to heal from both loss and trauma.

Whilst reading *The Myth of Normal*, I found something that may help understand the mechanism through which childhood trauma can be healed using drumming. Gabor Maté quotes Bruce Lipton explaining the state of brainwaves that dominates during early childhood:

"Delta waves, the brain's lowest frequency, predominate in our first two years, then theta waves ramp up until we are about six. 'A child under seven is predominantly in theta,' he told me. 'Theta is an hypnotic state and it's how you absorb all this stuff for seven years.' Just as under the spell of an hypnotist, you believe whatever messages you get. Only afterwards does the state of conscious awareness and logical thinking associated with alpha and beta waves activity comes online. 'We download our perceptions and belief about life years before we acquire the capacity for critical thinking,' Dr Lipton writes. 'Those perceptions and misperceptions become our truths" (Maté, 2024.)

Upon reading this, I was struck by the following hypothesis: could the drum's profound healing effect on trauma be linked to its ability to induce alpha and theta brainwave states? If these are the very states in which early childhood traumas are formed, by returning us to these brainwave patterns, drumming may allow us to access, process and ultimately heal deeply embedded traumatic experiences.

Pre-verbal experiences, which happened too early to be captured in words, might suddenly resurface. Traumas that were too overwhelming to process at the time may gently rise to the surface of our awareness. But this time, we're not helpless infants or vulnerable children. If we can approach these resurfaced experiences with our adult cognitive abilities, our expanded emotional capacity and in a supportive environment, this has the potential to offer a powerful opportunity for healing and integration.

It's no wonder, then, that people often report profound emotional releases during drumming sessions. Insights that have eluded years of talk therapy suddenly come up. The drum, in its simplicity, offers a direct line to our deepest selves, bypassing our well-worn mental pathways and defensive structures. This mechanism helps explain why, in the words of Gabor Maté, "Drumming can be powerfully helpful and healing in times of stress, anxiety and trauma."

Conclusion

The science of drumming is truly mind-blowing, corroborating what shamans and healers have known for millennia. From altering our brainwaves and releasing feel-good hormones to improving our physical health and fostering deep social connections, drumming offers a holistic approach to enhancing almost every aspect of our wellbeing. Its ability to address trauma, reduce stress and allow for emotional expression without words makes it a powerful healing tool.

As we continue to bridge ancient wisdom with cutting-edge research, drumming emerges as a testament to the profound impact rhythmic practices can have on our whole selves – body, mind and spirit. This growing body of evidence not only validates traditional knowledge but also paves the way for integrating drumming into contemporary Western healthcare, education and community settings.

In a world where we are increasingly disconnected, isolated and stressed, the drum offers a simple yet profound path back to ourselves, to each other and to a sense of belonging to something greater than ourselves. It is clear that drumming is much more than just a hippy practice – it's a powerful tool for healing, connection and rediscovering our innate rhythms.

5

DIVERSE FREQUENCIES: HOW DRUMMING SUPPORTS PEOPLE WHO ARE NEURODIVERGENT

"When I play drums, I'm free. Free to be me, to express my soul through rhythm."

Neil Peart

I was recently diagnosed with ADHD, aged fifty-three, shortly before I started writing this book. It has become clear to me, both from personal experience and from reading research, that drumming is particularly helpful to support both ADHD/ADD and autism, and yet most people are unaware of this.

When I analysed research and read about drumming and healing, it came as a complete surprise for me to discover that there were several people who had been using the drum to help neurodivergent kids and adults since the 1990s and yet I had never heard about it. I felt that, rather than including it within the chapter on science, this specific topic needed its own chapter to do it justice and to help neurodivergent folks discover how it may help them.

A couple of years ago, the thought of anybody being neurodivergent in my family had not even crossed my mind. Then my youngest child was diagnosed with autism. The reading I did around the subject led me to discover my own ADHD and I was diagnosed a year later. Finally, my eldest was diagnosed with autism in 2024. My husband, although not diagnosed, is also neurodivergent. The journey has been one of empowerment, because it helped me in becoming kinder to myself, more understanding and compassionate towards my children, and I started to understand my entire family's specific gifts and challenges.

One of the most important aspects of myself this process uncovered was to help me understand how hypersensitive we all are. There were always signs but I did not understand them before. For example, I am hypersensitive to noise. I get extremely distracted by even the smallest of noises and it stops me from being able to concentrate on anything.

People who are neurodivergent, because they are more sensitive to everything, also have a nervous system that gets more easily dysregulated. This is due to several key factors:

Sensory processing differences: Many neurodivergent children (and adults – but there has been more research on children) have atypical sensory processing. Atypical sensory processing means a person's brain handles information from their senses differently, which can make them more or less sensitive to things like sounds, lights or textures, affecting how they interact with the world around them. This can lead to heightened sensitivity to environmental stimuli, causing more frequent nervous system activation. (Delapiazza et al., 2020.)

Altered autonomic nervous system function: Research shows some neurodivergent individuals have differences in their autonomic nervous system function (the part of the nervous system that automatically controls involuntary bodily functions like heart rate, digestion, breathing and blood pressure), affecting their ability to regulate arousal and stress responses. (Porges et al., 2013, Bellato et al., 2019.)

Executive functioning challenges: Executive function refers to a set of cognitive processes that help us manage, control and regulate our thoughts and actions, especially in relation to goal-directed behaviour. Many neurodivergent people have difficulties with executive functioning, impacting emotional regulation and stress management. (Barkley et al., 2012.)

Neurotransmitter differences: ADHD is linked to changes in the dopaminergic, adrenergic, serotoninergic and cholinergic pathways, which affect attention and impulse control. (Cortese, 2012.) Autism may involve alterations in serotonin, glutamatergic, dopaminergic, cholinergic and GABAergic systems, affecting mood regulation and sensory processing. (Ramos et al., 2023.)

Stress vulnerability: Neurodivergent individuals have a lower threshold for stress and a smaller window of tolerance, making their nervous systems more prone to dysregulation in challenging situations. (Neff, 2024.)

Drumming's ability to soothe the nervous system and bring us into the present moment can help to shift our nervous system from states of hyperarousal or shut down into a balanced, calm alertness. Moreover, the act of drumming demands our full attention, anchoring us in the present moment. This focused awareness can interrupt cycles of rumination or worry, offering a respite from the mental chatter that often contributes to nervous system dysregulation.

The beauty of it is that it's pretty effortless, especially in the case of listening to calming or focusing drumming tracks in the background and it also requires much less effort than meditation. Drumming enhances the restoration of presence and safety by engaging the body's motor functions, making it an even more powerful tool for grounding and reconnection.

How drumming stills the mind

For neurodivergent minds, which often experience heightened analytical activity and sensory processing differences, finding moments of stillness and peace can feel particularly challenging. While neurotypical brains might naturally filter information, neurodivergent ones often process everything simultaneously, making inner quiet more difficult to achieve.

Imagine a murky pond with sediment and debris settled at the bottom. This represents the cluttered and rigid state of our analytical mind – the thoughts, beliefs and conditioning that get in the way of calm.

When you try to peer into the muddy depths directly, forcing and straining to make out what lies beneath, the sediment only gets stirred up. The harder you try to grasp at those answers and insights, the more obstructed your view becomes, just like furiously searching for a forgotten word makes it even more inaccessible.

When you drum, it's as if you are gently disturbing the surface of the pond with ripples. Only these ripples, instead of agitating the muck below, create a gentle movement to allow the sediment to gradually disperse.

As the water clears, you no longer need to strain to find the answers – they become visible of their own accord. Your inner wisdom and knowing becomes accessible by getting your analytical mind to relax and stop grasping.

The drum provides an effortless way to still the waters of the mind, allowing insights to become clear and available, as naturally as a long-forgotten word flows back after you stop frantically trying to recall it. The answers were always there, waiting for your mind to settle.

How drumming supports people with autism

In a crowded room, a group of autistic children and adults sit in a circle, each with a drum. As the facilitator begins a simple beat, hesitant hands join in one by one. Soon, the room is filled with a synchronised rhythm, faces lighting up with smiles of connection and joy. This scene, observed in one of the studies reviewed by paediatric occupational therapy clinician Zahava Friedman, exemplifies the power of 'connected rhythm' in therapeutic drumming for neurodivergent individuals.

Friedman's review about therapeutic drumming as an intervention to improve mental health in autistic individuals included seventeen studies (Friedman et al.2024). He explains that, *"The confluence of varied adversities faced by people with autism may contribute to statistically significant increases in co-morbid health issues, including challenges related to mental health [...]. The need to address mental health issues in this population is imperative, as research indicates that improvement in mental health has a positive effect on other functional domains, such as improved sensory processing and motor skills."*

In this paper, Friedman and colleagues also quote a study where a non-verbal autistic child began to vocalise rhythmically during drumming sessions, surprising both researchers and parents.

Friedman's review emphasises the positive social effect of drumming interventions. Across studies, participants repeatedly expressed joy during and after sessions. Drumming shows promise not only for autistic kids, but also for supporting autistic individuals across their lifespan. One study included autistic participants in their fifties, suggesting that drumming can be a meaningful activity well into adulthood. This is crucial given the lack of services typically available to autistic adults.

The review concludes that drumming can address multiple challenges faced by neurodivergent individuals. It can support mental health, social participation and sensory-motor needs simultaneously. The Friedman review highlights the importance of neurodiversity-affirming practices. Drumming allows neurodivergent individuals to express themselves creatively on their own terms, fostering a sense of empowerment and belonging.

In another study conducted by Litchke and Bracken (2018), a group of autistic children participated in a four-week group drum program. The researchers observed improvements in social interaction and engagement among the participants. The children showed enhanced communication skills, both verbal and non-verbal, during the drumming sessions. This is significant because social communication is often an area of difficulty for autistic individuals. The research also noted positive changes in emotional regulation. Participants demonstrated a better ability to manage their emotions, with reduced instances of anxiety and frustration during the drumming activities.

Jeff Strong's book, *Different Drummer,* also presents a compelling collection of case studies featuring autistic children and young adults who previously struggled with social engagement. Through his innovative approach, Strong demonstrates how carefully crafted drumming patterns can dramatically transform their ability to connect with their families and peers:

"Stacey's mother called me after 7 weeks, excited by an event that occurred the night before. She reported that Stacey had a sleep-over at a new friend's house, a first for her on several levels: First, Stacey had never been invited to a sleep-over before, second, she was able to separate from her mother to actually go on the sleep-over and third, the next morning she was able to describe in proper sequence what she did at the sleep-over. These were major milestones for her.

"When Jason began the REI Custom Program, he was 5 years old and had limited language abilities. He could say his name and ask for things using one- or two-word phrases. Over the course of the first two months, his language blossomed to two or three sentence phrases, and he was beginning to describe events in sequence."

In one dramatic case, 19-year-old Jim, who was also non-verbal, had a powerful response to the drumming. *"We had the CD made. We put it in during a session with his Craniosacral therapist and he responded instantly,"* described Jim's mother, Linda. *"His system was calming down: and to the surprise of his therapist, he started vocalising. We were like, hip-hip hurray."* Jim had been listening to his program CDs for about nine months when Jeff visited him. *"He is now starting to put sentences together. I'm very pleased,"* Linda added.

Jeff references many different situations in his book where drumming calms and reduces anxiety in neurodivergent kids and adults:

"Jonah, Garrett and Jim each had anxiety and related anxiety-based behaviors when I started working with them. Across the board, I attribute our non-verbal clients' improvements in language to REI's ability to lower their anxiety levels so that the client can find the words that are trying to get out. Anxiety seems to be at the heart of nearly all symptoms. I feel if I can reduce the anxiety, a door opens for language to start developing."

How drumming supports people with ADHD

From my first experience with the drum over ten years ago and every single time I've drummed since, before I knew anything about the science of drumming, I've always noticed that the drum loosens and softens my mind. It allows me to find answers or solutions that are normally elusive. I've often said that listening to shamanic or repetitive drumming feels like having a massage in your brain. Whilst I can get into the same state with other practices such as meditation or mindful movement, these usually take a lot longer. With the drum it is both quick and effortless. It provides a way to get out of my own way and to access a deep, relaxed presence.

Drumming is especially helpful for people with ADHD because it provides the following elements:

- **Rhythmic stimulation:** The steady, repetitive rhythm of drumming can help regulate the nervous system, improving focus and attention.
- **A physical outlet:** Drumming provides a constructive outlet for excess energy and the need for movement often experienced by people with ADHD.

- **Stress reduction:** The repetitive nature of drumming can be calming and meditative, potentially reducing stress and anxiety often co-occurring with ADHD.
- **Increased dopamine release:** Engaging in music and rhythmic activities can trigger the release of dopamine, a neurotransmitter often implicated in ADHD and associated with attention and motivation.
- **Mindfulness practice:** The focus required for drumming can serve as a form of meditative practice, helping to improve present-moment awareness.

Jeff Strong mentioned, when I interviewed him, that people with ADHD have more theta brainwaves than neurotypical individuals. This can seem odd because ADHD individuals are often referred to having "a Ferrari brain." This commonly used analogy highlights the ADHD brain's potential for powerful performance, quick processing and need for high stimulation – like a Ferrari's speed and high-octane fuel requirements. It also underscores the need for specialised management strategies, similar to the skilled handling a Ferrari demands.

Published research shows that individuals with ADHD have an elevated theta to beta (TBR) brainwave ratio. This means that they often have more theta waves and fewer beta waves than other people (Arnset al., 2013). This pattern is associated with inattention, slower cognitive processing and lower cortical arousal. It may contribute to difficulties in sustaining focus, challenges with executive functions and feelings of drowsiness when not motivated.

In hunter gatherer societies, neurodivergent people may well have been the seers, the medicine people, the artists, the wayshowers etc. Some studies have also found a similar higher prevalence of low brainwaves patterns in autistic individuals. Personally, I believe that this high theta state, a state normally associated with meditation and light sleep, may account for the fact that many people with ADHD have a 'blue sky thinking' or 'bird's eye view' way of thinking.

When attention is needed, however, drumming can easily be used to help arouse the neurodivergent brain and keep it alert and focused. Banging on a drum also provides the "fidget to focus" strategy that is a well-known tool for people with autism/ADHD (Strong, 2015).

In his book about ADHD, *The Drummer and the Great Mountain*, Michael Ferguson explains that people with ADHD have a "hunter-gatherer brain", characterised by heightened awareness of the environment, quick shifts in attention and the ability to hyperfocus on interesting tasks. On the other hand, people who are neurotypicals have a "farmer brain", which represents the typical modern mindset, suited to routine, structure and long-term planning and is associated with focused attention on single tasks for extended periods (Ferguson, 2014).

Evolution hasn't 'caught up' with the shift from hunter-gatherer to modern societies because evolutionary changes typically occur over much longer timeframes than the relatively recent advent of agriculture and industrialisation. The short time since these societal changes, combined with the lack of strong selective pressure against ADHD-like traits, the potential ongoing benefits of some of these traits and the complexity of the genetics involved, all contribute to the persistence of these traits in the population.

Lee Havenga is the creator of a drumming programme called Go Mad Music. He started the programme as a thesis for his Bachelor of Music degree and it grew into a fully-fledged curriculum aimed at children and young adults struggling to manage their ADHD. A pilot study carried out by the Go Mad Music founder showed positive results that even after one thirty-minute drum class, there were overall increased levels of cognitive performance across all participants (Havenga, 2024).

Havenga explains that, *"For someone with excess energy and difficulty concentrating, sitting behind the piano or guitar can be very frustrating and even boring; however, picking up a stick and banging on a drum will give the learner/player that immediate thrill and enjoyment and because of the natural rhythm in us, it will much sooner start to sound like they're playing something that could go on to form part of a song or solo; once again building confidence and self-esteem."*

Studies with elementary and middle school boys diagnosed with ADHD show that a course of twenty-minute treatment sessions with these rhythmic beats yielded results similar to the effects of ADHD medications such as Ritalin and Adderall (Saarman, 2006).

Jeff Strong tested one adult taking Ritalin using a standard test for attention, under the following conditions: 10mg of Ritalin taken 1.5 hours before the test, 20mg of Ritalin again taken 1.5 hours before the test and while listening to his REI recording. His test scores were significantly higher whilst listening to drumming than with either of the Ritalin doses (Strong, 2024).

"For children with ADHD, music therapy bolsters attention and focus, reduces hyperactivity and strengthens social skills. Music is rhythm, rhythm is structure, and structure is soothing to an ADHD brain struggling to regulate itself to stay on a linear path. 'Music exists in time, with a clear beginning, middle and end,' says Kirsten Hutchison, a music therapist at Music Works Northwest. 'That structure helps an ADHD child plan, anticipate and react.' Take this notion of how rhythm is so highly effective and combine it with the physical, primal, interactive innateness of banging the drums... and the results speak for themselves."

Lee Havenga

How drumming is helping me as a midlife neurodivergent woman

Discovering that I have ADHD has been extremely empowering. I'm able to understand myself so much better and most importantly, be kinder to myself:

- I understand why I get so easily overwhelmed
- I understand why over the last few years I've embarked on so many new activities which are known to raise dopamine levels and calm overwhelm (such as cold-water swimming and 5 Rhythms dancing and of course, drumming).
- I understand why trying to meditate whilst sitting still is something I find difficult and why drumming and movement meditation work much better for me.
- I understand why working with coaches who help me organise my time in a holistic way has been invaluable, and also why working with more mainstream coaches in the past only increased my sense of overwhelm.
- I understand why switching to a ketogenic diet six years ago has done wonders for my mental health (it has been shown to provide more stable brain energy, reduce inflammation and balance neurotransmitters).
- I understand why, even though I've put a lot of effort, tried so many life-style changes, complementary therapies, supplements and herbs, things

that seemed to be working for a while, were no longer enough to manage my symptoms as my hormonal profile changed further. (I've been peri-menopausal for twelve years).

- Most importantly, as I have been able to slowly put more strategies and hacks in place to manage my overactive mind, anxiety and overwhelm, to amazing results.

Since I was diagnosed with ADHD, I have been on a quest to find ways to hack my brain and stay focused on my work at will, not just when I have a burst of hyperfocus.

Here are the ways in which I use the drum/drumming in my life to help manage my symptoms and stay regulated and calm:

- I listen to Brain Stim Audio entrainment drumming tracks, which include things like help with focus, increasing energy levels, meditating and sleep. I listen to these daily whilst I work, almost exclusively using the range of focus I have noticed similar sensations in my brain when listening to these tracks to the sensations I get when I take ADHD medication. When used in combination with ADHD medication, the drumming tracks appear to increase the effect of the medication.

- I aim to play the drum daily (even if only for five minutes) and also play every time I feel overwhelmed or have a problem to solve. Drumming is more effective than meditation/stillness at calming my mind and reducing overwhelm. The daily practice brings a sense of calm and inner peace I was never able to achieve before.

- I drum to help rewire my negative thought patterns/bring more kindness to myself. This means that I use my drum or drumming tracks as a priority whenever I notice that I'm in a negative mindset or mood.

- I play the drum weekly with my drum sisters, monthly with my drum circle and every six weeks with my community as part of wheel of the year ceremonies. This provides a much-needed mood elevating combination of drumming and social connection which ticks a lot of my wellbeing boxes.

All my life, I've quickly gotten bored of things I have been undertaking. This has been especially true in my work and in the hobbies I chose. I strive for novelty; it makes my heart sing. I love learning new things. When I look back at my career, whether as a scientist or a self-employed educator, healer, doula and author, the only constant has been change and evolution. As a scientist I worked in about seven different organisations. The only reason I stayed for seven years in the same biotech company was because it grew from a startup of twelve to over one hundred employees and I had a constantly evolving role from bench scientist to group leader over my years there.

Over the course of my self-employment, I have grown from being an antenatal teacher, doula and babywearing instructor to evolving organically to teaching workshops to professionals, becoming a doula mentor, an energy and drum healer, to teaching online courses, dropping many outgrown roles along the way to make room for new growth. The one sign that tells me that I've outgrown something is boredom.

Therefore, it is a true credit to the power of the drum that not only I'm still going after eleven years, but that it is still growing in presence and power in my life.

The other aspect that strikes me as not being coincidental is that the start of my drumming journey coincides with the beginning of perimenopause, aged forty-two. Having ADHD means that I already have a dysregulation in dopamine production. Research shows that menopause can make ADHD symptoms significantly worse and that many symptoms of ADHD and menopause overlap (Newson, 2022). This is because oestrogen, which is known to promote the release of both serotonin and dopamine in the brain, decreases during perimenopause. This was certainly true for me, because my ADHD symptoms did not become unmanageable until my late forties/early fifties, along with when my perimenopause symptoms (sleep disturbances, night sweats, anxiety, and finding it harder to focus/brain fog) also became more challenging.

This time also coincided with my daughter's mental health crisis which I described in Chapter 1. It's easy to understand why the combination of multiple stressors made this a very overwhelming time for me. Despite everything I believe in (I'm more into natural remedies than modern drugs), when the combined symptoms became completely unmanageable, resulting in constant overwhelm, I decided to try HRT, shortly after my ADHD diagnosis, to help re-regulate my nervous system, with great results *(after eighteen months I stopped taking HRT due to increasingly problematic side effects, and found that once I stopped my previous symptoms did not return, probably as I had the time to get myself back into a re-regulated state by then, and my family's situation has improved).*

I find it very interesting to look back and see that, the more challenging the blended menopause/ADHD symptoms got, the bigger the role drumming took in my life.

Drumming and perimenopause

– Lucy H. Pearce

Shamanic drumming found me when I was experiencing a major autistic burnout, in early perimenopause. I had bought several drums over the years and even gone to a drum-making workshop run by a couple of autistic women for our autistic women's group, where we made them out of reclaimed materials – old sail cloth, rope and plastic tubs. Another women's group I attend had had a couple of drumming circles many years before and I had even organised one for our local arts festival. I loved drumming…but it had always been a communal activity. Drumming on my own…that was a stretch too far it seemed. I felt…silly. I hid the drums away, embarrassed, ashamed I had bought them and been unable to use them.

During the writing of my most recent book, Crow Moon, *I found my inner symbols and was surprised to find the drum was one of them. I took a leap of faith and recreated the crow from my book cover on the drum skin. There was something about this act that allowed me to claim the drum as my own. I started to use it regularly by myself – in my studio, in my garden – it quickly took me into a trance-like state where visions emerged quickly which became pieces of writing.*

I also began to meet with a member of my women's group. Sometimes on the beach, sometimes in her garden, we sit by a little fire and drum together – weaving in and out of each other's rhythms, sometimes adding improvised songs. These are some of my very favourite times I have spent in the last few years. I have let go of any rhythms I ever learned in drumming circles and just learned to go with what emerges. Without exception I feel blissed out and vibrant every time we do this. It flips some sort of switch in my neurodivergent brain and shifts me out of my daily stress, anxiety and overwhelm and into a deep, buzzing, ancient calm.

6

BEATING THE 'SHROOM: DRUMMING AS AN ALTERNATIVE TO PSYCHEDELICS

"What had become lost to us, due to the spiritual amnesia inherent within incarnation in the mundane world, is now directly accessible to us once again – through the direct experience of Shamanic Drumming!"

Jade Wah'oo Grigori

During the writing of this book, my drumming practice has intensified, revealing unexpected parallels with psychedelics. I've begun to notice striking similarities between the altered states of consciousness and neuroplastic changes (the brain's ability to rewire itself and form new connections throughout life) induced by microdosing psychedelic substances and those evoked through drumming. This exploration has unveiled a fascinating intersection between ancient percussion practices and modern psychedelic research, suggesting that both may offer pathways to profound cognitive and emotional shifts.

Psychedelics in prehistoric and Indigenous cultures

Human populations across the world have used psychedelics for medicinal, spiritual and cultural purposes for millennia. The oldest evidence of psychoactive mushroom use dates back from between 5000 and 7000 BC, in the form of cave painting/carvings called petroglyphs found in Tassili, Algeria. The petroglyphs, depict figures known as "mushroom shamans", with fists full of mushrooms and mushroom sprouting out of their bodies (McKenna, 1999).

In his controversial book, *Food of the Gods,* McKenna also introduces the Stoned Ape Theory: he suggests that early humans ingesting psilocybin mushrooms experienced enhanced visual acuity and cognitive abilities, which may have accelerated human evolution (McKenna, 1999).

Nearly a thousand years later, around 3780-3660 BC, Indigenous cultures in the Americas began their ceremonial use of peyote. Fast forward to the time of the Aztecs, between 1300 and 1521 AD, and we find evidence of mushroom consumption so revered that they called it the "flesh of the Gods". However, with the arrival of European colonizers came a shift in perspective; by 1500 AD, Catholic texts were dismissively referring to the sacred peyote rituals as mere witchcraft, marking the beginning of a long period of misunderstanding and suppression of these ancient practices (Visual Capitalist, 2021).

Understanding psychedelic substances

Before diving into the modern history of psychedelics, is it important to explain how they work. They temporarily change how your brain functions, affecting your thoughts, emotions and perceptions. It's like rewiring your mental pathways, allowing you to experience the world differently. The hallucinogenic effects mean you might see, hear or feel things that aren't physically present – like seeing vibrant colours, patterns moving or feeling unusually connected to your surroundings.

There are two main categories of psychedelic substances: entheogens, and synthetic drugs. Entheogens are derived from plants, while synthetic psychedelics are created in a laboratory.

Some of the most well-known psychedelic substances include:

- **LSD** (Lysergic acid diethylamide synthetic or from the Ergot rye fungus).
- **Psilocybin** (synthetic or found in magic mushrooms).
- **DMT** (Dimethyltryptamine synthetic or made from *Banisteriopsis caapi* vine and the leaves of the *Psychotria viridis* shrub, a brew known as Ayahuasca).

- **Mescaline** (found in peyote and San Pedro cacti).
- **MDMA** (3,4-Methylenedioxymethamphetamine, often called ecstasy).
- **Ketamine** (a synthetic substance).
- **Ibogaine** (found in the *Tabernanthe iboga* plant).

Psychedelic pioneers and prohibition

The nineteenth and twentieth centuries saw a surge in psychedelic discoveries, starting with the isolation of mescaline in 1897. This kicked off a wave of scientific breakthroughs: ibogaine in France (1901), MDMA's accidental creation in Germany (1912), and the synthesis of LSD in Switzerland (1938). Psilocybin was discovered in 1958, while ketamine was synthesized in the US in 1962.

As these substances gained popularity for recreational use, governments began to tighten regulations. The tide turned sharply in the 1960s and 1970s, with California criminalizing LSD in 1966, followed by federal US laws against psilocybin in 1968. The trend went global with the 1971 UN Convention on Psychotropic Substances, mirrored by strict national laws in the US and UK. This legal crackdown, part of the broader 'War on Drugs', effectively halted most legitimate research into psychedelics' medical potential for decades, despite their promising early results (Visual Capitalist, 2021).

The psychedelic renaissance

The twenty-first century marked a dramatic shift in the perception and use of psychedelic substances. After decades of prohibition, these once-vilified drugs are now being reconsidered for their therapeutic potential. Starting in 2017 with the FDA granting MDMA-assisted psychotherapy "breakthrough therapy status", a cascade of scientific, legal, and cultural milestones followed. Cities and states began decriminalising psychedelics, while research expanded rapidly, exploring their potential for treating mental health conditions and stimulating brain cell growth.

The industry has seen unprecedented growth, with public companies emerging and market analysts projecting a $100 billion potential. As of today, there are hundreds of active trials globally and increasing legislative support, psychedelics are poised to revolutionise mental health treatment and potentially address a wider range of medical conditions (Visual Capitalist, 2021).

Grassroots movements in psychedelic exploration

In parallel to these scientific and regulatory changes, we have also seen the rise of the psychedelics microdosing movement, driven by communities rather than corporations. Microdosing involves taking sub-perceptual amounts of substances, usually LSD or psilocybin, to enhance creativity, mood and productivity without experiencing hallucinogenic effects. Users report benefits such as improved mood, energy levels, cognition, creativity, and reduced depression and anxiety. Scientific research on microdosing is still emerging, with some studies showing small to medium-sized improvements in mood and mental health and some finding limited improvements (Polito and Stevenson, 2019).

The rise of citizen science in the psychedelics movement marks a cultural shift by empowering individuals to participate in research and knowledge creation, breaking down traditional barriers between scientists and the public, and fostering a sense of community and shared understanding around the therapeutic potential of psychedelics. This democratisation of research not only challenges established norms within the scientific community but also reflects a growing acceptance and interest in alternative healing practices, emphasising personal narratives and lived experiences as valid contributions to scientific discourse (Fadiman and Korb, 2019).

"There has been a huge rise in people and especially parents enquiring about how microdosing can help them. In the UK, I've noticed parents contacting me when they feel at the end of the road with mainstream medicine and talk therapy. These systems are failing them. They are looking for more. They don't want to talk endlessly about their trauma, they don't want medication long term that numbs their emotions. They want to feel more connected to themselves, their children, their partners. They want to feel better, but they want something deeper – a spiritual or at least a more meaningful life journey. Microdosing can help facilitate this."

Naomi Tolson, Microdosing coach

Personal experiences

I have noticed that drumming affects my brain profoundly in a positive way. When listening to drumming tracks designed to aid focus, I sometimes feel sensations inside my head which are similar to the ones I experience when taking ADHD medication.

I discovered the power of 'microdosing' drumming while writing this book. The practice is simple: set a timer for five minutes and commit to drumming for just that length of time. I chose five minutes because it feels achievable. I knew I'd be less likely to maintain a longer daily practice of, say, twenty minutes. The results surprised me. After a couple of weeks of this brief daily ritual, I began noticing previously unconscious negative thought patterns. Becoming aware of these patterns allowed me to interrupt and replace them with more constructive patterns.

The reason this experience struck me as similar to psychedelics, was because I had experienced exactly the same effect when I started microdosing psilocybin mushrooms to support my mental health a couple of years ago. Within a couple of weeks of taking the plant medicine, I started "hearing" a judgemental voice in my head which I hadn't been aware of before. I was in a dark place then. The combined weight of supporting my child through their mental health crisis, navigating the stormy waters of perimenopause and living with undiagnosed ADHD had left me struggling to keep my head above water.

A pivotal moment stands out in my memory: I was in the bathroom, feeling exhausted and overwhelmed, when an internal voice suddenly berated me. The voice felt like an overbearing parent, complete with an imaginary wagging finger. I became acutely aware of this thought pattern and how unkind and unhelpful it was and engaged in a conversation with it. This interaction marked the beginning of a transformative journey. I started recognising many judgemental and unkind thought patterns I had unknowingly hurt myself with for years. This was very helpful in starting to heal my relationship with myself, because the first step of healing is to bring up an unconscious issue to consciousness.

Experiencing the parallel above prompted me to do some research about the link between drumming and psychedelic experiences. I wondered if, as well as changing consciousness, drumming could also help rewire our brains.

Connections to other disciplines

Listening to mycologist Paul Stamets explain that low sound waves, such as the ones produced by drumming, stimulate the growth of mycelial networks, I could see a similar pattern of stimulation and growth, whether it's networks of neurons or networks of fungi.

I could also see the similarities between the shamanic state of consciousness and the state of consciousness during birth, when our own inner psychedelics, endorphins, help us enter this state.

In his course, "Beyond Shamanism", Jeff Strong explains that most cultures have historically used percussion to change consciousness and enter trance-like states, while the few that didn't develop percussion used psychedelic plants instead. Traditionally, he explains, only about 10% of cultures used psychedelics, while 90% used percussion.

When I interviewed Jeff, I asked him to explain this further. He shared that some cultures developed the use of psychedelic substances as an alternative to drumming, in particular when the practice of native religions and rituals was banned as part of the colonisation process. Using psychedelics as part of secret ceremonies was a lot more discreet than using drums.

Is it possible that the use of percussion to alter consciousness might be the norm for humans and a lot more common than the use of psychedelic substances?

Mircea Eliade, a pre-eminent scholar of shamanism, drew a distinction between authentic shamanic techniques and what he considered degraded practices. While he emphasised drumming as a central and legitimate method for achieving altered states of consciousness (along with dance, chanting etc.), he viewed the use of psychedelics as a corruption of genuine shamanic tradition. In his perspective, psychedelic substances served merely as shortcuts for less capable practitioners who could not access transcendent states through their own spiritual resources and traditional techniques like drumming (Eliade, 2020).

In his book, *Drumming at the Edge of Magic,* Mikey Hart explains that *"using drugs to access and manipulate these non-ordinary states was not a modern discovery. Classical shamanism was no stranger to the potentials of botanicals allies to amplify trance. Plants such as vine ayahuasca, the psilocybin mushroom and fly agaric mushrooms have long histories of shamanic use. And because we in the West have a tradition of altering brain metabolism with drugs, we are perhaps more sympathetic to the claims of shamans who use botanicals than we are to shamans who simply beat on a piece of horsehide stretched upon a willow frame."* (Hart, 1990.)

I also couldn't help but wonder: maybe it isn't either/or. When I was microdosing mushrooms, I also drummed many times after having taken a dose, and I found that it really deepened my experience. I was going within in an altered state that I did not reach with the microdosing or the drumming alone.

Shamans have long used drumming as a tool to alter states of consciousness, as part of ceremonies, facilitating spiritual journeys and healing practices. The trance-like state induced by the repetitive beat allows practitioners and communities to access different dimensions of awareness, enhancing their connection to spiritual realms and aiding in the retrieval of knowledge or healing. This practice is deeply rooted in many Indigenous cultures worldwide, serving as a means of communication with spirits and ancestors.

Studies exploring Aztec medicine, show that that music – especially drumming – has been integral to psychedelic ceremonies. The rhythm of the drums mirrors the heartbeat, helping participants enter a trance-like state that fosters creative expression (Cox 2024).

The ancient Greeks and Romans participated in seasonal rites, including drumming and dancing, and the use of a psychoactive drink called kykeon, which contained hallucinogens similar to LSD (Cox, 2024). The Bwiti of central Africa practice a powerful rite known as "breaking open the head," where they ingest iboga, a psychedelic plant central to their ecstatic tribal dances accompanied by rhythmic drumming. This ceremony reveals the Bwiti's deep understanding of inner work, a knowledge that resonates across cultures and throughout history. Similar elements of shamanic participatory rituals can be found in various traditions, highlighting a shared wisdom about the transformative power of these experiences (Moores, 2020).

It makes sense that the combination of drumming and psychedelics enhances the overall experience due to their complementary effects on consciousness. Both modalities can facilitate profound alterations in perception, emotional processing and cognitive flexibility. Psychedelics can induce intense visionary experiences, while drumming helps ground individuals and maintain a rhythmic focus, creating an environment that enhances the transformative effect of the psychedelic experience.

The neuroscience of drumming

As you may remember from the chapters on the science of drumming, the synchronisation of brainwaves with drumbeats is believed to be a key mechanism through which drumming modifies and expands states of awareness. This shift in brainwave activity facilitates neuroplasticity, allowing for the formation of new neural pathways and the rewiring of existing ones.

A study investigated the effects of drum training on brain structure and function. The researchers found that learning to drum induces long-term plasticity in the cerebellum and increases cortical thickness in connected brain areas. These structural changes were associated with improved drumming performance and enhanced ability to discriminate drum sounds, suggesting that drum training can lead to significant neuroplastic adaptations in the brain (Bruchhage et al., 2020).

Parallels and differences between drumming and psychedelics

Published research comparing psychedelics to drumming has found overlapping traits between the two states. However, whilst both drumming and psychedelic substances have the potential to induce altered states of consciousness and facilitate neuroplasticity, it appears that they work through different mechanisms.

- **Mode of action:** Psychedelics work by interacting with specific receptors in the brain, leading to profound changes in consciousness, introspection and sensory perceptions. Drumming works through auditory entrainment, rhythmic stimulation and the engagement of motor and sensory neural networks. The rhythmic input synchronises brainwaves, activates the body's natural reward systems and stimulates the release of neurotransmitters like dopamine and serotonin. Unlike psychedelics, the effects of drumming build gradually through consistent practice, creating lasting changes in neural pathways related to attention, emotion regulation and sensory-motor integration. The underlying neurobiology appears distinct and there are changes in brain activity which appear specific to the shamanic state of consciousness induced by drumming. Experiences such as complex imagery, experience of unity, spiritual experience and insightfulness appear to be greater for shamanic practitioners during trance compared to healthy controls under psychedelic compounds such as psilocybin, ketamine or MDMA (Huels et al., 2021).

- **Control and regulation:** Drumming allows for the ability to control and regulate the depth of the altered state by adjusting rhythm, tempo and volume, or stopping entirely. If anything unpleasant happens (think 'bad trip') one simply needs to ask for this to stop, become something else or open one's eyes for it to stop (Jeff Strong, "Beyond Shamanism" course). Psychedelic experiences using substances, once initiated, can be more challenging to control or terminate.

- **Predictability and effectiveness:** According to Jeff Strong's research, both drumming and psychedelic 'trips' are as unpredictable as one another in that, even if setting up the conditions and intentions, some experiences can be mystical and some disappointing. McKenna also discusses how shamanic cultures have used both drumming and psychedelics in their rituals. He notes that these practices often aim to induce altered states of consciousness, but the specific outcomes can vary (McKenna 1999). In the Netflix documentary, *How to Change Your Mind*, in various episodes, Michael Pollan also explores how 'trips' can range from mind-blowing insights to more underwhelming experiences.

- **Legal considerations:** The use of psychedelic substances is illegal in many countries, while drumming is a widely accepted and legal practice across cultures.

- **Access and cost:** Accessing psychedelics can be complex and expensive due to legal ramifications, while drumming tracks are widely available for free and drums can be inexpensive to acquire.

- **Integration and after-effects:** Psychedelic experiences can be intense and overwhelming, requiring careful integration and processing. Drumming, being a more gradual and controlled process, allows for smoother integration of insights and experiences into daily life.

- **Building new skills:** With psychedelics you need the substance to enter the altered state of consciousness. With drumming, over time your brain builds the skill to be able to enter that state at will, like when you train a muscle and eventually you become able to enter that state without the help of the drum (in that state, however, using the drum usually helps you go deeper).

While drumming and psychedelics share the potential for inducing altered states and facilitating neuroplasticity, drumming offers distinct advantages as a legal and more controllable means of accessing altered states. Drumming potentially provides a safer and more accessible avenue for personal growth, therapeutic benefits and expanded awareness.

If you would like to try for yourself how drumming can change your state of consciousness, a beautifully simple way to do so is to listen to a drum journey, a form of guided meditation accompanied by the drum. Many of my students report more success doing this than with meditation, because the sound entrainment requires no effort. There are several drum journeys available on my YouTube Channel and in the appendix.

In conclusion, this chapter highlights the powerful connection between drumming and altered states of consciousness, drawing parallels with the effects of psychedelics. Both methods tap into our brain's plasticity, allowing for emotional and cognitive transformations. While psychedelics offer intense, often unpredictable experiences, drumming provides a more controlled, gradual path toward inner exploration and personal growth.

Drumming, being legal and accessible, stands as a safer alternative to psychedelics for those seeking transformative experiences. It allows individuals to enter altered states at will, especially with consistent practice, enhancing mental flexibility, emotional regulation and creativity. Drumming offers a deeply spiritual and therapeutic avenue for those who may not have access to or prefer to avoid the complexities associated with psychedelics.

Drumming offers an approachable, yet profound, way to shift consciousness and tap into the brain's amazing capacity for healing and adaptation.

If you're curious, start with a simple drum journey, or grab a drum, and see where it takes you. It may well open new pathways of understanding within yourself. You might just stumble upon some hidden corners of your mind that you never knew existed. After all, if our ancestors could use it to commune with the spirits, who knows what kind of magic you might come up with?

7

SACRED CIRCLES: DRUMMING, RITUALS AND CEREMONIES

"Music can touch on strings you might not know you had. It can provide meaning, but it can also create moments which can't be defined. Moments which go to your core, that touch some sort of primal instinct and that put you in a trance-like condition. Music can confuse you. But it can also make you feel happy, uplifted or enriched. And maybe even more whole."

Mari Boine

Drums have been used as part of ceremonies for millennia, marking important life events and ceremonies. The centrality of drumming across cultures comes from the fact that the drums represent the heartbeat of life itself: the rhythms and vibrations have been used as means to achieve transcendence and communication with spirit. Even in our contemporary 'homo rationalis' society, we still have an innate understanding of the fact that drumming is an important part of rituals. I would go as far as saying many of us have a deep longing for this.

Even in our modern world, we still have an innate understanding of drumming's ritual significance. This can be seen in how drums remain central to many modern gatherings and celebrations – from music festivals to sporting events. People report feeling a deep, almost inexplicable connection to drum rhythms, suggesting that our bodies remember what our modern minds might have forgotten.

This longing for rhythmic connection manifests in various ways: the growing popularity of drum circles, the integration of drumming into wellness practices, and the increasing interest in traditional drumming ceremonies. People seek out these experiences for something deeper – a sense of connection, community and transcendence that our technology-driven society tends to lack.

This yearning might be explained by our evolutionary history. When we drum together, we're not just making music; we're participating in an ancient form of communication that speaks to something fundamental in our human experience.

This longing for rhythmic ritual also reflects a broader desire to reconnect with practices that ground us in our bodies and connect us to others in non-verbal, deeply emotional ways. In an age of digital disconnection and virtual relationships, the physical, visceral experience of drumming offers a powerful counterpoint to our increasingly mind based lives.

Drumming and bringing more sacredness to your life

I used to long for a more meaningful life, for a sense of connection to something bigger than myself. Drumming certainly helped with that.

I can still see myself witnessing my first closing the bones ceremony and wishing it was me on the floor receiving the ritual. I can still feel the excitement, as I attended my first doula retreat, how beautiful and sacred it all felt and then how much returning to my normal life, especially with two young children to care for, felt so bland, so lacking in connection and full of drudgery. I longed to go back to the feeling that this amazing, spiritual retreat gave me. I was holding an unconscious limited belief that this kind of magic only happened outside of normal life. When I attended women's circles, red tents, retreats and so on, something in me believed that the 'sacred' only happened in these special, out of normal life, spaces.

I was missing and longing for more sacredness partly because it is missing from most of our culture, but also partly because of my own unconscious and narrow definition of what the sacred was. It took me a long time to reweave a sense of sacredness into my daily life, in a way where it feels natural, normal and simple. The drum led me in the most gentle and powerful way.

I have been reflecting on the fact that all cultures around the world used to have three practices that belonged both to everyday life and to the sacred. These practices are singing, drumming and dancing. But here, today in the modern world, we think that only special people, gifted people can do them.

Having taught workshops and courses that involve a deep element of spirituality since 2014, I have witnessed the same longing in many women again and again, especially when leading people through circles and ceremonies. This longing I sense in others is why I want to offer more ceremonies, more women blessings, more drum circles, more healing gatherings and share more rituals. We need to create new rituals for our modern times. We need to make this normal again. A sense of spirituality is as important to wellbeing as eating and drinking.

As I have explored what sacredness means to me in my everyday life, I encourage others to follow their own journey of reintroducing sacredness to their own lives. If you feel the same longing in your heart and you want to create a more beautiful life for yourself, listen carefully to what your heart is telling you. We aren't meant to live such disconnected lives. You deserve a life where you feel more connected to yourself, to your community and to the world around you. Start small. Be gentle. Try things and see what works for you. Drumming can be an incredibly gentle and powerful way to lead you back into a more connected life.

Finding sanctuary

– Joanna Summers

In the embrace of the drum circle, amidst the primal beats, flickering flames, I've found a sanctuary – a place where souls relate, united by the rhythm of the earth and the whispers of ancient wisdom. Inspired by the teaching of the Q'ero and my own journey of holding sacred spaces for the past thirteen years, I've come to deeply understand the profound importance of acceptance and inclusivity.

However, this understanding was not without its trials. Despite our commitment to an open-door framework, tensions arose when comments were made that excluded an outwardly presenting transwoman. This experience served as a catalyst for change, prompting me to reflect on the true meaning of acceptance and the need for advocacy in all spaces.

In response, I made the decision to close the circles and return to university to retrain, where I encountered post-colonial diversity studies and advocacy work that ignited my passion to bring shamanism into academic spaces. Inspired by the teachings of Myira Khan, anti-oppressive practice, I embarked on a new path, currently advocating for inclusivity and acceptance within the LGBTQ+ communities.

In the tapestry of lived experiences, it's challenging to weave threads of love, dignity and grace, as we discover places to honour each other, embracing the universal rhythms that flow between us. With each beat of the drum, we flow closer to a world where inclusion isn't just something out there but becomes our reality and lived experience. Within the drum with all the relating challenges therein, as we give voice to values, principles and ethics – where every voice is valued, every soul heard and every heart free.

In the heart of the wild, where spirits roam free,
There lives a circle, under ancient tree.
With drums in hand and souls ablaze,
We gather 'round the fire, in a rhythmic gaze.
The World Drum spoke, its message clear,
Of love and peace, for all to hear,
In the shadow of the mountain peak
We alight our voices, strong and unique.

As the beat begins, a primal call,
Echoes through the valley, over hill and hall.
The frame drum sings, its rhythm pure,
While my tank drum joins, its voice is secure.

As the drums beat on, the rhythm swells,
A symphony of souls, where magic dwells.
We feel the pulse, of the cosmos' beat,
Uniting us all, in a dance complete.

For in the circle of the drum, we find our song,
A melody of love, that carries us along.

With each beat, we weave our tale,
Of unity, peace and where hearts prevail.

So let us drum, with hearts aglow,
Spreading love and peace, let our spirits flow,
For in the rhythm of the drum we find our way,
Embracing our lives as we embrace sacred play.

Drumming during ceremonies to mark a life transition

"I realised that I and others in our culture were being methodically starved of substance, that something was awry in some of the 'wisdom' of our culture, that it did not have our best interests at heart, that it saw those who are 'menopausal' as somehow less. It is not so; we are instead more. Much, much more."

Clarissa Pinkola Estés

Recently, I taught an intuitive drum healing course, during which I got the women to pair and share with each other what happened to them when they first had their period. I asked if they were celebrated. I expected to hear about a lack of celebration, but the women shared harrowing stories of not only no form of celebration but a total lack of kindness and preparation. Some had not been told about periods at all and were frightened and alone when they bled. One was only ten years old when she bled for the first time, whilst at a boarding school, and thought she was going to die.

After the sharing I asked them to work together to craft then enact a menarche-reclaiming ceremony. I had been nervous about this, worrying that they might not feel inspired, but I need not have worried. Together they co-created the most beautiful ceremony. It included walking a labyrinth made of flowers, accompanied by the drum and crossing a threshold whilst being welcomed and given flowers by an elder, accompanied with whoops and shouts of joy. Even though it had been crafted quickly and was short and simple, it was incredibly powerful. I found it deeply moving and so did the women present. It reinforced both the need and the power of holding such ceremonies.

As I write this, I am at the cusp of crossing the menopausal threshold and when this has happened, I am going to gather a group of trusted midlife women friends to create a menopause/croning ceremony for me.

The drum is beautifully suited to add reverence and accompany rituals that mark all important transitions in a woman's life.

As women, we go through tremendous changes during puberty, pregnancy, motherhood and menopause. Our bodies, minds and spirits morph to accommodate new phases of womanhood. Yet modern society lacks rituals to honour these pivotal thresholds or guide us through the transitions.

All over the world, diverse cultures have historically celebrated feminine rites of passage – blessing and welcoming girls into maidenhood, providing pregnancy blessings, postpartum nurture after birth and honouring crones. Colonialism and industrialisation disrupted these ceremonies, leaving us, modern women, adrift during these intense periods of change.

I believe reclaiming menstrual, maternity and menopausal rituals can heal women and society. Ceremony grounds us during liminal states, connects us to the cycles of nature and anchors us in community when we need support most. They also help bring the community together.

I want to encourage a movement towards recreating embodied traditions surrounding:

- Menarche/first blood
- Pregnancy, birth and postpartum
- Perimenopause/menopause.

A tale of two women

In our modern world, women's life transitions have been stripped of their power and meaning. The deep, transformative experiences that mark our journey through womanhood, from first blood to motherhood to the wisdom years, have been reduced to clinical procedures or ignored altogether. I've witnessed firsthand how this loss of ceremony and community support affects women deeply, often in ways they can't quite name but feel intensely.

I have written these two stories to illuminate the stark contrast between what a woman experiences in today's society and what her body, mind and spirit yearn for. These parallel narratives show us two worlds: the sterile, disconnected reality of modern life, and the rich, supportive environment our ancestors knew, one where every transition was understood and honoured.

A girl is born into a sterile hospital room, greeted by machines beeping rather than welcoming drumbeats and reverence. No wise familiar women are present to bless her arrival. The medical staff does not acknowledge the enormity of what has just happened. For them it's just another day at the office.

As she grows, her menarche goes uncelebrated. Only the practical is discussed: how to use period products. It is just a matter of facts. Not only is there no ritual, no celebrations, but her bleeding is shrouded in shame and secrecy. Something one does not speak off. Nobody helps her comprehend the momentous physical and spiritual transition she is going through, nor of the magical power that comes from her womb, a portal of life.

She is also not honoured when she becomes pregnant, as it seems that only her baby matters and she is just a vessel. If there is a gathering, it is a soulless event where all the presents are for the baby. When the time comes for her to give birth, it is treated as a medical procedure. She labours alone or with only her partner for support and the presence of hospital staff she has not met before.

With her baby's arrival, there is no joyous community celebration. Her status remains unchanged – she is just another new mother, others have done it before, what's the big deal about that? There is no special treatment during her recovery. She is sent home quickly, expected to care for herself and her newborn with minimal support. There are no experienced mothers surrounding her, no teachings on the art of nurturing her new baby. No rest, no massages, no wrapping of her belly, or specially prepared nourishing meals. She is left to fend for herself as her body, mind and spirit try to heal from the intense feat of growing and birthing a whole new person.

Alone, with internet searches and books as her only guides, she stumbles through those raw postpartum days. There is no community rite of passage to mark her transition into motherhood. She has become a mother, but there is no drumming, no ceremony, no village acknowledging her new role. She feels that something is missing but she doesn't know what and she blames herself for her struggles.

As the seasons pass, each transition and rite of passage she experiences goes unrecognised, unmarked by any traditions or rituals. When her fertility cycles end, there are no drums summoning her into her croning years. There is no acknowledgement that she is now a well of wisdom to be celebrated. Instead, society portrays this transition as an anomaly to be treated. Her menopause transition passes unacknowledged, just another uncelebrated phase of life.

Most of the important life transitions in a woman's life, menstruation, birth and motherhood and menopause, are systematically minimised, stigmatised and portrayed as weaknesses in modern society. These rites of passage, which should be sources of strength and empowerment, are instead either completely ignored or clouded in secrecy. The systematic devaluation of these experiences reflects and reinforces the disempowerment of women.

Jane Hardwicke Collings, the founder of the School of Shamanic Womancraft, says that, *"Anything to do with women, or the feminine that is put down, ridiculed, feared, or made invisible, is a clue that it holds great power."*

With the return of the drum to the hands of women, as a normal spiritual practice, I imagine another world, one where women would be supported and celebrated into their life transitions. This isn't just about nostalgia, it's about understanding why so many women feel unseen, unsupported and disconnected during their most significant life transitions. Through these stories, I invite you to imagine a different way, one where we can create new traditions for today's world – one where the rhythms of womanhood are once again celebrated, where community holds space for transformation, and where the drum guides us through the thresholds of our lives.

A girl is born. From the moment she takes her first breath, she is embraced by the rhythms of the drum welcoming her to this world. Wise women gather round, guiding her entry into the community with honouring rituals and blessings.

As she grows into a young woman, her menarche is heralded with drumming, ceremony and dance, honouring the deep transition her body is undergoing. Elders surround her and share their wisdom, preparing her for womanhood.

When the time comes for her to bring new life into the world, it is an event of deep reverence. Sisters gather around her. They wash her hands and feet and place a flower crown on her hair. They drum and sing, weaving a cocoon of support around her. Each gift is accompanied by blessings and shared wisdom. She is bathed in a warmth that goes beyond the physical, nourishing her spirit and fortifying her for the journey ahead.

When she goes into labour, gentle drumbeats guide her along in the journey into an altered state of consciousness as she brings her baby into the world, surrounded by familiar wise women.

With the arrival of her baby, the community comes together in celebration. Her status is heightened by bringing a new soul into the world. She is treated as sacred, a queen among queens. All her needs are tended to by loving hands as she recovers her strength. Experienced mothers encircle her, teaching the precious art of nurturing her newborn. She rests, receives daily massages, her abdomen is wrapped, nourishing meals are made especially for her with love – all this is lavished upon her to heal her body, mind and spirit.

Constantly surrounded by nurturing, experienced women, her transition to motherhood is easy. When, after a month has passed, she emerges ready to re-enter the world, she feels strong, seen and acknowledged in her new role as a mother.

So it continues, through the seasons of her life, each rite of passage accompanied by the drum alongside her journey. Drumming is part of her life, part of ceremonies that mark the turning of the year, part of regular gatherings created to release tension and bring the community together. The drum weaves the women together.

So it continues, through the seasons of her life, each rite of passage accompanied by the drum alongside her journey. When, finally, her fertility comes to an end, the drums accompany her transition to cronehood, a well of wisdom to be revered by the community, ready to support the younger women in her community through their own rites of passage.

There are many other moments of deep change and transition in our lives that also go unmarked, endings and beginnings throughout a woman's life that can be honoured with rituals such as:

- Moving away from home.
- After baby loss, miscarriage, stillbirth, abortion…
- In preparation for or after a hysterectomy.
- To support a fertility journey or conscious conception.
- To mark the end of breastfeeding or other big child milestones.
- Children leaving the nest.
- Marriage or entering a steady relationship.

- Losses, including separation or divorce, or the loss of a job.
- To honour and grieve not having been able to have children.
- New beginnings including starting a new job, or a new relationship.
- Healing including abuse and trauma.
- Death (creating a ceremony to either prepare for or mark a death).

RITUAL BLUEPRINT

Let me share with you how to create a simple ceremony and how you might incorporate drumming into it. This can be adapted to hold a woman through any of life's transitions: whether she's entering menarche, motherhood, the menopause, or navigating any of life's thresholds, here's how to weave magic and meaning into her journey.

Setting the intentions

Meet with the woman who wishes to have the ceremony. Invite her to share her vision, her intentions of what she would like the ceremony to look and feel like, and what she would like to achieve from it. Offer suggestions and ideas you think she might like. Be sensitive to her needs, her spiritual beliefs and what feels right for her.

Gathering your circle

Help her gather her friends and loved ones. Call in those who truly see her, who've walked similar paths, who hold pieces of the wisdom she's seeking. Keep it intimate – too many people can scatter the energy. I find that somewhere between six and twelve women creates the perfect container.

As you plan the day remember that less is more and create plenty of spaciousness in the ceremony.

Creating your sacred space

Create a womb-like space: soft, warm and nurturing. Think beautiful fabrics dotted around the space, fairy lights, candles, cushions placed in a circle. Your central altar might include crystals, flowers, oracle cards, art and objects/figures representing the transition the woman is going through, and/or the elements. You can also invite the guests to bring something to place on the altar. And of course, bring a drum or several if you have them and maybe some percussion instruments.

Welcoming everyone in

As the women arrive, invite them to drop into sacred space. You might welcome them with a smoke or scented spray cleansing ritual as they enter. If you have a helper to do this, you can play the drum in the space as they arrive, letting the rhythm draw everyone into their bodies and away from the rushing world outside. You could open sacred space by welcoming each direction and each element, and/or simply speaking your intentions for this gathering and the sacred circle you're creating.

Honouring her journey – the heart of the ceremony

Place the woman being celebrated on a special seat (you could set-up an armchair or other comfy seat, think throne rather than hard chair), and crown her with flowers. There's something so powerful about physically marking someone as special, sacred. You might invite guests to wash her feet or hands in a bowl with scented oils and rose petals, an ancient act of blessing that says "you are worthy of being tended to."

Have a circle of introduction, starting by sharing a few breaths together, and invite each woman to speak her name, and the name of her mother and grandmother, to invite the presence of ancestors in the space.

Invite guests to share a story, a blessing, a piece of wisdom, a strength they see in the woman. There are often tears! Let the laughter bubble up too. Share gifts that carry meaning beyond their physical form and the moment: a bead from each guest to share to make a communal necklace to keep and cherish, a shawl to wrap her in community's embrace.

Honour her body. Maybe share some gentle touch through massaging her hands and/or feet, or plaiting her hair in a fancy way. Whilst this is happening, you can also lead the group into a simple chant apt for the occasion, accompanied by the drum (there is a list in the Appendix).

You could also do some art together, a collage of wishes for the journey ahead, vision board style, using cutout from old magazines, with each guest sharing the meaning of their chosen picture once it is complete.

Make sure you're also planning the support that extends beyond the ceremony. Who's bringing meals? Who can she call at 3am? Who's checking in next week, next month? Write it down, make it real. This could be captured on a beautiful piece of paper or card, whilst people are doing the collage.

Weaving the web of support & closing the ceremony

Pass some wool or string around the circle and have everyone wrap it a couple of times around their wrist or ankle. Once everyone is bound by the thread, pass scissors around to cut it and have everyone knot the thread, with an invitation to keep it until a certain milestone has happened (in the case of a mother blessing, when the baby has been born).

You could also gift everyone a tealight, with an invitation to light it and send good wishes to the woman being honoured at an agree time. This might be the beginning of labour, the morning of a significant surgery, the anniversary of a loss, or before starting a new chapter such as the end of a significant relationship or moving home.

Then, when the time is right (a good couple of hours is a nice length), have a final sharing circle, maybe some drumming and singing, then announce the end of the ritual, and close sacred space.

Grounding the sacred with a feast

After the sacred time and before people leave, share some food together. The practice of sharing food helps weave the sacred experience back into ordinary life, reminding us that ceremony and daily life need not be separate. It could be as simple as tea and cake, or you could ask each guest to bring a dish to share and have a feast.

Remember, this is just a framework – a basket to hold your own creative offerings. Each ceremony will be as unique as the woman it honours. Trust your intuition, follow what feels right, and don't forget to document the magic (and take photos if she's comfortable with that).

The key is creating space where a woman feels truly witnessed in her transition. Where she knows, deep in her bones, that she is not alone on this journey.

My hope is that we might rebirth new customs into accessible practices supporting women and making it the norm once more. Though we may not have much practice in this in our culture, I believe we all have an innate understanding of what is needed to craft a meaningful ritual.

My journey with the drum

– Jane Hardwicke Collings

I made my first drum during my shamanic training in my early thirties. I loved the process, and I used my drum in our ceremonies and for drum journeys in my home birth midwifery practice.

For many years, I celebrated the seasonal sabbats with a local community, comprised largely of families who had homebirths, many of whom I served as their midwife. I had my menopause rite of passage with this community and our youngest son had his puberty rite of passage, his welcoming to manhood ceremony within this community.

Each year at Beltane the community would gather to honour and celebrate the girls whose menarche happened that year and the boys who turned thirteen that year.

During Jackson's welcoming to manhood ceremony, I tearfully drummed farewell with the other mothers as we watched our boys walk into the bush with the men and the other boys for their ritual. As I watched Jackson, I really felt the power of the moment and the stretch on my mother's heart, letting go.

As I was drumming, seeing him get smaller and smaller in the distance, my drum split in half! Thirteen years ago, I had painted the inside of that drum, with the blood from his birth and the drum split at his puberty rite of passage into manhood!

Fast forward to the School of Shamanic Womancraft…

The drum plays a central role in the School of Shamanic Womancraft.

We use the drum making process as deep inner work.

The opportunity is to figure out the pattern of your birth and how to work with it, rather than be worked by it.

"If you don't do the work, the work does you."

We hold the drum making process like a prayer, a ceremony. The women mindfully choose their animal hide, or the hide chooses them.

They commune with the animal through a drum journey to connect and express gratitude for the honour of making a drum.

Many women receive particular instructions for the process during this journey.

Some women even receive a name for their drum.

Many women decorate the hoop with written words and symbols.

And the hide soaks often overnight in water under the moonlight.

Some women choose to make their drum with canvas rather than animal hide.

There are many parts of the drum-making process that reflect the energy of a mother giving birth. We see that when the women retrieve their wet hide from the soaking water with the reverence, they would give a newborn baby. And at the completion of the process, the care they give their newly birthed drum sometimes provides a healing opportunity for those who were separated from their mothers as newborns, or had their own newborn separated from them.

We embrace the healing power of the drum.

In the Shamanic Dimensions of Pregnancy workshop, we use craft for the women to experience their birth imprint and a drum journey to teach single pointed focus – a technique known to decrease pain of childbirth and to connect with the baby inside. Some women use the journey to connect with the baby's spirit they feel nearby to ask what they need to do to prepare for conception. Others connect with babies they have lost.

Drum making is a reclamation, a healing and a remembering.

Drumming during wheel of the year ceremonies

Another spiritual practice, accompanied by the drum, which is connecting me ever so deeply with nature and the cycles of the seasons, has been taking part in Celtic wheel of the year ceremonies.

In Celtic cultures,we used to celebrate eight festivals during the year: the two equinoxes, the two solstices and the four times in between.

- **Samhain** (October 31st): This marks the Celtic New Year and is considered the most important festival. It's a time to honour the dead and the start of the dark half of the year. It also marks the end of the harvest season.
- **Winter Solstice** (Around December 21st): Celebrates the rebirth of the sun as the days begin growing longer again after the longest night.
- **Imbolc** (February 1st): An early spring festival associated with the first signs of spring. It celebrates the returning fertility to the earth.
- **Spring Equinox** (Around March 21st): Marking the beginning of the fertile spring season when day and night are equal lengths.
- **Beltane** (May 1st): A celebration of the full bloom of spring and the fertility of the earth.
- **Summer Solstice** (Around June 21st): Celebrating the longest day of the year and the power of the life-giving sun.
- **Lughnasadh** (August 1st): The first of the three autumn harvest festivals, marking the beginning of the harvest season and gratitude for the bountiful earth.
- **Autumn Equinox** (Around September 21st): The second harvest festival, signalling the start of autumn when day and night are again equal.

These eight festivals formed the basis of the ancient Celtic calendar system and marked the key points in the agricultural year.

Over the last four years, I have progressed from first attending these ceremonies as a witness, to becoming involved in co-creating some of them and finally over the last couple of years, since I was crowned May Queen for the year at Beltane in 2023, I have become deeply involved in co-creating and running each and every one of these ceremonies. This has given me a deep attunement and appreciation of the changing energies of the seasons.

Every six weeks, I have had a powerful reason to pause, reflect and tune-in as I sit in a circle with like-minded souls to dream and co-create the next ceremony together. This has given me precious time out of the busyness of life to really appreciate the individual energy of each cycle, as well as a deep and fulfilling way to serve my community.

Last Imbolc, I reflected that, for the first time in my fifty-four years on this earth, I had not dreaded winter, but welcomed its slowing down and going-within wisdom, instead of fighting it and feeling like it was just a fleeting, changing moment.

Each ceremony is unique and designed to embody the energy of each specific time of the year. Over the last year we have created candle spirals, walked blindfolded around a circle of living willow with arches representing the eight gateways, whilst reflecting on the past year. We have sung songs, gazed at and jumped over sacred fires whilst speaking intentions, letting go ritually of what no longer served us. Every time we have drummed as we processed around the land and formed a circle around the fire as a community. It is simple yet powerful and it is grounded in reverence for nature and a deep sense of belonging and community.

In May 2024, my 'reign' as May Queen came to an end. As part of the ceremony for Beltane, a symbolic death was enacted for the previous May King and Queen. It was inspired by the fact that Des Crow, the druid who helps co-create and lead our ceremonies, had found two dead crows a day or two before the gathering, in the exact space where the ceremony was to take place. He was guided to create a death ceremony for us. A woman embodied the spirit of the Cailleach, the Celtic goddess of winter, and led us to a dug-up earth pit, where we laid on the ground and released our roles as King and Queen into the earth. The rest of the community sang and drummed as we did this. I had the most profound experience, as I released my May Queen mantle into the earth, and the drumming and singing faded completely. The earth spoke back and told me of the importance of sacred rest and to make the practice of lying on the earth a regular part of my life.

As I write this, I still carry within me the beautiful energy of the last Lughnasadh community ceremony which took place a few days ago. We sang and moved to a song and circle dance I had created for the occasion, accompanied by the drum. I never knew I had it in me to write songs and dance, and this illustrates the power of these gatherings and of the drum stirring the connection and creativity within.

I came across this amazing story from fungi expert Paul Stamets which blew my mind because it shows that these kind of land honouring community ceremonies may have more than just an energetic and spiritual effect on the land. He explains that research shows that low-frequency sound waves stimulate mycelial growth:

"It dawned on me that drum circles, whether of Indigenous people, pagans, or those celebrating harvests, weddings, or births, all coming together in community drumming – the long wave sound frequencies are literally going into the mycelial networks underneath and in the immediate surroundings. Just like strings on instruments, the mycelium reverberates from the thunderous beating, causing the networks to grow, adding nutrients and helping other life cycles flourish with more potential fruits, berries, nuts – the effects emanating throughout the ecosystem.

I realised this may actually be a feedback loop where the celebratory communal music communicates with and resonates the mycelial fibres, which respond by fruitfully acknowledging our presence and reciprocating with greater sustenance. An obvious yet profoundly underappreciated intersection of not just light, carbon dioxide, oxygen, temperature and water influencing growth, but our very thunderous footsteps upon the soil resonating communication to the underground fungal community that knows we are there, wakes up to our existence and when we respectfully reinvest into those mycelial networks around us, they replenish us because they understand we are involved together in the cycle of life." (Stamets, 2022.)

And so, when we gather to offer gratitude to the earth, when we drum and dance during these gatherings, is it not just a spiritual, but a real, physical effect that our ceremony may have on the land around us.

Drumming through the labyrinth

– Natanya Apfelbaum

The first time I went in the labyrinth, it was three weeks into my time in Palermo. A group of about a dozen of us holding tambourines, we threaded in.

High up on Palermo's sacred mountain, it was the pilgrimage day for the patron saint of the city, Santa Rosalia. We had come to pray. And pray I did.

Guided by our teacher's driving rhythm, we stepped and played. Tambourines high and loud, tambourines low and soft, we played in unison as the sun slid down the sky.

I let the rhythms bubble up the pain and trauma of the past year, uncomfortable sensations pushed through by the beats. Prayed for these earthy rhythms to return me to my body.

We walked back through the woods single file in the total dark. The only sound was the crunching of our feet.

I had come to Sicily from the United States in search of grounding myself in rhythm through frame drum and dance, entering into this program of study without knowing much of what to expect. This was the opening weekend.

The next time I came to the labyrinth it was nearly a year later. The labyrinth meanwhile had lodged itself firmly into my mind, but I did not actually know where it was. Luckily, at a fork in the path two hikers appeared and helped me find the tiny trail.

Again, I prayed in the setting sun, frame drum held aloft, bare feet tracing grooves known in my inner mind. This time I prayed for connection. To know my own way in relationship with others. I drummed through my cluttered thoughts.

Back in my apartment, I received my response, a reassurance really, of what I know to be true.

This past time I drummed in the labyrinth; it was the spring equinox. This time, I knew exactly where to go.

I prayed for the sharing of the skills I had cultivated and the healing of my root. I drummed and sang my way through the labyrinth.

That night, I received two dreams. In the first, my ex, who had not understood my body, was kissing me. This time, he got it right. In the other, I took a soft yellow car, like a Citroen, from near my childhood home. Then, I realised it was not mine to take. I wanted to return it but was not sure how. Was it showing me that it was time to let go of Italy?

In the afternoon, I went to the local park, frame drum in hand. A shirtless caramel-coloured man sat meditating in the sun. As I sat and drummed, he did headstands in the grass. The sun moved to the west.

Afterward, he approached and thanked me for my playing. He remarked on the beauty of him holding down the masculine and me the feminine. Then he left. A moment later he returned, bearing a soft yellow flower. I took the flower home and placed it on my altar.

Ancient memories

– Tracy Turnell

An unexpected series of events four years ago found me standing at the edge of an ancient Roman temple site in Harlow, about to attend my first drum circle. I was super nervous, completely out of my comfort zone and wasn't even sure what a frame drum was, but in that moment out on the land, I found a deep connection to the drum and to myself.

I'd been on a healing journey for eighteen years following a diagnosis of breast cancer, but the drum brought with it a different level of healing, something deeper, something I hadn't experienced with any other healing modality, this was it, this was what I'd been searching for! With the drum came a tribe: a tribe of women I hadn't known existed; a tribe I hadn't realised I'd longed for. I'd always been the weird one, the misfit, not fitting in and not really wanting to, but in that space of non-judgement with a group of yet unknown women, I found deep peace.

That night I slept deeply and dreamt that I was standing in the centre of a circle of joyous playful children, a circle filled with laughter and love, my arms outstretched holding a drum. It was profound and so much more than a dream, it was a gift, a deep inner knowing that I had been both a mother and drummer in previous lifetimes.

Just two weeks later I found myself back at the Roman temple site, this time to birth my own drum, a beautiful gift from my sister. The entire experience was incredibly powerful and deeply significant. I was unable to birth my own children, but with the birth of my drum I felt an inexplicable connection to each of those children in my dream. Drumming became a constant source of support and healing, a strength, a guiding light.

I found myself signing up to train in the Reiki Drum technique. My drum collection grew, as did my tribe and it wasn't long before I found myself on stage at festivals performing with The Sisters of The Drum.

When life is shining bright, the universe often throws a curveball and in 2022, my world was once again tipped on its axis with an unexpected diagnosis of thyroid cancer. A diagnosis that led to an ever-deeper journey working with my throat centre and the drum. I enrolled on a four-day shamanic retreat where, whilst drumming, I received a message, a very loud clear message – the drum is your voice. Not long after that message, I underwent surgery for a second time and sustained a surgical injury that took my voice leaving me nearly silent – it was then I knew, the old voice, the timid, shy, suppressed, unheard voice of my past-self had to die for a new more powerful voice to emerge.

I was determined to heal and found myself signing up to train as a sacred women's drum circle facilitator – I had no idea why I was signing up, I had no voice, but I kept hearing the same message repeating over and over – the drum is your voice, the drum is your voice.

My voice reemerged fully in August last year, different but stronger, more powerful and just six weeks after the facilitator training. The drum had indeed become my voice, helping me heal and rediscover my true self.

It was then I began thinking, if the drum was my voice, how many other women could it help to be heard, to find that voice, to explore their truth. I'm in awe of the power of this ancient instrument, my journey with the drum has led me here; to share the magic of the drum with like-minded souls and explore the transformation it could create in your lives.

One of the main reasons I decided to write this book is because I feel that humanity is going through a major shift, and one of these shifts is that knowledge will no longer come through teachers or "gurus" but directly from source. We are shifting away from reliance on external authorities and towards direct access to our inner wisdom. I have felt and known this for several years. It came first in a meditation, in which I was shown that the main cause of our collective suffering is disconnection. Disconnection from ourselves, from each other, and from the earth.

8

THE RHYTHM OF NEW LIFE: DRUMMING TO SUPPORT THE BIRTH JOURNEY

"Drumming for women during pregnancy and labour is a skill and tool to be reclaimed, this is something women have been doing for much, much longer than they haven't."

Jane Hardwicke Collings

My journey with the drum has taken me to unexpected places. From those first hesitant beats to drumming in birth rooms – a path I never imagined, yet one that feels deeply right, as if the drum always knew where it was leading me.

Being present at births reignited a longing to explore my connection to the divine further. It was witnessing those first moments when a baby emerges, this liminal space where the veil between worlds thins, the phenomenal sense of energy and power in the room, which reignited my longing for exploring and understanding the work of subtle energies and my sense of the sacred. In these moments, time seemed to pause, and I felt something vast and ancient. I had visions of the soul coming in, squashing itself into a tiny body. It was a call I couldn't ignore; it was this visceral experience of life's biggest threshold that led me to the drum.

Over the last twelve years, working as a perinatal educator and doula, I have repeatedly witnessed the lack of humanity present within maternity care, the lack of continuity of care, of time given to develop true connections.

More upsettingly, I have also seen an ever-rising tendency to coerce pregnant women to comply to strict medical guidelines, designed for an average population, which never take into account each woman's individual circumstance. As Jane Hardwicke Collings says, modern maternity care is *"Institutionalised acts of abuse and violence on women and babies masquerading as safety."*

As I explained in the introduction, we simply cannot outsmart or outthink a structure designed to keep us doubting ourselves. Over my years working as a doula, I have seen many women trying to beat bullying obstetricians at their game by arguing for their birth choices using scientific publications. This approach never worked, because few medical professionals take kindly to being challenged in this way, so they picked holes in their research, became defensive, or bluntly stated that "This isn't what the guidelines say."

It took me years to understand that modern maternity care functions like a medieval church: government medical guidelines are issued, then the system expects everyone within it to follow them without questioning, losing track of the fact that the guidelines aren't legally binding, nor do they represent 'the truth' (as opposed to the opinion of a panel of scientists). Not only are people discouraged to question the guidelines, but those who question them, or actively ignore them, are often punished or removed.

The reason drumming offers a unique potential to support and empower and heal during pregnancy, birth and the postpartum period, is because it supports a different way of thinking, one that is the opposite of what the system offers. It also helps restore a sense of sacredness, ritual and reverence during the pregnancy and birth journey. In today's modern healthcare system, where many births take place in hospital settings and the sacred aspect is completely absent or ignored, it is essential to find ways to re-infuse the birthing process with a sense of sacredness. Adding a ritualistic element, such as drumming, can positively impact this.

"The healing power of the drum and the capacity for transformation that labour and birth hold for a mother can shift beliefs and fears that have been long held."

Jane Hardwicke Collings

During birth, the brain undergoes a modified state of consciousness, due to the effect of birth hormones such as endorphins. Despite studies demonstrating this, this is not recognised within the modern medical model of maternity care, and neither is the rite of passage or spiritual process of birth. Not only is this completely ignored, it is also actively disrupted by the way the hospital is set up.

I've come to a startling conclusion: the disruption of natural birth processes may not be merely incidental, but purposeful – although I believe this is done unconsciously. The system seems designed to interfere with one of life's most potent rites of passage. Why? Because a woman who has experienced birth as nature intended – complete with its profound shift in consciousness – emerges transformed, empowered and with an unshakeable belief in her own capabilities.

Why modern maternity care actively disrupts the birth trance

The idea that our culture unconsciously interrupts the birth trance to exert control is rooted in the larger context of how power dynamics and social norms influence birth. It can be broken down into several aspects (Messager, 2024):

Medicalisation of birth: Modern cultures, particularly in the West, have increasingly medicalised birth, shifting it from a natural process to a highly managed, clinical event. This medicalisation is often framed as being for safety, but it also transfers power and authority away from the birthing person to medical professionals. The "birth trance" – a deeply instinctual, altered state of consciousness many women enter during labour – can be disrupted by interventions like bright lights, frequent monitoring and verbal instructions. These actions interrupt the natural rhythm of labour, reducing the birthing woman's autonomy and reliance on their own bodily wisdom, effectively placing control in the hands of others.

Cultural anxiety around surrender and vulnerability: Birth is a profoundly vulnerable and intense process that requires a certain surrender to one's body and instincts. Our culture tends to be uncomfortable with states of surrender, especially when it comes to women's bodies. Society often encourages control, predictability and structure. Medical protocols, constant monitoring and interventions – though presented as necessary – also reflect a cultural bias toward controlling a process that might otherwise appear chaotic or unpredictable.

Fear of female power: The birth trance represents a powerful state where women can experience immense physiological and psychological transformation.

Patriarchal structures have often sought to suppress expressions of female power, particularly in relation to childbirth, which is an inherently female, and thus potentially threatening, experience to male-dominated systems of power. By interrupting this trance, cultural norms may unconsciously aim to suppress the power women hold in this deeply primal moment, reinforcing existing hierarchies where medical professionals or institutions hold authority over women's bodies.

Disconnection from nature and instinct: Modern society places high value on intellect and technology, at the expense of intuition and nature. The birth trance is an instinctual, bodily experience that connects a woman deeply to her natural rhythms and ancestral wisdom. By interrupting this process, society reinforces a cultural disconnection from the body and nature. This serves to maintain control over birth by privileging external, scientific authority over internal, intuitive knowledge.

Economics and efficiency: Hospitals and medical systems are structured around efficiency and managing large volumes of patients, often within tight timeframes. Allowing women to enter a natural birth trance, which can slow labour down and make it less predictable, conflicts with these priorities. As a result, interventions like labour induction, C-sections, and other forms of control are encouraged to keep the process on a manageable timetable. This commodification of birth serves institutional needs at the expense of the woman's natural process, further reinforcing a culture of control.

A natural birth experience, undisturbed by unnecessary interventions, is nothing short of alchemical. It changes a woman at her core, awakening a primal strength and wisdom that cannot be easily dismissed or controlled. The ecstatic altered state of consciousness that accompanies physiological birth isn't just a side effect – it's a critical part of this transformation.

A woman who has touched this power, who has brought forth life through her own strength, is far less likely to doubt herself in other areas of life. She is less likely to blindly accept authority or to silence her own inner knowing. She becomes a force to be reckoned with.

And here lies the threat to the status quo. A population of empowered, self-trusting women would fundamentally challenge many of our societal structures. It's far easier to manage and control a population that doubts its own wisdom, one that looks to external authorities for direction.

This does not just affect the mother, it affects the child too, because modern maternity care also interferes with the subtle mother-baby dance, both with interventions during labour and in interfering with the precious first few minutes after birth with a lot of 'doing'. Cutting the cord too soon, taking the baby away for 'checks', putting a hat on the baby's head, trying to 'help' the baby latch onto the breast in disrespectful ways, and chatting during what should be a reverential time. This disruption of the birth process and immediate moments after birth then can be seen as a form of social control – one that begins at the very moment of our entry into the world. It's a sobering thought, but one that underscores the revolutionary potential of reclaiming our birth experiences.

Reintroducing drumming has the power to restore inner wisdom and sacredness to the profound rite of passage that is birth, re-infusing it with a power that resonates deep within our cellular memory. But its impact reaches far beyond the birthing room. The drum becomes a bridge, spanning the chasm between modern medical practices and the timeless wisdom carried in women's bodies. This resurgence of ritual would not just change the landscape of birth; it would have the potential to shift the very fabric of women's lives and the world. As the late birthkeeper Jane Parvati Baker said, "peace on earth begins with birth."

The birth journey offers a blueprint to other big transitions in our lives: we do not just give birth to human babies; we give birth to ourselves and to new projects over and over through our lives. What I am sharing here applies perfectly to other big periods of changes during our lives, the many endings and new beginnings.

How drumming supports the birth process

"Drum journeys often provided the women with wonderful information, sometimes for the pregnancy and sometimes for the birth. They also felt deeper connection with their baby inside. And drumming during labour has many benefits and positive effects like reducing pain, calming the nervous system and facilitating a trance state."

Jane Hardwicke Collings

I've already shared the many ways drumming positively impacts our body, mind and spirit in the science chapters. The aspects that are particularly relevant to birthing are:

- Drumming naturally shifts our state of consciousness, much like the altered state that should unfold during labour. While birth is designed to produce endorphins that help women enter this powerful state, modern hospital care often disrupts this delicate process. The drum can help restore this natural rhythm, offering a pathway back to the primal state that supports birthing. This modified state of consciousness also facilitates connection with the woman and her unborn baby.
- Drumming has been shown to stimulate the release of endorphins and oxytocin, both hormones which are required for labour to unfold as nature intended, as well as provide pain relief and feelings of wellbeing.
- Drumming promotes relaxation and reduces anxiety.

I want to show you exactly how drumming can support you through pregnancy, birth, and beyond. Here's your step-by-step guide to bringing the drum's medicine into each phase of the birthing journey – whether you're the one birthing or supporting others through this transformation. If you would like to learn more, I offer an online course called "Drumming for Birth," which is available on my website sophiemessager.com

I published an article in the *International Journal of Birth and Parenting Education* about drumming and birth in 2023, which is available to download as a PDF at IJPBE.com, and I also wrote an article about the same topic in the Green Parent magazine issue of February 2024 (issue 117, available to purchase as a digital download).

Drumming during pregnancy

What drumming offers that is particularly helpful during pregnancy:

Connection with the baby

How did we get to a place where women think that the only way to communicate with their babies is through a machine? Doesn't that sound completely crazy? Through the years I have seen maternity care professionals dismiss women at every turn, when they felt their babies were OK, but were told they weren't and the exact opposite, when women were dismissed when they felt something was wrong.

Drumming offers a unique opportunity for pregnant women to connect with their unborn child. The shift in consciousness enhances spiritual communication. Whether it is drumming themselves, listening to drumming, or doing a drum journey, engaging in drumming sessions can strengthen the bond between mother and baby and help the mother trust that she doesn't need machines to communicate with her baby. This would also apply to conscious conception, or to communicating with a baby after loss.

I interviewed former midwife and founder of the School of Shamanic Womancraft, Jane Hardwicke Collings. She said that once women have done a few drum journeys to meet their babies, it kind of opens the channel and after a while they can carry on communicating with their babies without doing the journey. (A drum journey combines two powerful tools: guided meditation and steady, rapid drumming at four beats per second. This combination naturally shifts your consciousness, making it easier to access deeper states of awareness.)

Drum journeying during my pregnancy allowed me to go deeply within, into my womb to journey and meet my baby… I felt as though I touched my baby before the birth, our souls connected on a deeper level. The ability to travel to the womb was very sacred. I was able to visualise my baby after each drumming journey with more clarity – this enhanced my communication with the baby.

Sophia, via Jane Hardwicke Collings

Drum journeying in pregnancy can offer the mother a regular opportunity to ritually connect with her baby and her body to receive information for her pregnancy, labour and birth.

Melinda via Jane Hardwicke Collings

Throughout pregnancy, as I chose freebirth, every morning I would drum. I didn't have maternity care or scans, so this was my connection. The drum was like an express train between me and baby, like a bridge between both of our souls.

Raffi

Increasing connection between the pregnant woman and her supporters

I remember feeling excited when Ailsa's message landed in my inbox: she wanted a doula to drum at her birth. As someone who had come full circle from being a closet spiritual practitioner, this felt incredibly validating. I had no idea about the journey that we would go on together and how much supporting Ailsa would teach me about presence and trust. Ailsa was a shamanic practitioner, which is why she wanted the support of the drum during her birth journey. Her first birth had been traumatic, and she was keen to have a more empowering experience this time round. The traumatic feelings from her first birth made it difficult for her to even talk about it at first, or to discuss her wishes for her future birth.

Drumming played a big role during her pregnancy, as a healing tool, but also as a way to get the pressure of discussing things out of the way. Since Aisla found it hard to discuss her future birth without becoming upset, we decided to drum together instead. Within ten minutes of drumming, Ailsa put her drum down and declared that she was ready to talk about her birth.

Over the course of her pregnancy, we used the drum on several occasions for healing. We had a lovely session towards the end of her pregnancy, when she had gone over her "due date" and the hospital was pressuring her to consent to having her labour induced. The most beautiful part of the drumming journey we had together was during her birth, when my co-doula and I drummed and sang together as she laboured in the birthing pool. It really felt like we were bringing the sacred within a clinical space. Ailsa's birth was straightforward, beautiful and healing.

Stress reduction and relaxation

Pregnancy often comes with heightened stress levels due to hormonal changes, physical discomfort and the anticipation of birth and motherhood. Drumming, with its steady and soothing rhythms, has a calming effect on the mind and body, inducing a state of relaxation, and lowering stress hormones. This relaxation response can lead to improved sleep quality, reduced anxiety and an overall sense of well-being for expectant mothers.

I had some gentle drumming at the beginning of pregnancy. I found it very calming and healing. The effect lasted a couple of weeks.

Leigh

Spiritual and emotional nourishment

Pregnancy is a time of profound emotional and spiritual changes. Drumming can provide a space for introspection and self-discovery. It allows expectant mothers to explore their inner thoughts and emotions, facilitating a deeper understanding of their changing roles and identities and accessing their intuitive wisdom more easily. This spiritual connection can lead to a more profound sense of purpose and a heightened awareness of the transformative journey they are embarking upon. It can also help women know what's right for them and their babies and stand up to the disempowerment that is rife within modern maternity systems.

Bringing back a sense of sacredness

As I've mentioned before, drumming can help bring back the sense of sacredness that is lacking within maternity care. It can be accompanied by other rituals (for example making an altar for the pregnancy and birth journey). Having regular drumming sessions can help bring a regular 'checking-in' time of connection with herself and her baby, away from the hustle and bustle of everyday life.

I wanted a doula who could drum for me during pregnancy and birth for many reasons, to mark a huge initiation, a reminder of the vast context of the process I was going through.

Ailsa

When I found myself rushing around in all of the 'doing' that comes with preparing for a new baby I would pick up my drum and after only a few minutes of drumming I felt as if I was coming back into my body.

Lizzy, via Jane Hardwicke Collings

Community and support

Participating in drumming circles or group sessions can provide expectant mothers with a sense of community and support. Sharing this practice with other pregnant women fosters a supportive environment where experiences can be shared, advice exchanged, and a sense of camaraderie built. Such connections can contribute to reduced feelings of isolation and increased self-confidence during pregnancy and beyond.

I went to the drum circle every month throughout my pregnancy. I felt accepted and supported. It was special to see my growing bump and connect with the circle every month.

Jessica

Drumming towards the end of pregnancy

As labour draws near, drumming can beautifully support this transition time, promoting relaxation, trust, intuition, easing the entry into the separation stage, when she starts to nest to prepare for labour and separate from normal life (Reed, 2021). Many women feel tense and anxious as they wait for their labour to start, and drumming promotes relaxation and can reduce any anxiety or fear about the upcoming birth. It grounds the mother in her body, helping release any mental blocks.

A drumming ceremony or journey could be used as a ritual closure to pregnancy and readiness to welcome the baby. The mother could participate in a drum circle at this time, uniting her with other women for emotional support. It is particularly useful to support post-dates stress and the maternity care pressure that comes with it. It can help the mother feel confident enough to decline an induction of labour.

I remember going to do a drum healing session with Ailsa. She was close to forty-two weeks pregnant and did not want to have her labour induced. She was experiencing the typical pressure that maternity care puts women under when their babies are 'late'. It was a beautiful healing session, and I could see how much more relaxed and confident she was at the end of the session. I believe that time with the drum helped her tune into her intuition and stick to her wishes.

More recently, I invited a forty-one-week pregnant woman to attend my drum circle, as she was being pressured to have her labour induced, yet wanted to give birth at home. She looked completely different after the circle: more glowing and relaxed. She went into labour that night.

In my ten years as a doula, I have lost count of how many times I have supported mothers who became really stressed, because our system treats women past their due dates as ticking time-bombs. I offer a session called "When labour needs to start" but the goal of this session is to relax the mother rather than to stimulate labour. I have often used rebozo massage* and guided meditation as soothing tools. I didn't systematically offer drumming, because for many years I shied away from it for fear of it being seen as 'out there'. If I could go back, I would incorporate drumming within this session as standard, because I know it would deepen the relaxation and the inner knowing.

I have also used drumming in all the motherblessing ceremonies I offer. A mother blessing is a mother centred alternative to a baby shower. It usually takes place during the third trimester of pregnancy and the activities are designed to make the mother feel celebrated, nurtured, loved and reminded of her strength, in preparation for the birth. They can be significant and powerful for everyone involved.

I drummed right up until my birth, would you believe that! But on the day I went into labour, it all kind of subsided for me and I just went with my playlist which had some drumming on it.

During pregnancy I would drum a lot, most mornings I would drum softly to myself and my baby. Even if it was for a few short minutes. Drumming really brought me into the present moments and helped me focus. I believe this practice really helped me with my whole birth journey, which was beautiful. I was very much able to connect with my body during the whole birth and it made things so much easier as everything progressed.

On one of our first online sessions with you, you did a drumming meditation that brought us to our womb space. During this I saw a baby boy, he was a fine baby (big baby) and fair haired, with blue eyes. At this time, I didn't know the sex of my unborn baby. Beau, my beautiful baby boy, was born and he was small to me, smaller than expected, and his hair was jet black, but as

* A *rebozo* is a Mexican scarf, often used to rock and relax a pregnant woman during pregnancy and birth.

I sit here typing this with Beau beside me, a big buster, fine big baby now at thirteen weeks and his hair has completely changed, he has fair hair and still his eyes are blue. This is the little face I saw. I'm in amazement sitting here. The power of energy vibrations and sound. It can change so many things and take us many places.

Robyn

Drumming during mother blessings

I've become acutely aware of the irony that doulas, and many women in caring professions, excel at nurturing others yet struggle to extend that same care to themselves. This self-neglect reveals a painful disparity between their capacity to give and their ability to receive nurturing.

To remedy this, I started offering mother blessing ceremonies to local doulas when they were pregnant. Mother blessings are a mother centred, more spiritual alternative, to a baby shower. They are also, as I explain in my book *Why Postnatal Recovery Matters*, the perfect place to start putting the mother, instead of the baby, as the centre of the circle of support. For a step-by-step guide and more detailed ideas, explore the ceremony blueprint I've shared in Chapter 7.

Every time I lead such a ceremony, I am touched to witness how the beauty of these ceremonies flows both ways. When we gather to honour a pregnant woman, witnessing her as the goddess she is, something magical happens: every woman in the circle feels that same reverence and love reflected back to her. Deep down we all know that we are meant to sit in sacred circles with each other. Our minds may have forgotten but our bones haven't. These ceremonies have a way of reminding us of our own sacred nature.

How drumming supports labour and birth

Drumming during early labour

Drumming at the beginning of labour can support many aspects of the process: It supports the separation process: leaving the everyday, mundane life tasks behind to enter the birth space, letting go of the mind, provides pain relief and relaxation and supports entering an altered state of consciousness.

I felt that the time had come to call upon the universe, to disperse distractions and non-essential tasks. My intention as support/husband/father was to create an energetic space that was welcoming and safe, to clear away the daily distractions, hold our older children both in presence and energetically in a calm open welcoming place and not interfere with the birthing process.

Dan, via Jane Hardwicke Collings

It can be especially helpful to promote trust in the process, in particular if things take a while or doubts creep in, for example with:

- Long early/pre-labour (when contractions start and stop for a while before a contraction pattern gets established).
- If the waters break before labour starts, especially if there is pressure to induce labour.
- During a long early labour.
- When labour takes twists and turns (slowing down etc.).

During labour, journeying deep within to the beat of the drum, the mother easily experiences the altered state of consciousness that is part of the birth process. As the labouring mother focuses on the rapid drumbeat, her brainwaves alter, and she shifts her awareness deeply inward to the place where physical pain is reduced and fears are gone. She taps into an inner knowing of how to best flow with the labour and often she feels a connection with all women who have birthed before.

Jane Hardwicke Collings

I was beginning to feel disheartened that the labour was progressing slowly and longer than I had expected. My focus on working with the waves was there though always in my periphery, was the thought that it was taking 'longer'. The drum, the beat, was like the pulsating of the heart. It was pulsating energy through me and through the space. I felt grounded and alive, primal and rhythmical.

Samantha, via Jane Hardwicke Collings

It can work remotely too, and I have supported people in this way, drumming for them with an intention of clarity and support. It would be powerful to call upon a group of women to do this together.

Drumming during established labour

When labour really gets going, the mother naturally enters a state of liminality and modified consciousness. Traditional rituals around the world have included drumming to support this process. During this stage, the mother needs reduced sensory input (low light, not being spoken to, quiet space etc.) to avoid disturbing her process. Modern maternity care has no concept of this and tends to activate the cortex with bright lights, questions, loud speaking, monitoring etc.

Playing the drum then can help bring back the atmosphere needed for sacred reverence, not only for the mother, but also for her caregivers, because having drumming discourages chatter and the modified state of consciousness will apply to everyone in the room.

Drumming offers the mother and her support people a "tool" to use in labour and birth that provides information via "internal enquiry" without the need to physically enter the mother's body or disturb her instinctive behaviour at any time. This encourages the mother to bring forth her own answers and maintain a sense of autonomy and empowerment throughout her experience.

Melinda

Being in that space and following the drumbeat, I could take away the rest of the situation and just focus on me and what was happening and what I was doing. When I followed the beat, I ascended and met my son's consciousness. My consciousness was circling upwards at the top of my head, and I met and merged with my son's consciousness and brought him into the physical reality. Meeting him in that way made what was happening in my body mine, a knowing, not the consequence of some other person, it stopped me being traumatised because I knew the person that was causing that pain, and it wasn't just some random unknown person.

Ailsa

Drumming can also help during transfer (to the hospital), delay in the labour pattern or transition. Drumming can help access inner power and help find what may impede labour as well as give strength.

At home, I felt in my own space but in the hospital, I felt at the system's mercy and a lot of vulnerability. The drumming stirred up the empowerment and standing up for myself. The drum calls upon strength and authenticity and celebration. The drumming felt like when you are jogging and you have power music on, it gave me a power boost, like it was saying, 'Open up, relax, trust your body, have faith in the journey.' It made me feel more confident in my abilities.

Leigh

My partner drummed for me for a while in my labour. I stopped thinking while he was drumming. I felt really relaxed. He was drumming slowly, I wanted it faster, it wasn't matching the intensity of the contractions. I was in the late first stage and I wanted the drumming to match the intensity.

Jess, via Jane Hardwicke Collings

Drumming during the pushing phase of labour

During the second stage (pushing phase) of labour, the drum provides the same support as during the previous stages: focus, calm, comfort. Women who have had the support of drumming during this stage mention its supportive power.

The first birth I drummed at was a homebirth. Malwina had hired me, after discussing how her first birth had ended up in an unwanted and non-medically justified transfer from home ending in an emergency caesarean. Malwina is very spiritual and bringing drumming to her birth felt completely appropriate. When I joined her at home during labour, she seemed to be managing the power and sensations of her contractions very well, so I did not get my drum out as it did not feel necessary. When she started pushing her baby out, however, I felt that she needed more support, so I started gently drumming in the corner of the room. Her baby was born soon after and it was a beautiful healing birth. When I asked her what the drumming felt like, this is what she said:

During labour, when the contractions were on top of each other and I had no break in between, it felt like the speed of the labour was taking over. When I heard the drum I thought, 'Oh I could have done with this from the beginning'. The drum acted as a background rhythm that I could hold onto, held me open, soft, it was like singing a song, I could feel that I was holding onto the rhythm of the drum, and I felt much calmer inside of myself.

Malwina

Interestingly, Ailsa, who had hired me to drum during her birth and for whom I drummed several times during pregnancy and during early and established labour, asked me to stop when I picked up my drum as she was pushing. It just did not feel right for her at this time. Often with pushing comes a lot more focus and presence and a return to a less modified state of consciousness, which might explain why it wasn't helpful at this stage for her. For me, it was a helpful lesson in always respecting the mother's wishes.

I've seen in my practice as a doula the wonderful way the drum enables women to relax, access and release the issues that have been blocking their labour from progressing. The drum almost effortlessly shifts and transmutes the negative energy or fears.

Cattalia via Jane Hardwicke Collings.

Drumming at the moment of birth

Drumming may or may not be appropriate during the very moment when the baby emerges. My instinct and a poll I did online showed that the majority of people feel silence is required at that moment. When I drummed during the pushing stage during Malwina's birth (the first birth I drummed at), I instinctively stopped as the baby emerged. However, it's up to the preference of each individual woman and something I would recommend discussing during pregnancy.

Drumming rhythms for the birth journey

People often ask me what type of rhythm I use for birth. Studies of shamanic rituals and research have shown that a fast tempo (around 3-4 beats per second or 180-240 beats per minute) is most effective at slowing brainwave patterns into deep relaxation and altered states of consciousness (Maxfield, 1990).

However, I've discovered that the most powerful drumming comes from simply listening – to the room, to the mother's needs, to the moment. The rhythm wants to be fluid, like birth itself, rising and falling in both speed and volume as needed. I often feel like the drum is playing me rather than the other way round, taking on a life of its own, through a process that requires no conscious decision on my part. The most powerful drum rhythm during labour is an intuitive one that responds to the ever-changing energy of birth.

Similarly, there is no set or right time or location for when to drum during the birth journey. I have drummed for women during pregnancy, during early labour, established labour, during the second stage of labour and during the postpartum. I have drummed at home, in the birth centre and in the obstetric unit. With some clients, drumming was included during every stage of the pregnancy, birth and postpartum, for others it was only during one particular stage.

For labour, the ideal drumming is live: a drum and an intuitive drummer who you know and trust, who you feel comfortable to have in your birth space. This way the actual vibration of the drumbeats will help reduce the pain of the contractions. If that isn't possible, you can reach the same level of focus with a recorded drumbeat played in the room or through headphones (Hardwicke Collings, 2011).

There are four main ways in which drumming can be used to provide support during the transition to motherhood journey:

- **Sound bath:** when someone simply drums near the person, encouraging them to relax and enjoy. This provides the benefits of the sound and vibrations.

- **Drum journeying:** where the intention is to get an answer to a question, or guidance (for example, connecting with the baby, or asking where the best place to give birth would be). The drumming is accompanied with guiding words (like a meditation) at the beginning, followed by a period of pure drumming.

- **Drum healing:** drumming over the person with an intention of healing. This combines the sound with a more direct effect of the drum vibrations on the body.
- **Listening to recorded drumming tracks:** if no live drumming is available, this can provide many benefits. Some women listen during pregnancy then take their tracks to support them during labour.

Drumming during the postpartum

When looking at birth as a rite of passage, the moment of birth corresponds to an emergence (Reed 2021). The mother comes back from the altered state of consciousness she needed to be in to birth, there is an adrenaline surge that causes a sudden increased alertness. She regains connection to the world. What she needs most of all is a quiet holding presence and physical support (if needed) from her supporters.

"In many cultures, midwives may enlist spiritual aid before, during and after birth, thus they are shamanic healers in their own rights."

Barbara Tedlock, *The Woman in the Shaman's Body*

Originally, midwifery was rarely acknowledged as a shaman's art. The understanding of midwifery as a shamanic practice evolved significantly with the rise of women ethnographers and feminist perspectives in anthropology. Early ethnographic research was dominated by male researchers who had limited access to women's space, and missed the deeper spiritual and ritualistic aspects of birth. The emergence of feminist anthropology brought crucial corrections to this imbalance, allowing for the documentation of midwifery's sacred dimensions and women's lived experiences of birth across cultures. This shift led to a more nuanced understanding of midwifery as a spiritual art (Tedlock 2005).

Drumming during the golden hour (the first hour after birth)

I have felt frustrated at most births I have been at by the lack of reverence during this time. This is a magical moment, something that cannot be recaptured. The mother (and her partner if she has one) meet the baby for the first time. It feels sacred and should be treated as such. Yet modern maternity care tends to interfere during this time with a lot of 'doing' and a lack of patience, things such as wanting to clamp the cord as soon as possible, managing the birth of the placenta, disturbing the mother (getting her out of the pool for example), talking, touching the baby without consent, putting a hat on, etc.

I know this is all driven by hospital policies and 'efficiency' rather than the fault of individual maternity care practitioners, but still, one could carve out a little time for quiet and patience.

Some cultures have prayers and chants that are the first things the baby should hear. I cannot help but wonder if some gentle drumming in the background during that time could help to support at least a bit more quiet reverence and slowing down. Maybe it is something to consider adding to the birth plan as part of your religious needs?

Drumming during the fourth trimester

The first six to twelve weeks after birth are a sacred window – a time when a woman needs deep support as she recovers from the monumental task of growing and birthing a new human. During this time, she's not just healing physically; she's also processing her birth experience and stepping into her new identity as a mother.

Cultures worldwide traditionally honoured this delicate time with a month of supported seclusion. New mothers would rest and bond with their babies, freed from all other responsibilities. They received nourishing, specially prepared foods for recovery and healing bodywork including specific postpartum massages. I explore these traditional practices and their importance in depth in my book *Why Postnatal Recovery Matters*.

The four pillars of postpartum recovery are social support, rest, food and bodywork. Even though this used to be a normal part of Western culture too, less than two generations ago, we have completely forgotten this. What we have now, is, if at all, a very short integration period (two weeks leave for the partner, who is expected to provide all the support), virtually no support for the new mother, and a very unhealthily obsession to go back to 'normal' as soon as possible, as if it was a sign of strength.

During the postpartum, drumming can be part of the recovery, by supporting:

- **Emotional wellbeing:** Mindfulness, reducing anxiety and depression, providing an emotional outlet, community support, drum circles.
- **Physical wellbeing:** Stress relief, releasing tension or trauma, providing a form of self-care (drumming/listening to drumming) and bonding with the baby (babies love drumming!).
- **Spiritual wellbeing:** Helping make the time sacred, reconnecting with intuition, a time for the mother to just be and as part of a healing postpartum ritual (such as closing the bones).

It felt so natural and normal to have the sound of the drum during the ceremony (closing the bones). It gave me the same feeling as when I rode a horse, when you and the horse are in the same rhythm together. Sophie didn't have to have her hands on me – with the sound I could feel her presence and good wishes. The song of the drum allowed me to soften, trust and surrender.

Malwina

A week after giving birth, I had the closing the bones ritual, with the drumming. I wept and released something, really opened up the gates to my connection as a mother and the realisation that I'd arrived as a mother – really landed. It was beautiful, I cried tears of joy.

Leigh

Drumming during closing the bones rituals

Very early on, I started adding drumming as part of the closing the bones massage ritual I offered to new mothers. However, I learnt this ritual at the same place and time that I was first exposed to the drum. Although drumming wasn't taught as part of the original ritual, as I shared in Chapter 1, a year after learning the ritual, back in the same retreat space, I gave the ritual to someone as part of a group ceremony. A woman drummed as we carried out the ritual and it felt like such a supportive and beautiful addition to the ritual that I felt drawn to offer it myself.

Having massaged hundreds of women for over ten years, some as early as twenty-four hours post birth, as well as having trained over a thousand holistic professionals in offering this ritual, I know the following to be true: a closing of the bones provides a space for physical nurturing, but also, perhaps more importantly, it holds a space for whatever needs to be expressed, witnessed and released. It is different for every person, depending on what has happened to them. For some it is a joyful honouring, for others it is a space to acknowledge and let go of difficult emotions. It is also a wonderful way to honour and support women through other important life transitions, to celebrate endings and beginnings, as well as help heal trauma, loss or shock. It helps to remind the body what it feels like to be safe.

When I felt confident enough to include drumming in all of my closing the bones (and other healing rituals), women repeatedly told me how much they loved the drumming, how deep it took them and many shared experiences such as, "I felt like I was in a temple", "I felt like my ancestors were with me." Recently, Laura, who attended my training, shared this: "I was really surprised by how much the drumming enhanced the experience. The sound resonated inside my body and spoke to something primal in the depths of my soul."

When I teach closing the bones, I lead my students through a ceremony where one woman is being cocooned with several rebozos, from her head to her feet. The women around her are holding the ends of the rebozos. Once she is wrapped, I read a poem and lead the group through a chant called "Let it Go", based on a poem by Michael Leunig. Whilst they carry on holding her, I stand up and drum over the woman and the group. This way my students not only experience how beautiful and powerful taking part in such a ceremony is, but they also experience, witness and receive the sound and the vibrations of the drum themselves.

People have often shared how this experience led them to want to take up drumming themselves. At the end of the ceremony, often many of the women are in tears, sometimes this also includes me. I'll never forget doing this once, and the woman next to me said, "I've had nine children and nobody has ever done anything like this for me", or the one who said, "I've had five children, and this is the first time I feel proud of my belly." This is so needed, and we need it back.

Drumming to support baby loss

Closing the bones is a beautiful way to honour the loss of a baby at any stage of pregnancy. My deep connection to this work comes from personal experience – I am the sister of a stillborn baby and have experienced four miscarriages myself. Through these experiences, I came to understand how the lack of recognition and ritual, especially for early pregnancy losses, can make grief more difficult to process. Society often minimises or overlooks these profound losses, leaving parents without the acknowledgement and support they need to heal.

Through offering this ceremony to others, I've witnessed how this ritual creates a safe, nurturing space for the emotions to be expressed, witnessed and healed. Women who have received this ceremony report feeling held, supported and able to process their loss in both physical and emotional ways. The ritual acknowledges what many of us know intuitively: that the depth of grief cannot be measured by weeks or months of pregnancy, and that every loss deserves to be honoured. As Brené Brown says, moments of collective grieving create powerful connections between us, allowing for deep healing and recognition of our shared human experience.

Having the closing the bones massage helped me to accept my baby's loss and start to move forward and also forgive my body and let go of all the negative feelings.

Claire

My friend Rosie whose baby who was diagnosed with a life limiting syndrome during pregnancy, passed away when he was five months old. She came to the closing the bones training a year later, and received the group ceremony at the end of the training. This is what she shared:

I laid down to receive my massage fairly reluctantly towards the end of the ceremony. As I was being rocked, deep shudders started going through my body and as the rebozo was pulled tight around my pelvis I felt a huge emotion that even now I am not sure what to call it. It felt as though the protective bubble I had formed around myself moved away and with that my baby – as if I was releasing him. Sobs racked my body. All the grief, the anger, the exhaustion, all the disbelief of what had happened came pouring out. I hadn't realised how much I was holding on to. I felt the women form a circle around me and felt what it was like to have a safe space held for me, allowing me to just be there in my wild tumult of emotion. I heard someone singing the most beautiful song and someone stroking my hair, hands touching me sending love and support. Gradually the emotions were spent, and I was left to gather myself. It was a true healing experience and much needed so I could move on through the grief process. But also, an awe-inspiring experience to be held like that and to not have to explain myself to anyone present. To have done that would have negated the whole experience. It showed me what a truly powerful ceremony Closing the Bones is.

Rosie also shared this poem about her experience:

Today I was healed
I was closed and I was healed
I was held, the pieces of me
Were held together, so I could
Let my grief out.
In all its glory, its noise, its mess
To be surrounded by women
Who understood and didn't understand
Today I was accepted for all that I am
My journey acknowledged
No explanation necessary

You can read more about this in my blog post, "How closing the bones can help after baby loss", which is available on my website.

Contemporary birth stories

Drumming during pregnancy, birth and postpartum can provide numerous benefits – physiologically and spiritually. More research is needed, but many women's accounts speak to drumming's value in bringing calm, focus, community and trust to the journey of pregnancy and birth. Science is catching up on what shamans have known for millennia and the modern world is hungry for more connection.

I wanted to finish this chapter with some stories from women who have experienced drumming as part of their birthing experience.

Drumming for the birth of Ylvar

– Nienke Claassen (who drummed for herself during her labour)

I chose to have my labour induced in the hospital. At this point, I was attached to the Pitocin drip, and I had a need to connect deeply to my son to communicate with him and also to sink into my body. The drumming gave me exactly that, following the beat, deeper and deeper until the contractions started coming like strong steady waves, my baby moving on the beat lower and lower. It was as if I drummed myself into this sacred birthing space. The hospital faded and it was just me and him. I kept with this until the space I created seemed stable and secure, then I put aside my drum and stayed in the magical birthing zone until I gave birth in only nine and a half hours. I believe the drumming helped to have the perfect hospital birth.

Beau's birth story

– Robyn Browning

Beau's birth was beautiful and perfect. I went to 42+2 weeks, but I knew in my body that everything was fine, drumming, daily meditations and affirmations are what kept me in my body and connected to me and my baby's journey.

Beau came on the 28th of October with the full moon. I wrote this date in my journal twice, back in February and May of 2023 I felt the baby would come on the 28th. The body still amazes me with our intelligence and power once we are connected.

During pregnancy I would drum a lot. Most mornings I would drum softly to myself and my baby, even if it was just for a few minutes. Drumming really brought me into the present moment and helped me focus. I believe this practice really helped me with my whole birth journey, which was beautiful. I was very much able to connect with my body during the whole birth and it made things so much easier as everything progressed.

I drummed right up until my birth. But on the day I went into labour it all kind of subsided for me and I just went with my playlist which had some drumming on it.

Holding space with the drum

– Anna Watts, doula educator and mentor

The medicine drum has been a steady and trustworthy companion to me for over thirty years. One of my early experiences of a shamanic drum journey was sitting in women's circle when my daughter was a toddler, she rested on my belly as we relaxed into the rhythm of the drum together. Since then, I have gained many insights through the shamanic drum, the heartbeat rhythm reconnects me whenever I feel scattered or out of alignment with my soul path. Thirteen years ago, I crafted my own drum under the guidance of a dear friend and shamanic Womancraft practitioner. My drum is named Beartha, and she provides an intrinsic element to my work in sacred birth circles, as a doula trainer and mentor, facilitating rituals and ceremonies.

I enjoy sharing creative ways for doulas to offer a true holistic perspective to the mothers and families they support, for them to discover different pathways to exploring the inner realms of pregnancy and birth in their own learning and growth as a space holder. Drumming can become a beautiful anchor in prenatal sessions and provide a deepening of connection between the doula and the mother/baby bonding experience.

Drumming at a birth is a profound gift of presence as a doula, for me it is the ultimate space holding experience to stay centred and connected with the healing rhythm, as the birthing woman and her baby ride all the nuances of labour supported by the unwavering heartbeat of the drum.

Drum journeys

– Marie Louise Lapeyre

I have learned the ritual application of drum journeys through the teachings of Jane Hardwicke Collings.

As a home birth midwife, I would ask from time to time, when the time felt right, if the woman was open to have a conversation with her baby while I would play the drum I made in a fast rhythm. I still have pregnant women come to me for this journey.

The first time I did this was profound, because I realised that this was a missing link. Many people talk to their babies but not many listen to the quiet still voice, which means that sometimes babies have to increase the intensity of physical sensation or difficulties to try to get through to one or both parents. I will tell the stories from my own perspective.

E. was having her first baby, she was a creative and kind person, near the end of her pregnancy she developed high blood pressure, and it became obvious that she needed more help than I could provide. She was admitted to hospital. There she took blood pressure medication but refused to be induced. The hospital staff, not used to strong women making their own decisions, were distressed and at times showing anger. I visited her regularly, bringing food and helping wherever I could. At one point she more or less said: "I'd rather die than to be induced." This worried me. I asked her to begin a conversation with her baby by writing at the beginning of a page: "Dear Baby," and then write everything she had on her mind and in her heart with as little censorship as possible. On the second page she was to write "Dear Mummy," and write what came as the answer from her baby. Her baby came through with a lot of certainty, he said: "No matter what happens I want you to be my mum." She then cried an ocean. That night she went into labour and gave birth beautifully with only midwives and no interventions.

S. came to me late in the pregnancy. As sometimes happens, she realised that she was not going to be able to advocate for herself in labour near the end of her pregnancy. We did the usual history taking and gathering of information. At forty-two weeks there was no sign of baby, so she agreed to do a drum journey. She asked her baby, "Why are you not coming?" The baby's answer was, "I am ready and have been for a while, there are somethings you need to address before I can come." There were tears, she understood that she didn't feel safe having her baby Earth side because of a long and difficult history of anorexia. She understood that her baby's journey through life would be different than her own. She forgave herself and gave birth that night.

9

TUNING INTO YOUR INSTRUMENT: FINDING A DRUM

"I have learned that the drum is coming into power again to awaken our hearts, for we must now learn to live from the heart. The heart is the place of balancing and awakening to our wholeness; the heartbeat is one of the reasons people so naturally and strongly connect to the drum. After all, each of us comes into the world having spent nine months listening to a heart drum in the womb. We are imprinted with rhythm from the very start and rhythm is the heartbeat of life."

Michael Drake

I hope that by sharing the contents of this book, I have instilled a desire to start your own drumming practice or dive deeper into drumming. If you are new to it, you may be wondering how to go about choosing a drum for yourself.

There are many types of drums available around the world, probably too many to count.

There is a wide range of options and prices to choose from. You will probably be familiar with the most iconic: the drum kit and the African Djembe, but there are many others, from every single continent, with a huge variety of shapes and sizes. Big and small ones, round ones, square ones…percussion truly is universal. To me, it really doesn't matter, a drum is a drum.

Frame drums are easier to play than say djembe drums, or even frame drums played by hand, because the latter require more complex skills to produce the range of sounds and beats required. However, other drums can also be used to similar effects. You can even produce the same entertainment phenomenon typical to percussion by shaking a rattle or even tapping on your body or a book.

Because the frame drum is the kind of drum I use, because it also happens to be the type of drum that shamans and healers use, because it's easy to carry and also the easiest to learn to use, here I'm only going to talk about frame drums, the kind of drum that is held in one hand and on which the sound is made with a beater or stick.

A frame drum is made from a thin circular wooden hoop (although you can also find some that are egg shaped, hexagonal, octagonal or even square), typically ranging from 10 to 22 inches in diameter, though some can be larger or smaller. Generally, the bigger the drum, the deeper the sound. The hoop is usually about 2-3 inches deep and forms the frame that gives the drum its name. Many different types of woods can be used for making the hoop. I have drums made from ash, hazel, aspen, pine, jackfruit, oak and larch. I'm sure many other woods are used, depending on the region. The wood can vary in colour and grain and can be decorated with carvings or drawings. Traditional designs can include spiritual symbols or nature motifs.

Stretched tightly across one side of this wooden circle is a thin membrane, traditionally made from animal hide, such as goat or deer skin, but now also often crafted from synthetic materials. This drumhead is what produces the sound when struck. Its surface is smooth and taut, with a slight give that you can feel if you press gently.

The other side of the drum is open, allowing you to see the interior of the frame and the underside of the drumhead. Some frame drums have small metal jingles or cymbals embedded in the frame, adding a different quality to the sound. There is usually a handle to hold the drum on that side, made from either hide lacing or cord.

I currently own over twenty-five frame drums, six of which I made myself. In this chapter, I'm going to help you choose a drum, by telling you about the different categories of frame drums available, the pros and cons of each and the wide range of prices available (including some unexpected bargains). I'm also going to tell you what to avoid, as sadly there are some really poorly made drums, and even some fake ones on the market.

This is based on my experience and is by no means exhaustive, as there are many other drums out there, many of which I have not even come across.

The first thing you need to be aware of when buying a drum is that frame drums come into two main categories: the ones made of animal skin and the ones made of synthetic skin (plastic material or fabric).

A good minimum size to start with to have a deep enough sound would be around 12-14 inches. Remember that the bigger the drum, the deeper the sound. However, you'll need to bear in mind the ease of holding your drum depending on what you want to use it for, as really big drums can be heavy to carry or unwieldy to hold. I have a couple of drums which are quite big and too heavy to do drum healing over someone's body for example. You will also need to consider how practical it will be if you plan to travel with it.

Synthetic drums

I have four synthetic drums: a 16-inch Remo Buffalo drum (this is a misnomer as the drum is made of plastic), a 16 inches Remo Bahia Bass one, a small 8 inches Remo frame drum (which I mostly use for display, as the sound is too high pitched for my liking) and a 20-inch drum made of yurt fabric.

Advantages

- Synthetic drums from reputable companies usually have a good, reliable, quality sound
- The sound/pitch remains the same regardless of weather/water/temperature
- If you play outdoors like I do, especially in a cold country like the UK, you might be grateful to have a synthetic drum. It does not need to be warmed up to play, and you can play it in all weathers without fear of it being damaged, even in the driving rain, which is a big advantage in unpredictable weather. I have even taken my synthetic drum inside sweat lodges and saunas with no ill effects.
- These drums are an excellent choice for those seeking alternatives to animal-based materials.

Disadvantages

- Remo drums are made by machines in a factory. Although all drums have their own spirit and you can connect to the spirit of a drum even if it is made from synthetic material (after all, even synthetic materials are made from the earth), I personally feel that they have less 'spirit' than handmade skin or synthetic drums.

Cost:

- About £115 for a 16-inch drum.

The German drum company Thomann, who sell a wide range of percussion products worldwide, has sound samples available for different drums, including Remo ones (and many others) on their website.

Drums made of fabric

I have a synthetic drum made from yurt fabric, made by French drum maker Philippe Jalbert. It has similar weather impervious qualities as a synthetic drum, with the addition of a bike tyre inner tube built into the frame, which allows to modulate the pitch with a bicycle pump.

I know of three manufacturers of drums out of fabric/canvas in France and I was lucky to try out all three in a percussion shop called Djoliba in Toulouse (they also sell online at djoliba.com) The one whose sound I was most impressed with was made by Laurent Saulnier at tambour-en-toile.fr

Drums made from animal hide

There are as many hides as there are animals that are big enough to make drums from. I own drums made from buffalo, cow, deer, goat, horse, monitor lizard, reindeer, stag and wolf hide. I have seen drums made from bear and salmon and even one made from tiger shark skin! I crafted a small drum using human amniotic membranes. The hide you chose will also carry the unique medicine of the animal it came from.

As well as the animal from which the skin has come, the way the animal died is important to the energy of the drum. The people I have made drums with only use skins where no animal was killed just to make a drum, but were killed for another purpose (being killed for food or for sustainable culling), where the hide would have otherwise been wasted.

Similarly, the hoop of the drum may be made from different tree essences, each with their own unique spiritual properties. I have one made from the wood of a larch tree that was hit by lightning. Other tree essences are available depending on the country the hoop comes from.

Skin drums advantages:

- They are unique, beautiful, individual drums.
- Many are handmade by cottage industry businesses.
- Each one has a unique spirit and energy.
- You can make your own, or have one made, to your own preference and style (including adding symbols, crystals, paintings on them etc.)

Skin drums disadvantages

- The quality can vary a lot and unless you know the maker, it's difficult to assess quality online. There are many mass-made drums from India for example, which do not necessarily sound great.
- They are sensitive to weather and temperature. In cold or damp weather (from around October to April in the UK) you need something to warm the skin up (like a fire) in order to play outdoors (and ideally a shelter against the rain), otherwise the skin tends to be slack and does not sound resonant.
- Skin drums can get damaged by heat or moisture (you cannot play them in the rain, or leave them in the back of a hot car).
- Because they are handmade, they tend to be pricey (from £150 to £300 or more).

One affordable skin drum option is the Irish bodhrán. Whilst not officially designed as a shamanic drum (although historically this is what it was used for), it works very well for this purpose.

Bodhráns are usually sold with a small wooden stick called a tipper. You may prefer a soft beater instead, but these are very easy to make (a foraged stick and a stuffed sock or piece of felt attached to the stick with a string or elastic will do the job, or you can buy a beater online, there are beautiful handmade ones on Etsy). New bodhráns start at 130 Euros, however I have found such bodhráns available second hand on eBay or Facebook marketplace for as little as £20-40.

Here is a list of people from whom I have purchased drums and/or made drums with:

- Melonie Syrett, Thedrumwoman.com (UK).
- Jonathan Weekes, Heron Drums (UK).
- Lusio Art, Etsy (UK).
- Veleslav Voron, Shaman Drums, on Etsy or Instagram, (Ukraine).
- Juha Jarvinen, Yxpila Art, on Etsy or Instagram (Finland).
- Ayas Irgit, on Facebook (Russia).
- Malachy Kearns, bodhrán maker, (Ireland).

A few other people I have seen drums made by in person (some run drum birthing workshops and also sell kits to make your own drum) include:

- Driftwood hollow drums (UK).
- Rachael Crow drums, Etsy (UK).
- Shammantrommer (Denmark).
- Hollie Hope (USA).

Some instruments shops that sell drums and other musical instruments:

- www.knockonwood.co.uk
- www.soundtravels.co.uk
- www.thomann.de (ships worldwide).
- djoliba.com, France, (ships worldwide).
- Another well-known bodhrán brand is Waltons.

This is by no means an exhaustive list. I am only comfortable recommending drum makers I have personally been in contact with. There are many other drum makers around the UK and the rest of the world. I suggest you ask for local recommendations and find someone you resonate with. There are many drum makers who sell handmade drums on Etsy. If at all possible, try to get to see and hear the drum you'd like to buy, ideally in person but if not, at least on a video. You can ask the drum maker to share a sample of the sound for you.

Handle or not?

There is another style of frame drum that has no cross or handle at the back. This type of drum is usually played using the hands and fingers to hit the drum head, instead of a beater. Hand frame drumming requires different techniques to hit the drum to create different rhythms and sound and therefore more complex skills to produce a good sound. Beating a drum with a beater is the easier skill to learn and immediately produces good sounds.

However, it does not matter which drum you use and whether you prefer to hit it with a stick or your hands, the resulting effect on your consciousness is the same. Remo Drum makes simple synthetic frame drums without a handle at the back, which are very affordable. For example, a 12-inch Remo Renaissance Frame drum costs around £35. There is no reason why you cannot use these with a beater. However, I personally find shamanic style frame drums (with a handle to hold the drum at the back) easier to hold than frame drums without a handle.

Making your own drum

Out of all the drum options available, by far the most powerful one, in my opinion, is to make your own drum. There are many reasons this is the ultimate experience. You can select wood and hide materials with personal significance. The process of making the drum is very deep and meditative. You can decorate it with symbols and designs of your liking. You will have the pleasure of knowing you crafted it yourself. Your drum will be imbued with your unique intentions for it, your energy and spirit, and, perhaps most importantly, the process of creating it will provide the medicine you need, and this medicine will keep working with you as you use it. I think it's not by coincidence that people refer to making your own drum as "birthing a drum."

The first time playing your handmade drum can often feel especially meaningful. Some people like to meditate with their drum, and ask the drum to tell their story. Each drum has a unique story to tell, the story of the tree that gave the hoop, and of the animal that gave the hide, and of its making.

During the writing of this book I commissioned a drum made of wolf hide (one of my power animals) from shamanic master drum maker Ayas Irgit in Russia. When I first held this drum, he told me, "I'm going to take you to the top of the mountain", reflecting a vision I often had when present at births. I could also see which tree it had come from, even though Ayas had not yet shared this information with me, and that this tree was hit by lighting, which was confirmed later on.

There are a couple of options should you decide to make your own drum:

- **Buy a kit online from a drum maker.** This usually contains the already cut hide and lacing, and instructions. A kit in the UK costs between £125 and £200 depending on the size of the drum.
- **Attend a drum birthing workshop.** Some workshops are one day long (which is plenty of time to make a drum). The costs are around £250 to £300 for a one-day workshop. Some people offer longer workshops or drum pilgrimages, which can last several days. I have made some drums over a day and some over a four-day long training.

In the UK, I recommend drum maker/drum birthing workshop leader Melonie Syrett at thedrumwoman.com.

Drum birthing as a mirror

– Melonie Syrett

The process of birthing a drum starts somewhere with the person who wants to do it receiving a call to make their own drum. Some people have no idea why they're there. They've paid their money, they've joined the group, or they're on a one-to-one workshop or a retreat, but they don't know why, and they really can't work out what made them book.

Other people have been dreaming about a drum for a long time, thinking about drums for a long time, hearing about drums for a long time, and that calls them. Other people just see it and go, "oh, I'd like a drum" and then they book it.

And some have been avoiding it for a long time because the sound of a drum, just a couple of beats, really reaches somewhere deep in and makes them emotional and want to stop hearing the drum but slowly, slowly, they've realised there's some medicine in that.

The drum birthing starts there when the person books onto the workshop.

On the day, they come into the space where a range of hoops are set up and an altar. They've collected any crystals that want to go in their drum and a stick for their beater. They've thought of something for the altar and they arrive with this perception of what their drum is going to be like, what it's going to be made of, what size it's going to be and everything like that.

I work in a way that hopefully enables a dropping out of the head where we say, "I want this, this and this," to dropping into the heart where we can hear, feel, see, know and imagine the nudges of the wood and the hide and the crystal and create what's actually supposed to be coming to us, as opposed to what our heads say we want.

We begin with a meditation to ground us and that lets go of anything that's been walking into the room with us – any worry, any fear, any kind of ungrounded energy – and we set an intention in that space. This is like putting a call out to the universe or a ripple through time and space to bring the things that are supposed to be coming towards us. We've said yes to the infinite pool of possibility and the energy that's all around us that's been trying to catch our attention for that time.

From that space of meditative grounding, we share. Maybe the first spot of healing is stepping through the door and grounding and then sharing. Things come out that we didn't expect when we get that opportunity to speak from our heart and our womb space or our guts or whatever it is that's coming in. It might bring things up that we didn't know.

Then we choose our hoops and there is a range of sizes and woods. People come with a desire for this and that, but as soon as they've opened their eyes from the meditation there's a hoop that keeps catching their eye or there's an energy around one or they pick one up and it will fizz or build up a load of emotion. It's like that hoop chooses you. And it might not be the size or the wood that you expected as you planned your drum in your head. A lot of people want the biggest one possible and they end up making a small one, or people want a small light one and they end up making a bigger, heavier one because the hoop has called them and there is medicine in that hoop, in that wood. There is magic in it that will be with every beat of the drum and when the drum is in the house or wherever the person is, and with that energy radiating out to them it will bring a lot to them.

Choosing the hoop is the first set of connection. Then we'll connect into that hoop and see if it needs anything from us. It might want to go and dance out in the sun, it might want some plants rubbed onto it, it might want oiling, it might want a crystal grid in the middle of it and it's like it's bringing a deeper connection to you and your hoop.

People have written in their hoops, words like 'love' or 'protection'. People put symbols that mean things to them and that is an expansion of that energy. Somebody wrote recently something along the lines of "I trust myself." Every time you look at that drum it's radiating that energy because the hoop is like a boundary of a crystal grid, you know, there's going to be lacing all through it and so that writing and anything that we put in the drum is being amplified with every beat.

Then, when you start working with the hides, they are all put out and people get an opportunity to go round and touch them and go with the one that seems to call them. That in itself is a journey of connecting back into the land, into the natural world, into the stuff we don't see. We don't get to see a raw animal hide often. We get to go to the shops and buy prepared meat, or buy a handbag of leather – we don't see it in its raw form. This is like deeply coming back to yourself, to ancient times, to times before everything was taken away and prepared for us.

Once they've chosen their hide, like the hoop, it might be that the hide sends a wave of emotion towards them or says, "Don't move away from me." Some people think, "I'm going to work with this" and then they go over to that hide and it feels horrendous and they exclaim, "No, I can't work with it!" because the energy knows what's coming for you.

Horse, which is a fast and transformational energy and is going to give you a challenge. It won't call the people who don't need that, it will push them away. And the deer that brings the heart energy and the grounded energy and the forest energy will call those who need it. And the goat that brings resilience and playfulness and joy – it will bring it to those who need it. They all have their own medicine. So you get connected with what is supposed to be with you.

As you start to cut it and make the drum head and punch the holes you get to know it, it becomes part of you, like the hoop becomes part of your story, your journey. It brings out so much in different people that you can't help but have some of that pattern that you've laid down through life and probably from being really young gently eased out, maybe dropped or brought right up in front of you so that you can see it.

It gives me an opportunity to reflect that back at people and just ask them, when they're fearful over and over again that their hide will rip, whether that's been part of their life: the fear of things breaking again and again. And then ask what would happen if it did break? So I reframe what has been holding us hostage all our life – what would happen if it did break? Nothing, we can put it back together again, all is good.

Some people's lacing will snap three times and then when you gently invite them to talk about these snaps and what was going on as it snapped, you find that they've had three divorces or three massive life changes or three bereavements. It mirrors back what has been moving through us in life.

And then as we start to bring it all together, we can weave in intention. If we've been nervy all the way through, we can start changing those words. Recently, a lady was making a drum and she just kept saying, "What happens if, what happens if, what happens if?" And then there were a couple of breaks but they were all in really easy to fix spaces.

She said, "What if, what if?" and I was able to hold space and say, "Okay so let's not weave this into your drum, 'there's going to be a break, there's going to be a break' – let's reframe it". With every weave and wrap we can say, "I am strong, I am strong, this drum is strong." The words that are going to change the pattern.

As I watched her do it, I could see her energy move and shift as she imprinted new patterns of the things she'd been telling herself. Instead of it being, "I'm going to break, I'm weak, everything's going to go wrong," it was, "Everything is going perfectly and I am strong," weaving that into her life instead. That drum will radiate that out.

As they weave that drum together, it does the same thing as cutting the lacing. It can bring up inner child energy. Often there's a fear, a confusion, a muddled feeling because this is new to them and they say to me, "You're so good at it and I'm not." Well, yes, I am good at it, I've been doing it for nearly eight years, this is muscle memory and expertise. For you this is brand new and it's okay to be doing something brand new, not knowing what you're doing, and to ask for help. We're so good at not asking and we're so good at holding back because we tend to be holding the fort for everyone as women. To ask, "Can you help me?" is huge.

Putting the crystal into the drum is a wonderful thing, that energy of the crystal is beautiful. A lot of people bring lots of different crystals and their head says, "Oh, I really like this rose quartz," but it doesn't feel right and it doesn't sit right under their hands. And actually there's a piece of tourmaline or malachite or something that just goes in perfectly. And that's as if the crystal had been saying, "Bring me, bring me because I hold a key here to this drum, I hold a key to this crystal grid that you're making, I hold a key to every beat with this under your hand vibrating through you." Maybe it is something that you weren't ready for, or you didn't know about or maybe it wasn't conscious for you that you needed this energy as opposed to that rose quartz energy.

The birthing of the drum itself is just such a huge magical thing – you pull the lacing through itself and it leaves an umbilical cord for you to cut. The pulling of it through itself reflects so much to the person. Sometimes they just slide through and the person exclaims, "Wow, wow, look at that!" and it gives a huge affirmation of "I can!"

Other people really struggle, and when speaking to them I find out that in life, giving birth to babies, they've had a breech baby or they had lots of interventions and ended up having big tears or an emergency caesarean. It is reflecting this – the hide stuck inside, there's only a bit coming out, it's really pulling, I'm having to support you – and to pull it through is a huge release and rebirth and rewriting of these stories.

Even for those who've not had children, there's a whole challenge in it of something that's been going on in their life. Some remark on the 'birth' they've had and become emotional.

The joy and the relief and the elation that I see once they make their drums, that's why I do it. It's just so beautiful because you just watch all those layers and all those things you've told yourself just fall apart and break off into pieces all over the floor and this new person is reborn. It is just magical.

It's really so much more than making a drum. That drum will be your guide – it will be with you radiating that energy every time you touch it. You'll remember all the things you did, felt, said, collected and dropped and it becomes this massive being in your life that helped you move into the next phase of being you.

Drums are great healers, and that's even before you start to play them and they know what you need as you play them.

Rebirth through creation

– Hollie Hope (from the book *The Sacred Healing Drum*, 2024)

My first experience making my own sacred healing drum was in a beautiful forest in Northern Utah, with pine needles underfoot and a flowing river nearby. I knelt in the dirt, barefoot and ready for what I thought would be a once-in-a-lifetime experience.

Working with the slimy rawhide lacing, I struggled with limited instructions as the instructors were preoccupied with others. Frustration began to flow as I didn't consider myself 'crafty,' and I felt an immense pressure to connect with Spirit for guidance on my new life path. As I wove, feeling inadequate and unnoticed, a sense of independence began stirring within me.

As I worked through my emotional state, something magical happened. A tiny, bright green caterpillar appeared, inching its way across my lacing. Then another appeared, and another – three times I helped these little visitors back to the earth. Looking up at the waving pines above, I laughed, "Okay, message received!" I understood that though I felt small and unsure, I was already on my path of transformation.

When my drum dried, I discovered what looked like a mummified caterpillar in the drumhead – actually a piece of cottonwood seed creating a perfect ripple. As I drummed, images emerged in the hide's patterns, revealing a butterfly. I painted the words that spoke to my heart: "From the darkness she discovered her light and flew beautifully."

What I see as women birth drums

– Rachael Crow

What I see in women as they birth their drums is a deep remembering, an excitement and an embodiment of courage. Holding their drum as an instrument of power and an instrument of warriorship and in this I mean the drum is almost like a shield, a tool they can use to support them in stepping out into the world and support them in being seen. In some ways they can hide behind their drum, until they are fully ready to step out fully into their power. Once they step out, it seems like there's no stopping them! I have witnessed women who were so shy, who could only drum in their bedrooms – somehow finding the courage, finding their inner strength to sing in ceremony, to hold space for others…all through the strength that came through the connection to the drum. Of course, we know now really that strength was there inside them all along, the drum helped coax it out!

When a hoop breaks
– Jo Drew

My first drum, Deer, encourages strength through gentleness. A challenge when previously I had seen my gentleness as a weakness. My Deer drum is a guide leading me to understand my true nature and purpose.

Then years of relentless trauma, my drum leading me to my guides and to a daily ritual of release. An intense time…the drum my friend. Until…the hoop broke! Tragedy.

I discovered that when a hoop breaks it signifies a great change, transformation, rebirth. I journeyed to the spirit of my deer drum who advised a new drum to mark the start of a new journey. Miraculously, the money appeared at the same time that a new drum called me, a Stag drum! The hoop on my Deer drum was fixed but she wasn't the same, she was wounded. She remains with me, resting. I have such gratitude for her lessons, and she adorns my wall.

The Stag drum has taken me on a new journey to start to live my life's purpose. He accompanies me to the astroshamanic journeys that I deliver in the community. Leading participants in astroshamanic journey and dance.

The Deer, the feminine helped me to heal the inner wounds and manage a period of trauma. A dark night of the soul, possibly a necessary part of my healing. The Stag, the masculine brought me closer to my soul's purpose and gave me confidence to share my astroshamanic training to the community. The stag and deer together, the masculine and feminine represent my journey to wholeness.

Whilst I was writing this book, a woman called Anna, who regularly attends my drum circle, contacted me asking for advice about buying a drum. She shared that she had just separated from her partner. She said, "Sadly my drum also snapped this weekend." The skin of her drum has broken, where it was attached to the lacing. She mentioned it was terrible timing, but for me, this was not a coincidence, but rather a powerful reminder of drums as living allies, and representatives of our lives.

What to avoid when buying a drum

Sadly, there are a lot of poorly made and fake drums around. A lot of the drums sold via Facebook ads, eBay or Amazon are poor quality drums made in China, where someone has often copied a real drum-artist's pictures and printed it on a cheap plastic drum.

For example, the stunning drums made by Velenslav Voron of @shaman-drum_org, are so distinctive in style that I instantly recognised one of his designs on a Facebook ad advertising them for only £30. I contacted him and he told me about the stealing and the cheap copies and of not being able to do anything about it. I have seen these drums in real life, they are very small, and they sound so poor I wouldn't even give them to a child to play with. You can also find the same drums for under £10 on AliExpress. Remember: if it seems too good to be true, it probably is. Get recommendations and if possible, try to see and try a drum before you buy.

However, I have also found amazing bargains of good quality on eBay or Facebook Marketplace. But these weren't copies or cheaply made, simply good quality second hand drums.

If you can attend a drum circle near you, many facilitators offer the option to borrow drums to play during the circle. This offers you a chance to try different drums and find out what kind of drum you enjoy playing the most.

THE ETHICS OF DRUM MAKING

When considering the ethics of drum making, it's important to look at the entire journey – from animal to finished instrument. This includes how humanely the animals were raised and killed, whether the skins are by-products of the food industry or ethical culling rather than primary products, and whether natural or harmful chemicals were used in processing the hides.

The human aspects are equally important: were the craftspeople paid fairly and working in safe conditions, especially in developing countries where mass-produced drums may involve exploitative practices? The same ethical considerations apply to the sourcing and shaping of the wooden hoops.

Ethical drum makers will be transparent about their supply chain and honour both cultural traditions and craftsmanship. Don't hesitate to ask questions – any reputable maker will be more than happy to share their process.

The 'wrong' drum

– Kathy Labrum McVittie

I'd met my Power Animal at a group dance workshop in 2015, where a Russian-born shaman had drummed us on a trance journey through The Opening. In the safety of our circle a dozen of us rested with our feet towards the circle's Centre, where he had laid the totems of his ritual.

There was fierce power in his voice as he declaimed the beauty of his vision. A mere, gentle, boyish person transformed into the doorkeeper of dreams. Afterwords [sic.] he held gently whatever insights we'd gleaned and accompanied our interpretation.

For months I was euphoric from meeting my animal soulmate, Brown Hare. In awe of the ways he'd already been present at my edges, for long decades. Then on a solitary retreat in 2016 I encountered an incomplete Hare skeleton above Gartymore, Sutherland. On the strength of that I followed a dream to move north.

I spent 'Coronapause' as a solitary in the Far North of Scotland; my human contact was largely online. I joined 'The Way of the Buzzard' Mystery School and ordered a skin drum 'Courage', birthed by Anglezarke Hallows at Samhain Full Moon 2020.

By a fluke, 'Courage' was sent to a woman who had ordered 'MagicK'. She instantly fell in love with her 'wrong' drum, made for me and I was left with a choice: waiting for a duplicate 'Courage', or accepting 'MagicK' – making her my own.

My relationship with MagicK has been both bittersweet and stormy. Awe-ful and awful. Often she sulks and so do I. Sometimes we rock.

She has danced with me online and I've soul-sung with her. She accompanies ritual and earths The Wheel of the Year. We're invited on Buddhist retreats in Gairloch Youth Hostel.

She's held 'Writing our Way Whole at Home©' sessions with her presence, sounding across a healing landscape where therapy horses roam. In 2023 a Cormorant flew up that valley where I sat with the Young Healer beside her Firepit and circled her therapy room three times before continuing on its way.

I am learning to discern others' intentions, with this Drum I bear. I recognise my changing moods reflected in her Hare-face. In a dark period during the healing of my mastectomy scar in 2022-23 I was reluctant to release her voice – or my own. Indeed, I feared she might never speak again.

Now I believe this mysterious silence represents inherited ambiguity about my roles as Maiden, Mother, Crone. That clears my way towards facing into the symptoms of a second menopause, brought on by my continuing treatment for oestrogen-sensitive breast cancer.

Thus, I open my heart for healing of ancestral trauma, with Wolf alongside. I stand stronger in the support of those very ancestors and their kith: flawed, brave, singular women (and kindred men also).

The drum MagicK has now travelled south with me to meet soul-kin in Cambridgeshire and is to accompany me on a Voice Medicine workshop in Devon, her reindeer-skin resonance steadying our blood's pulse.

Getting to know your drum

If you get a drum, have fun playing with it with no preconceived ideas. Remember that there is no 'wrong' way to play it. Try different ways, there are many simple tutorials on YouTube if you'd like to get new ideas to try.

A beautiful way to connect with your drum more deeply is to do a drum journey to meet the spirit of your drum. There are many available on YouTube and I recorded one myself which you can find on my YouTube channel, in my drum journey playlist.

In the Appendix, I have included links to tracks and videos you can watch or listen to if you'd like some inspiration about ways to play the drum, shamanic style.

I hope the following chapter helps you get started on your drum journey.

10

RHYTHMIC PRACTICES: WAYS TO WORK WITH THE DRUM AND DRUMMING

"I always giggle when someone tells me they can't drum – I say to them, 'Of course you know how to drum…the very first sound you ever heard was your own mother's heartbeat when you were inside her womb… drumming, drumming and drumming… You know how to drum!'"

Carol Weaver

I want to share the many ways you can use drumming in your life, it's easier than you think!

You do not even need a drum to benefit from the consciousness changing power of the drum, as there are many tracks (see Appendix) available for free on YouTube or Spotify. All you need is a way to listen. You don't even need headphones, nor to set quiet time aside to listen, just playing it in the background will do its magic for you.

However, experiencing live drumming and working with your own drum will bring a different, more powerful experience, because you will experience it live (with more powerful vibrations and sound) and also develop a relationship with it.

Regardless of whether you have had a drum for years, just got one and don't know where to start, here are some ideas to get you started, or deepen your practice.

Setting the space and intentions

The concepts of 'set' (one's mindset) and 'setting' (the environment) have long been emphasised as pivotal in determining the effects of psychedelics (Golden et al. 2022) and because drumming works very much in the same way, by altering our state of consciousness, using the same principles when preparing to drum also increases the effects of the drumming practice.

Setting the environment:

- Choose a place where you feel safe, will not be disturbed and maybe also somewhere where you know you will not worry about disturbing others.
- If this appeals to you, add ceremonial elements such as burning incense, lighting a candle (scented or unscented), diffusing essential oils, making a simple altar, saying a prayer or mantra, or whatever appeals to you.
- Close or cover your eyes so that you can enter the lower brainwave state more easily.
- Keep a notebook nearby, so you can jot down your experience. You may also find that keeping a simple journal, like people do when they use microdosing, will also help you enhance your experience, to find out what works for you.

Here are some simple ideas for journalling (that can be done in as little as a couple of minutes):

- Mood
- Physical sensations
- Sleep
- Work

This will help notice any changes over time. You could also ponder this question: Did anything occur today, that was different from what you would expect to happen?

I made this simple so it's not off-putting by feeling like too much, but you could expand on each of these areas if you wish:

Setting intentions:

- **Connection to purpose:** setting an intention helps focus the mind and drum with a specific purpose.

- **Amplifying energy:** having a clear intention amplifies the energy and vibrations created through the drumming. The intention acts like an energetic directive, shaping and guiding the drum's effects.
- **Creating sacred space:** setting an intention can be part of creating a sacred ceremonial space. It signals to the drummer that they are entering an altered state of consciousness.
- **Manifesting goals:** setting an intention can simply help manifest a desired outcome, whether creative inspiration, emotional release, or sending energy towards a goal or person.
- **Personal meaning:** on a personal level, intentions infuse the act of drumming with deeper meaning and mindfulness.

Practicing on your own

Whilst getting tuition from more experienced people is valuable, there is a risk when you follow someone else's ways and beliefs, that they may take you down a path that's not yours. There is value in exploring what a new modality feels like for you without preconceived ideas.

I personally feel that there is a lot of value in learning to play with your drum intuitively, so you learn what feels good and you can become familiar with your drum. If you start with a constrained idea that you don't know what to do and that you aren't doing it 'right' or learn from someone who has rigid ideas on the subject, you may spend years believing that you aren't good enough and carry impostor syndrome and shame.

The maverick in me also enjoys the idea of giving the finger to the patriarchy, encouraging each person to learn things their own way. Later in this chapter I mention drumming techniques, because it can be fun to try new ways to do things, however, I really encourage you to play with your drum and have fun and get to know it without any preconceived ideas. Shamanic-style drumming is very simple and easy to do, and you cannot really do it wrong, especially as we are all rhythmic beings.

Here is a simple way to start:

- Sit or stand somewhere quiet where you won't be disturbed.
- Take a few deep breaths and ground yourself, maybe imagining roots

growing from the soles of your feet.

- Once centred, hold your drum in your non-dominant hand and the beater in your dominant hand (or you could try the other way round).
- Play with your drum: approach it like a child would, with wonder and curiosity, trying to set aside any thoughts of right or wrong. Just intend to play with it and see what happens.
- As you explore your drum, you will find that when you strike it on different spots with your beater, it will produce different sounds. Experiment with that and you may find some sweet spots in your drum, which when hit with your beater, produce the most beautiful sounds.
- Let the drum respond and guide you.
- When you have finished, notice how you feel and maybe write something in your journal about it.

Getting to know your drum

As well as playing with your drum intuitively, you may want to develop a deep spiritual relationship with it and get to know its energy and spirit. Again, there are no rights and wrongs about how you go about this. You can simply hold your drum and feel its energy, or ask it if there is anything it wants to share with you, or what its medicine is. None of it is set in stone and can change with time.

Another beautiful way to get to know your drum is to sit down holding it and listen to a drum journey to meet the spirit of your drum. A drum journey (more on that below) is like a guided meditation with the drum. I have recorded a journey to meet the spirit of your drum, which is available on my YouTube Channel. Simply set aside about fifteen to twenty minutes where you can sit quietly with your drum and see what comes up. You may want to have a notebook ready to write down about your experience afterwards, as journeys are a bit like dreams, and we tend to quickly forget what happened if we do not capture it.

If you like the idea, you may also want to make an altar dedicated to your drum practice. This could be as simple as a candle and a card or picture on a shelf, or could be a lot more intricate, with drum art, drum figures or a mini drum (there are some gorgeous ones on Etsy) depending on what resonates with you. I especially like the work of Sophie Maliphant, a linocut artist, who creates and prints drum art depicting women and frame drums (something that is quite rare to find). Renata at Wispywool (also on Etsy), created a custom needle felted wool figure of me drumming on my request, and she now offers these in her shop.

Drum journeys

Doing drum journeys is a powerful way to experience the transformative effects of the drum.

Drum journeying is a shamanic practice that involves using the rhythmic beat of a drum to induce an altered state of consciousness. It enables you to embark on a symbolic journey for personal growth, healing and spiritual exploration.

Here's how drum journeys can contribute to personal development and familiarity with the effects of the drum:

- **Accessing the subconscious mind:** The trance-like state induced by the repetitive drumbeat allows the conscious mind to relax and the subconscious mind to become more accessible. This can help individuals explore their inner landscapes, unveil suppressed emotions, gain insights into their thought patterns, beliefs and behaviours and find solutions to problems. Journeying gives you the amazing ability to become your own coach/therapist/spiritual advisor!
- **Symbolic journeying:** During a drum journey, people can experience vivid imagery, symbolism and encounters with spirit guides or power animals. These symbolic experiences can serve as metaphors for personal challenges, strengths or areas that require attention, providing opportunities for self-discovery and growth.
- **Emotional release and healing:** The altered state induced by the drumbeat can create a safe space for individuals to process and release emotional blockages, trauma or unresolved issues. This can lead to a sense of emotional cleansing and healing, enabling personal growth and transformation.
- **Enhancing intuition and creativity:** The trance-like state can open up channels for intuitive insights and creative inspiration. People can

experience heightened intuition, artistic expression, or innovative solutions to problems during or after a drum journey. These days when I encounter a problem, I make a mental note to "drum on it".

- **Familiarity with altered states:** Regular participation in drum journeying can help individuals become familiar with the effects of the drum and the experience of altered states of consciousness. This familiarity can aid in personal exploration and the integration of insights gained during journeys into daily life.
- **Connection with nature and spirituality:** Drum journeying is often associated with connecting with nature spirits, animals, ancestors or spirits, depending on people's belief system. This can foster a deeper sense of connection with the natural world and spiritual realms, contributing to personal growth and a sense of belonging. The elusive feeling of oneness can also become a lot easier to access.

If you practice regularly, over time, you may become able to get yourself into an altered state of consciousness without the drumming. You will also become able to enter this state as you drum, however in my experience this takes quite a bit of practice and time, because when you drum you are using your brain's motor centre, which somewhat distracts your brain from entering the altered state.

After many years of active drumming practice, I can easily get into that state by just thinking about it or whilst drumming, but I almost always go deeper if I'm just relaxing and listening to someone else drumming (or a recording of myself drumming). Therefore, as you start, if you want to enjoy the full benefits, you will have an easier experience just listening to someone else drumming, whether live or recorded, to enter the altered state of consciousness that characterises journeying.

Listening to different drum rhythms

As well as doing drum journeys (you can try mine on YouTube, or simply search for some on YouTube or Spotify, or look at the links in the Appendix), you may want to try listening to different drumming tracks, from shamanic ones to some designed to stimulate and modify your brain state and mood, like the ones created by Jeff Strong. Jeff's work demonstrates that specific drumming rhythms can influence the brain and behaviour in various ways:

- The concept of entrainment refers to the synchronisation of brainwaves with the underlying pulse or tempo of the drumming rhythm. Playing rhythms at certain tempos can shift the brain into corresponding brainwave states.
- Complex, unpredictable rhythms can stimulate and activate the brain, resulting in increased cognitive abilities.
- Traditional drum healing techniques from various cultures used rhythms to alter consciousness, affect behaviour or synchronise groups. Jeff drew from these traditions to develop Rhythmic Entrainment Intervention (REI).
- Different rhythms can induce specific responses like calmness, increased focus, boosting creativity, decreasing anxiety, or agitation. Even subtle changes in rhythm, tempo and orchestration impact the listener differently.
- Strong has used REI drumming rhythms to reduce anxiety, improve language, eye contact and socialisation in children with autism and other conditions.

Jeff Strong shows drumming rhythms can entrain and influence brainwave activity, cognitive function and behaviours through the principles of auditory driving and neural activation/entrainment.

Listening to people's experiences with the drum

I'm sharing this because even though it's not the same as listening to drumming, you may enjoy broadening your knowledge and hearing about aspects of drumming you may not have thought about.

- My podcast, The Wisdom Messenger, is full of interviews of women drummers. It is available on YouTube, Spotify and Apple Podcasts.
- The Emerald podcast by Josh Shrei, has several episodes featuring drumming, I particularly like his episode called "Give the Drummer Some."
- There are several TED talks about drumming and healing on YouTube (see Appendix).
- There are several videos of the late Layne Redmond on YouTube.

Playing with different rhythms

There are many different kinds of drums and many different ways to play them, but here, the main goal in mind with your frame drum is to slow your brain down and enter a deep meditative state of consciousness.

Typically, this is done using a rhythm of approximately 3-4 beats per second, or 180-220 beats per minute, which is quite fast. You can find many examples of this online, by simply searching for shamanic drumming tracks, or look at the Appendix. You will find tracks lasting a few minutes or much longer. Since it's such a simple rhythm you can pick it up in no time.

When you start practicing with your drum, after you've done this intuitively and if you would like to experience playing with different rhythms with your drum, you can go on YouTube and search for "how to play the shamanic drum" and play along with the videos, or look at the links in the Appendix.

With a shamanic drum and beater, you can create different rhythms in two different ways: 1) by striking different parts of the drum head with your beater, 2) by varying the tempo, 3) by combining the two.

If you experiment with striking your drum on different spots on the drum head, you'll notice that, especially with a skin drum (I find this is less noticeable on synthetic drums), depending on where you hit it, it will produce different sounds. Some lower pitched, some higher, some more resonant, some more flat. People often describe their drums having a sweet spot, which produces the best sound. So, during a drumming practice, simply making a conscious effort to strike the drum on different spots will produce a variety of sounds.

As well as where you strike your drum head with your beater, the way with which your beater makes contact with the drum will also influence sounds. For example, you can let the beater rebound, or you can let it sit on the head as it lands. This will result in more resonant or more muffled sounds.

When varying the tempo, you can move from 4 evenly spaced beats per second, to making accents (making one of the beats stronger than the others), or beating alternatively strongly and softly in rhythms of 2, 3 or 4. Another simple way to play is to drum at the rhythm of your heartbeat. There are many videos available online that you may use for inspiration in the Appendix.

Do not worry too much about getting it perfect or 'right'. As drummer Jeff Strong explains, the minute irregular variations in tempo created by the imperfect human drumming (this applies even to very experienced drummers) actually make the drumming more effective in terms of brainwave entrainment, because it bypasses our brain's tendency to tune out repetitive patterns. This is also why, according to Jeff, binaural beats do not work as well as drumming to change consciousness, because our brains tend to tune them out after a while. Jeff has a video explaining this on his YouTube channel.

Experiment with different strokes and speeds to discover your drum's voice and also what sounds and tempos you enjoy best. Trust what the drum is doing to guide you. I have found and so have my students, that once you get a bit more confident, it can sometimes feel like the drum is drumming you rather than the other way round. The speed, sounds and tempo can change almost without you having control over it. When this happens, I find it very enjoyable, like I am truly in tune with my drum and what's happening around me.

If you read all of the options above and it makes you feel overwhelmed, simply start with what feels more appealing or exciting to you.

Drumming and singing

Singing accompanied by drumming is an ancient practice that resonates deeply with our human nature. This combination has been used for millennia in various cultures for spiritual, communal and healing purposes.

I absolutely love singing accompanied by the drum. I do this often and I always finish my drum circle with a song. (I have included a list of simple drumming chants in the Appendix.)

I share a simple chant and teach it by ear, call and response style. Voices join in, hesitant at first, then growing in confidence. The drums start again, a soft beat supporting our song. Rattles shake, adding a crisp, energetic layer to our chorus. Our individual voices blend into one, rising and falling with the beat of the drums.

The energy in the circle intensifies. We're no longer individuals, but a unified whole. The boundaries between us seem to dissolve and for a moment, we are one voice, one heart. Time seems to stand still, and we're connected to something greater than ourselves.

Something magical happens when we sing together. It feels like a deep reclaiming of something we are all meant to do. There's something deeply emotional and powerful about it, a connection to something ancient within us.

As our chant comes to a close, I look around at the glowing faces around me. Eyes shine, smiles are wide and there's a palpable sense of joy and connection in the air. This, I think, is why I do this. This is the magic of singing together with the drum.

If you ever get the chance to experience this for yourself, don't hesitate. Join a drum circle and let the rhythm and singing carry you. I promise, it's a journey worth taking.

Learning from others

One of the main reasons I decided to write this book is because I feel that humanity is going through a major shift and one of these shifts is that knowledge will no longer come through teachers or gurus but directly from source. We are shifting away from reliance on external authorities and towards direct access to our inner wisdom. I have felt and known this for several years. It came first in a meditation, in which I was shown that the main cause of our collective suffering is disconnection. Disconnection from ourselves, from each other and from the earth.

What we need most at this moment in time, to heal ourselves and to heal the earth, is to support women to stand in their true power. The power that resides within us, in our ability to trust ourselves and know what's right for us, rather than abdicating knowledge and power over to the system. What we need is to support a feminine way of accessing knowledge.

Modern culture has a tendency to gatekeep knowledge, especially in the healing field, by centralising and controlling access to these domains through established institutions, authorities and systems. This reflects a cultural belief that healing and knowledge must be strictly controlled and dispensed only through approved, centralised channels. It disempowers individuals from accessing their own inner wisdom and taking authority over their wellbeing.

Our culture conflates formal education with genuine competence. We place academic qualifications above practical experience, creating a culture where diplomas and certificates are prised more highly than the hard-won wisdom gained through years of hands-on practice.

While formal training certainly has its place, it's only one aspect of skill development. True mastery often emerges from a combination of theoretical knowledge and practical application, honed through trial and error in real-world scenarios.

Unfortunately, our current system tends to overemphasise standardised credentials, sometimes at the expense of recognising the depth of knowledge and skills that comes from direct experience. This leads to overlooking highly skilled individuals who may lack formal qualifications but possess deep, nuanced understanding of their craft.

This lack of self-trust is more pervasive in women, the drum feels particularly important because it offers a way to relearn how to access our own wisdom, one that is easy and fairly effortless. Drumming offers a way back in through the layers of parenting, education and societal conditioning that have eroded our self-knowing. Reclaiming this knowing is critically needed in a culture that conditions women from childhood to seek truth outside rather than within.

When I work with women and the drum, I see exactly this happen. The drum gives a voice to inner emotions and feelings and acts like an inner pilot light, putting women back in touch with their unique expression, voice and power.

I experienced this myself, with impostor syndrome feelings, having trained and learnt to offer many aspects of my work, especially the ritualistic aspects, through exploration and experience, rather than through formal training.

A shift from outer to inner-centred wisdom

The shift I see happening at grassroot levels challenges the top-down model, a de-institutionalisation of knowledge and healing – enabling direct access to source wisdom within each person rather than relying on external authorities and systems as intermediaries.

For me, this shift has manifested itself in a reluctance to learn from others and explore things for myself, after several years of training obsessively with as many teachers as possible. I do still train but I only pick mentors who work in the same, empowering and unique way, offering not their own path, but encouraging others to carve their own. I have shared the names of these teachers throughout the book.

I no longer want to teach drumming the way I was trained, which is the Reiki Drum system (where you channel Reiki through the drum). The learning path follows a rigid system: you have to train at two levels of Reiki healing before you can train to become a Reiki Drum practitioner.

Whilst I loved learning to offer and teach Reiki and Reiki Drum and still do and whilst this was a big part of my personal growth journey, today I prefer to offer something which gives permission to people to offer drumming to one another straight away. I believe that we can all do it. I believe that healing and drumming are innate abilities present within all of us. When I offer the opportunity to women to do this, I always see that this is true.

In my evolving approach to healing, I've shifted away from relying on the idea that I, as the practitioner, am the source of healing. Instead, I'm drawn to use my drum as a space holder and a facilitator of self-discovery and inner wisdom. My role has transformed from that of a 'healer' to a guide. This approach honours women's unique journeys and empowers them to be active participants in their own healing process.

Drumming with others

"The drum has many powerful properties. One of the most important qualities of the drum is that it is a healing instrument. It has the power to heal, I believe, because it can take us out of our waking mind to a deeper level of consciousness, especially when drums are played in groups."

Carolyn Brandy

As well as drumming alone, it can be a wonderful experience to drum with others. This can take many forms:

- **Drum circles:** Shamanic drum circles are gatherings where people come together to drum in a communal setting. These circles typically have a facilitator or leader who guides the group through meditation and intentions. It can be a wonderful way to experience different ways to drum, how drumming facilitates unified consciousness, and it can be really joyful and life-affirming as well as connecting you with like-minded people who like to drum. There are drum circles all over the world, just search for one in your area, or ask around people for recommendations.
- **Drumming ceremonies:** You could attend wheel of the year or other ritual gatherings that include drumming. Or you could create your own and invite others. These ceremonies are usually led by a spiritual leader

and often also involve singing or chants and intentions related to a particular tradition. Or invite others to join you in an impromptu drumming session at meaningful places or times.

- **Shamanic journeying events, or drum sound baths.** Experiencing this live is usually more powerful than doing it with a recording on your own.
- **Drum healing gatherings:** some people use drumming in healing circles, where the drumming and vibrations help restore balance, release negative energies and promote physical, emotional and spiritual healing.
- **Drum conventions:** In the UK, Melonie Syrett, aka The Drum Woman, runs a twice-yearly drum convention, near Colchester, with workshops, stalls, drum workshops and circles, in April and November. Melonie also runs regular drum circles near Colchester and in Harlow, UK and there is a schedule for these on her website. Melonie also runs the UK Association of Women Drummers, Makers and Players. Membership includes a quarterly magazine which includes drumming articles, events and drum circles. In the US there is a 3-day convention held by the Percussive Arts Society International Convention in Indianapolis, Indiana, each November.
- **Nature-based drumming:** Some people prefer to drum outdoors, connecting with the natural environment and the rhythms of nature. This can involve drumming in sacred spaces, such as near bodies of water, in forests, or in any other natural settings that appeal to you.
- **Online drum circles:** online drum circles have become more popular, allowing people from different locations to drum together virtually, guided by a facilitator.

My drum story

– Melanie Wright

I feel like drumming came to me sideways, found me when I wasn't watching yet needed it most. I've always been musical, singing in choirs and bands and playing in orchestras my entire life. My battered guitar has been dragged all over the world to hundreds of campfires. I have always loved nothing more than gathering a group of people and making music together. But drumming wasn't really on my horizon.

In 2009 I heard a taiko[*] drum performance at a conference in California and was deeply thrilled by the vibrations, attending a workshop the group was holding the next day which was wonderful. But returning home I could find no taiko groups near me, so the impulse waned.

A few summers later, visiting my family's cabin near the Mille Lacs Lake Ojibwe reservation, I very nearly bought a frame drum made by a local artist, but I had no way of transporting it home, nor did I know how to play or what to do with it.

By this time, I had switched careers from quantitative social scientist and data analyst to birth doula and was slowly shedding my skin to discover the 'woo' underneath. I took a class from Sophie on Reiki for Birthworkers where she drummed as part of our attunement process.

During Covid, I saw a women's drum birthing in the wild event advertised by a fellow birthkeeper. We camped in an ancient woodland in Kent and made frame drums. It was so special! I began to appreciate how drumming can be used to build and sustain community.

I began attending local drum circles and online drumming with Melonie Syrett (aka The Drum Woman) and became part of a loose group of devoted drummers who call ourselves Sisters of the Drum. We began playing and singing and giving workshops at Pagan events and performing at fairs and handfastings. We meet monthly at the site of a Roman temple to Minerva (built on the remain of an earlier Celtic temple to Sulis) and we drum for ourselves, for humanity and for the land.

We have also travelled to ancient sacred sites across the UK, drumming at standing stones and ancient springs, temples, wells, forests, tombs and other places of power. We drum to heal the land and its people, to feel connected to the deep history and power of the place, but also to love and support one another.

Becoming part of this drumming community has transformed my life. Finding deep soul friends is so much harder as an adult and harder still as an older person once kids are grown and natural connections of the school gate and kids' activities disappear.

For me, drumming is like church. When I was a kid growing up in the

* A large traditional Japanese drum.

American Midwest, everyone went to church of one stripe or another every Sunday. Churches functioned not only as places of spiritual practice, but places of community and identity, of support and fellowship. In a drum circle, we take time to settle and ground ourselves, to open ourselves to the magic of the universe and connect to each other through a guided meditation. We share candidly what is up with us, how we're feeling, what has been happening in our lives. From the sharing circle, we find common themes that become the intention of our group drumming. We set the intention in our hearts and minds, and we begin – a simple beat which slowly diversifies and becomes a narrative, a song, a polyrhythmic prayer. The rhythms weave in and out and for many images appear in the mind's eye. Sometimes voices ring out, songs, words, sounds. All is welcome; all is necessary. The drumming goes through a swelling and contracting (or several) before eventually and as organically as it began, it ends. We sit in the vibrations for a while and then people who are inspired to, share things they experienced during the drumming. It's delightfully surprising how many times the same images, thoughts and feelings are experienced by multiple people. We do this a few times with different intentions and then we close the circle with another guided meditation, giving thanks and gratitude for all we experienced, for each other, for the power of the universe we encountered.

What is different from church as I knew it growing up, is that drum circle is all about connecting to the divine directly, unmediated by a set theology, liturgy, or clerical structure – hooking in directly to the universe, to source, to spirit, to Love, God or the goddess or your highest self or whatever it is you experience in the drumming. There is no right or wrong and your experience will be different from everyone else's. You don't have to follow codes or commandments or memorise prayers or face certain directions; you don't have to be taught how to do it, or ask a priest or saint to intercede on your behalf, or receive attunement from a lineage of master practitioners who came before. It is a direct and utterly personal line to the transcendent.

And at the same time, it happens within community, the music of it builds the circle into a single instrument as the drumming around me dances with my drum, weaving together a whole far greater than the individual drums and drummers. The circle, the group, the community is where the magic happens.

Drum circles

How drum circles support personal growth

> *"When you take your drum to a rhythm circle and play it with your community, healing happens. It does not matter if the group's focus is purely social or ritualistic. If you come and drum, the healing is compounded because everyone is putting their spirit into their drum and their hearts are open. You get and give a rhythmical massage that is compounded by the number of people in the circle and the energy they are sharing with each other."*
>
> **Arthur Hull**

As you will know from the science chapter, drum circles impact us on many levels. A drum circle provides much more than just drumming together and it is difficult to separate the effect of each part of the process. And to be honest, I don't think we should.

Western culture tends to compartmentalise and analyse things in fragments, breaking down wholes into component parts. This approach fails to capture the synergistic effects that arise from the combination and interaction of those parts.

A drum circle is a multi-layered experience that impacts us on physical, emotional, psychological, social and even spiritual levels. As explained in the science chapter, attempting to isolate and study the effects of just the rhythmic drumming alone neglects the synergies created by the wider drum circle dynamics.

When we drum together, we connect beyond words, beyond our different experiences, social status, culture or beliefs. The multisensory and physical experience of drumming as a group grounds us in the present moment, something that is rare in the modern world. Our minds might drift a little, we may worry whether you we are doing it right, especially when we are new to the process...but just as we are told to go back to the breath when meditating, we can just go back to the beat of the drum, and it helps quiet our minds and helps us be present and in our bodies. It helps us be both focused and relaxed in our presence which is quite extraordinary, creating a sense of belonging, a deep sense of shared humanity. It gives us a felt experience that we are all one.

*

As participants arrive in the woodland clearing, the geodome stands like a beacon amongst the trees. People approach, carrying with them the concerns and stresses of their day. There's a feeling of anticipation and tension in the air.

Entering the geodome, they're greeted by the scent of incense. As they settle onto cushions arranged in a circle, there's a gradual unwinding – shoulders drop, breaths deepen and faces soften. Soft light filters through the trees, through the dome's entrance and into our space.

To mark the transition from the outside world and into this sacred space, we start with a meditation accompanied by the drum. Then we share our collective intentions for the drumming. The first gentle drumbeats begin, like a heartbeat, gradually picking up speed.

The beat of our drums reverberates through the dome. The thick canvas of the dome's walls cocoons us in a womb-like space, muffling the outside world, reverberating the sounds of our drums and intensifying our experience. As we drum, the boundary between our sacred space and the surrounding woodland becomes blurred. The beats of our drums blend with the sounds of nature filtering through the fabric – the wind rustling through the leaves, the calls of birds.

As our beaters strike our drumheads, the deep sounds ground us in our bodies and the tempo brings our consciousness upwards. The rhythm picks up, growing in intensity and power. A rattle joins the chorus, its staccato sounds weaving through the deeper drum tones, adding layers of texture and energy to our sound tapestry. Some people start to sway, or move around the space, some hum or sing. Energy swirls around the dome, building with each beat and the space seems to vibrate with unseen power.

As the session peaks, it feels as though the dome itself has become a living entity, pulsing with our shared vibrations. In this liminal space, cocooned yet connected to the world outside, the ordinary falls away, leaving only the power of rhythm and nature combined.

As the final beats fade away, a profound stillness settles over us. There's a collective exhale, as if the space is releasing the built-up energy. People sit in quiet reflection, their faces now serene and open, a stark contrast to their arrival. The sense of connection – to the self, to others, to nature, is beyond words. As people slowly stir and we move into social time, there's a reluctance to break the spell. They move with a new rhythm, unhurried and grounded. Conversations are soft, peppered with warm smiles. Many of us were strangers when we started, but now we feel like life-long friends. Each person carries with them a renewed sense of peace, the heartbeat of the drum circle still echoing within them as they step back into the world.

*

Drumming calms the nervous system. Beyond the scientific evidence showing this, I have noticed time and time again how a drum circle group settles down from each round of drumming to the next. This is clear in the energy and behaviour of people. When they arrive, they are still full of their day and their energy is somewhat wired. They are all in their heads. It is often clear in the intentions they share prior to the first round of drumming too.

Newcomers (I usually have a handful at each drum circle) are often feeling slightly nervous. After the first round, which acts as a light cleansing, a gentle removal of the top layer of distraction, people are more settled and have 'arrived' a little more. They are calmer and more present.

With each successive round of drumming, this effect deepens, becoming more pronounced and palpable. I often feel that, as we drum, it is similar to layers of an onion being peeled away. Each round of drumming strips away another layer of everyday consciousness, allowing individuals to go deeper within themselves. The beat serves as a constant, grounding presence, creating a safe container for this deepening exploration.

By the end of the circle, the difference is palpable. Everyone feels more peaceful, more open, more present. The drums provide a sense of deep connection that does not require words and that link us together in a common process. This creates a sense of community and belonging that transcends beliefs, origins and social status, which feels amazing and is healing and transformative in its own right.

I run my drum circles without set rhythms, inviting people to drum as they feel. This is important because I prioritise connection and expression over perfection, and it also gives people space to express themselves fully. And yet during rounds of drumming, our beats usually synchronise in the most natural and beautiful way.

I find that Sophie holds the space in a way that is liberating and very open. To be able to hold both of these qualities in the same circle is a very powerful ability. Sophie does not direct, but she provides enough preparation (including cleansing and protection work) and gentle guidance for each of us to bring our own gifts into the circle. This can be anything, positive or negative. After the circles I feel that I have fully expressed myself and been seen, not by other people so much as by myself!

SJ

Drumming as part of a group not only helps bring us back into the present and into our bodies and for some people it can also re-regulate their nervous systems and reteach them what it feels like to be safe in their bodies.

I recently led an impromptu drum circle on the top of the hill that overlooks Cambridge, as part of the Global Drum Gathering initiative. I started a WhatsApp group about it just a few days before, inviting people to join me. I was pleasantly surprised by the turnout, as about twenty people met me at the bottom of the hill. It was beautiful to watch our colourfully dressed selves walk up the hill together. The drumming was powerful as we connected with the energy of the hundreds of other drum circles taking place across the world that day. What I loved most of all was how easeful and informal it felt for me to lead the drumming, in a way that only comes with enough years of practice, when you feel that you no longer have anything to prove.

What drum circles do energetically/spiritually

I was raised a Catholic and I've often felt that, since I rejected the Church in my teens, I was left adrift without a sense of spirituality in my life. I remember reflecting that, beyond churches, there were no sacred buildings to be in. At some point in my forties this manifested into a deep longing, which was felt when I attended spaces steeped in spirituality, such as the retreats I attended once a year. Over the last ten years, I've been on a journey to reclaim my spirituality and crafting my own spiritual practice, one that feels true to me and does not belong to any named or set religion. Drumming has been a big part of this process. I believe that attending a drum circle fulfils this need in others too, whether they are aware of it or not.

"Spirituality is recognising and celebrating that we are all inextricably connected to each other by a power greater than all of us and that our connection to that power and to one another is grounded in love and compassion. Practicing spirituality brings a sense of perspective, meaning and purpose to our lives."

Brené Brown

When I run a drum circle, I always set up sacred space first to imbue the atmosphere with supportive energy. I create a central altar; I cleanse the space with smoke or sound before people arrive and I call to the seven directions and to some spirits of the land and my guides. Sometimes I also invite people to cleanse each other with smudge or rattles and invite them to take part with their drums in my calling the sacred directions.

As drumming softens our state of consciousness, from that place our thoughts are more fluid and flexible. It makes it possible to not only gain a sense of inner peace and presence, but also, because we set intentions for each round of drumming, we are literally 'drumming our intentions', which helps bring more of what we want in our lives. When we drum together, our brain's rhythms synchronise into a unified consciousness.

I wrote this song about drumming and sung it at one of my recent circles:

We drum together, our rhythms combine

Our hearts beat as one, our minds align

In sacred circle, our spirits renew

Our connection grows, strong and true.

The drum circle's magic

– Malwina Idzik

Where I live, we have this woodland, where people come to recharge and reconnect to the Normal Frequency for Human Beings. One evening of the month a group of people gather to Drum.

I join them sometimes but last night my partner was late. Normally, when "my plan" doesn't come easily I get very anxious, but not that evening… I recognised it and thought "interesting".

My kids went from being challenging to becoming playful before bed and I joined them; at 7pm I rarely have any playful energy left but that night it was different.

My partner arrived closer to 8 and found us in contact improvisation movement pillow fight, I was bursting with laughter…we all joined family silly before bedtime…

I thought: should I go for the drumming…there is still an hour left? Or should I stay and see what this amazing energy is shifting for us?

The ease, the laughter, the fun, the feeling of togetherness…

I know for sure that having a group of people drumming in our space in the woods brought a difference – one that I was searching for a long time.

I got to experience the goodness of the drumming circle from afar – the drummers do not only bring goodness for themselves but for all that are in the area.

Thunder, drums and transformation

– Helen Ni Mhaireid

In June 2023, I started working towards realising a dream or vision of mine to become a birth doula and yoga teacher full time.

My first medicine or shamanic drum came to me through several synchronicities, chances, coincidences and me following my intuition. These all led me to a local woman who makes and sells drums. She has a process where you visit her workshop and sit with her and her drums. She plays the drums to you and you feel into the drum and the sound and the call and what you feel, if anything. I went with an open mind about whether she would have a drum for me or not, and. whether I would be a keeper for one of her drums or not. One of my diary entries from 2023 reads:

"A wonderful and amazing thing has happened. I have found my drum and I feel whole. I walked away from M's on Sunday and I have never felt so strong and so centred and so whole. I have found the missing piece. I have found what I have been searching for forty-odd years and it is the right thing!

...as I held her [the drum] I started crying...but there was no question that I was going to take her home."

Finally, I started a drumming circle. It took me a few months to find the right women. There are lots of circles locally to me and a few offering drum journeys but not one where we all drum together. We managed to find a day and time which suited us all and agreed on half an hour, to meet, do a little gratitude, maybe sing a little and drum. Half an hour and done!

We arranged to meet by the creek close to where I live. As I was walking from home, I could see a storm starting over to the west. As we met and started walking to the creek together the rain started and the thunder and lightning was getting closer. By the time we had found a spot next to the creek we were already drenched (handy to have a synthetic drum at this time). As we started to drum a kangaroo on the opposite side of the creek was seeking shelter under some trees. He stopped to watch us drum.

It was absolutely amazing. We were drumming, the sky was drumming. Every time someone changed the beat the sky would flash. If we slowed down the thunder would speed up. Meanwhile in the centre of town they were experiencing snow and flash flooding which the whole town was talking about for days!

It was truly an awesome inaugural circle. And we ended up stripping off and jumping in the creek because we were so wet already, baptised with thunder and lightning and our drums.

Starting your own drum circle

When you first step into facilitating a drum circle, remember that every experienced holder of space started just where you are. Let me share how I've learned to create and hold these sacred gatherings, and to help you find your own way.

The magic begins before anyone arrives. Getting to your space – whether it's a woodland geodome like mine or a community hall – at least thirty minutes early is essential. This gives you time to set the space up physically but also energetically. As you arrange your central altar and lay out drums and percussion instruments around it, you're already beginning to create the container. Use this time to ground yourself too – you'll need this to hold space for others.

Clear timing helps everyone feel secure. I let people know exactly when to arrive (for example, from 6.30 for a 7pm start), and I ask people to arrive on time to avoid disturbing the sacred space. I'm specific about late arrivals – they need to wait quietly until a round finishes before joining. It might feel strict, but I've found this clarity actually helps people relax.

When it comes to the circle itself, starting with a grounding meditation helps immensely. It doesn't need to be complex – just guiding people to connect with their breath and feel the earth beneath them works beautifully.

You can use a talking stick (in this case, one of my drum beaters) for the rounds of sharing, and explain that only the person holding the stick will be talking, and that sharing is optional. This removes the pressure to share whilst also giving people a chance to decide whether they want to share or not.

Share some simple rules about the circle, such as confidentiality, speaking from the I (as in for oneself instead of others), and from the heart (waiting for the talking stick to come to join before deciding what you will share so you can listen to others).

Follow this with a brief sharing circle, giving each person about two minutes to speak. You can use a rattle as a gentle timekeeper, reminding people if they share for a bit too long you will gently shake it – this helps to keep boundaries lightly, and often brings laughter.

The sacred space flows naturally from here – opening directions together, cleansing with rattles or smoke in pairs (depending on whether smoke is appropriate and/or comfortable for people – always ask if anyone is sensitive to smoke). You can then start setting individual intentions, and use these to weave in a joint intention. Trust your intuition with the joint intention – you'll be surprised how naturally it comes when you're in the space.

For the drumming itself, invite people to join you into a gentle heartbeat rhythm to start with, then to trust their hearts and hands when guided to do something else. The beats often evolve from cacophony to beautiful synchrony over the course of the drumming round.

I find three rounds work well – two for personal needs and one for the world/wider community. Each round will have its own character, its own energy. Do not try to control this – let it flow. Some rounds will be gentle, others powerful. All are perfect.

Closing is just as important as opening. You can lead the group into a closing song (find a simple chant that resonates with you and your group – I prefer something easy that everyone can join in), and then allow time for chatting and sharing refreshments. Never underestimate the power of cake and informal connection to help integrate the experience!

If you're just starting out, begin simply. Start with smaller groups – maybe eight to twelve people max. Keep your structure basic: meditation, brief sharing, drumming, closing. Ninety minutes is a good length to begin with. As your confidence grows, you'll naturally find ways to expand and adapt.

Remember that challenges will come – late arrivals, varying experience levels, different energy needs, emotional challenges. Meet them with grace and clear boundaries. Trust that the drums will help harmonise the group.

Most importantly, know that this is your journey. While I've shared my way, you'll develop your own style, your own rhythm. Start where you are, trust your intuition, and let the drum guide you. Each circle will teach you something new. Reflect on each circle, and what there was to learn for the future.

The key is creating a safe container where people feel free to express themselves through the drum's voice. Hold the space lightly but clearly, balance sacred with social, and trust the process. Before long, you'll find your own way of weaving these elements together.

Remember, the drum has been calling people into circle for thousands of years. You're not alone in this journey – you're part of an ancient tradition that continues to evolve. Trust the drum, trust yourself, and most importantly, enjoy the journey.

Drum circle reflection

– Philippe

Drumming is a transformative practice with multifaceted effects. A typical drumming session lasts two hours, but the process begins even earlier as I arrive and prepare. The initial arrival at the woods, setting up and meeting my friend Sophie is already a relaxing and centring experience. I cherish the opportunity to meditate, walk in the forest and let go of tensions and desires that pull me away from being present.

Even before the drumming starts, I find myself feeling more centred, fluid and streamlined in my thoughts. As the session begins and people gather, there is an air of sincerity among the ten to twenty participants united in purpose, which carries its own power. However, there is also uncertainty, especially with new people, as we are all occupying and influencing each other's energy fields.

I often experience doubts during the first round – Will I be able to keep rhythm after not drumming for a month? Will my pride or desire to be seen become overbearing? Will I overextend myself? Will it be boring? Will I be able to sing? These distracting thoughts and uncertainties are palpable.

Initially, I find myself judging others' level of presence or sincerity, which is regrettable but a pattern I've developed over the years. However, as the drumming progresses, I almost always end up with a sense of brotherhood and sisterhood – the dropping of layers of separation between individuals and a coming together as a collective. This transformation from separateness to unity is profound.

On a spiritual level, there are also felt effects, as we create a space for both human and spirit realms to converge.

One of my key struggles has been a lack of self-belief, doubts about my worthiness and the value of my being. However, I find that through the creative expression of drumming, where I can go a bit wild, hit the drums harder, try new patterns and move freely, I receive validation and a sense that my expression is valuable. The drumming circle reflects love back to each person, supporting our individual creative uncertainties.

As each person feels comfortable and validated, it creates a circular effect, amplifying the sense of collective being and frequency. Even the most anxious participants tend to find greater self-strength and expression through this process.

While the first round is often accompanied by fears and doubts about how to drum properly, these tend to dissipate by the second or third round as we become immersed in the experience. The drumming practice helps me break through self-limiting ideas, uncover challenges and find the courage to express myself more freely.

CONCLUSION: ECHOES INTO THE FUTURE

"When 8000 sacred drums sound together, an intense healing of Mother Earth and Our Peoples will begin and more Peace will come."

500-year-old Otomi Toltec Prophecy

When the idea of this book first germinated in my mind, I thought I was going to write about birth and birth alone. Then it became clear that it needed to be a lot broader than that and it sure did.

Writing it has expanded my mind beyond belief, from reflecting on my own journey, to the history of women and drumming, to finding out about so much exciting drumming science.

I've shared my journey, the history and contemporary use of women and drumming, the science of drumming, how drumming supports neurodivergent folks, social transformation, the birth journey, altered states of consciousness. I've shared the stories of many women, how to choose a drum and the many ways you can work with drumming and the drum. In fact, I've shared everything I know about starting your own unique journey with this sacred tool, something I wish I had known when I started my own journey: that there is not one right path, one right way, but many unique ones, because your way into the drum will be as unique to you as your life.

I hope I have made a strong case about the power of the drum and how it can help women heal, hear their inner voice and reclaim their power. But most importantly, I hope to have inspired you, to have ignited a desire to bring drumming to your life, or, if you are already a drummer, to grow the presence that your drum plays in your life.

We've explored how drumming can transform our experiences of the world, of our life and of its transitions, from birth to menopause and beyond. As we come to the end of this journey, I invite you to reflect on the profound power of the drum to reconnect us with our innate wisdom, our communities and the sacred rhythms of life.

I invite you now to pick up the drum, to feel its heartbeat and to let it guide you back to your own inner knowing. Whether you're navigating a major life transition or simply seeking a deeper connection to yourself and others, the drum is waiting for you.

I imagine a world where every woman's journey is honoured, where the wisdom of the feminine is celebrated and where the drum's rhythm weaves us all together in a tapestry of support and understanding. This world is not just a distant dream – it's a reality we can create, one woman and one drum at a time.

As women, we need the transformative power of the drum at this moment of time, more than ever. If you discover drumming, or love drumming, please share your experience with others. Better still, take your friends to drum circles, drum journeys and drum gatherings. Only by experiencing its power can people truly understand what it brings.

My invitation to you is simple: start with just five minutes a day. This small commitment can transform your life and ripple out to others too. Whether you work in the healing arts, education, business, or any other field, you can be a catalyst for change through drumming. Lead a drum meditation at your workplace, bring drumming to your community group, or simply share your practice with friends and family.

If you're called to go deeper, consider:

- Creating or joining drum circles in your community.
- Incorporating drumming into ceremonies.
- Sharing the drum's power with other women through workshops or informal gatherings.
- Using drumming to mark transitions in your own life and supporting others to do the same.
- Adding drumming to your professional practice.

Remember, you don't need to be an expert to share the gift of drumming.

If you worry that you do not know enough, remember that even drum masters were once where you are. You only need to be willing to start, to share, and to hold space for others to experience the wonders of drumming.

As you close this book, remember: the power of the drum, the wisdom of your body and the strength of sisterhood are always within you. Let the drumbeats guide you home to yourself, and let them ripple out to create the more connected, conscious world we all long to belong to.

I am going to leave you with this vision of women and drumming:

The sun peeks over the horizon, a group of women walks up a hill together, carrying drums, their faces glowing with anticipation. The morning air is crisp, filled with the promise of a new day. Trees sway gently in the breeze and wildflowers are scattered through the grass, their petals still heavy with dew.

At the top of the hill, the women form a circle. They hold hands and share a few breaths together. One by one, they speak their intentions for the drumming. There's a moment of stillness, before the first beat rings out.

A heartbeat-like drumbeat starts, steady and strong. Each of them joins in, each with their unique sound and their unique tempo. The sounds weave together, creating a tapestry of rhythm that resonates through the air.

The women begin to move, swaying and stepping in time with the beats. They sing, their voices rising and falling like waves. Their eyes are closed, and they are lost in the shared energy of the moment.

As the rhythm builds, so does their connection. The beats flow between them like an invisible thread, binding them together in this modern version of an ancient ritual.

They dance and play, celebrating the dawn, their bodies, the earth beneath their feet. The rhythm of their instruments matches the rhythm of their hearts, of their breath, of the seasons, of life itself.

Gradually, the tempo slows. The beat softens until only a single drum remains, its heartbeat-like rhythm echoing like the pulse of the earth. One by one, the women fall silent, until the sounds of nature can be heard again – birdsong, rustling leaves, the distant babbling of a stream.

As they stand together after their shared ritual, a profound silence envelops them, rich with unspoken understanding. Their eyes meet, conveying more than words. All barriers of age, background and personal history melt away, leaving only pure connection.

They sense a collective lightness, as if the rhythms and movement have washed away their worries and stresses. Shoulders that arrived tense and hunched now stand relaxed and open. Furrowed brows have smoothed, replaced by soft smiles and clear eyes.

Each woman feels the invisible threads that bind them. What they have just shared reaches beyond the constraints of language and social norms. In this circle, they are not defined by their roles as mothers, daughters, professionals, or partners. Here, they are simply women, connected to each other and to the earth.

The anxiety they might have carried in – the arguments left unresolved, the deadlines and the many tasks to be done, the fears for the future – seem to have been absorbed by the earth, transformed by their collective energy into something manageable. They stand taller, breathe deeper, feel more alive in their bodies.

In this shared experience, they have found a peace that doesn't need to be named or explained. It simply is, as they simply are, whole and complete in their connection to each other, the drums and to the world around them.

They gather their instruments and prepare to return to their daily lives. This gathering, once forgotten, has once again become a normal and integral part of their lives – a time to connect, to heal, to honour themselves, each other and to weave the rhythms of nature and womanhood together.

Appendix

Drum rhythms and drum tracks resources

Things to listen to:

My podcast, The Wisdom Messenger, has several episodes about drumming. It's available on Spotify, YouTube and Apple podcast.

My YouTube channel has a playlist full of drum journeys.

Josh Schrei's podcast, The Emerald, has several episodes talking about trance and about drumming.

Jeff Strong's YouTube channel has many drum journeys, videos about drumming and shamanism, videos that show in real time what happens to the brain when you drum. You can listen to many of Jeff's drumming tracks for free on his YouTube channel (he has collections for sleep, for attention and focus, for creativity and problem solving. Tracks are also available on his website (Stronginstitute.com), on Spotify, or via his (paid) website Brain Stim Audio (which you can try for free for two weeks without providing a payment method).

Sandra Ingerman is a shamanic teacher, and you can find a lot of drum journey videos with her on YouTube.

If you search for shamanic drumming on either of these platforms, you will find plenty of varied tracks to listen to.

TED talks on YouTube

"How traditional djembe drumming can help heal trauma", Francis Agyakwa. TEDxMileHigh.

"The Healing Drummer", Toby Christensen. TEDxCincinnati.

"Drumming and Your Brain: Magic and Science", Cornell Coley. TEDxJamaicaPlain.

Shamanic drumming teaching lessons videos on YouTube

Margaret Harmer has a playlist of shamanic drumming video lessons.

Lee-Anne at Temple of Balance on YouTube has some lessons to get you started with your drum.

Veleslav Voron at Shamandrum.org

Simple drum chants on YouTube or Spotify

"Deep into the Earth I Go", Tarisha.

"We are the Women, We've Come to Drum", Lisa Dancing-Light.

"Mother I Feel You", Windsong Dianne Martin.

"The River is Flowing", Lindie Lila.

"We all Come from the Goddess", Lindie Lila.

"Wisdom in my Bones", Heather Pierson.

"Sacred Circle", Heather Pierson.

"We Shall be Known", Mamuse.

"May The Love We Share", Šárka Elias.

ACKNOWLEDGEMENTS

I am grateful to Lucy Pearce and the Womancraft Publishing team and community for their encouraging support, for making this book possible and for helping me create a much more powerful book than it would have been if I had created it on my own.

I am grateful to Bridget Supple, who encouraged me to attend Womancraft Publishing's prospective authors Zoom call, and to expand this book from focusing solely on birth to a broader perspective.

I am grateful to my parents Michelle and Jacques for supporting my outspoken spirit and for being such strong supporters of my ever-meandering work, my forever-new passions and my seeking of personal development, especially through my professional conversion from a prestigious career as a scientist to becoming a self-employed birth worker, educator and healer, and now taking a journey towards even more 'alternative' work. Thank you for encouraging my curiosity, my questioning of power, and for loving me and supporting me as I am.

To my husband Chi, thank you for your unwavering support in my life directions. You married a scientist, and now you live with a hippy healer woman, and our house is full of altars and drums. I'm so grateful that you have been able to embrace my ever-evolving self with support and understanding, even when my path takes me into directions you do not share or understand. I am full of gratitude for our journey together.

To my children, Sebastien and Jin, your births changed everything. Thank you for stretching my heart, my mind and my soul. You know who you are and are such kind and sensitive beings. I am very proud of you and of the young, empathic and compassionate adults you are becoming.

I am profoundly grateful to the women who guided me on my drumming journey, each one highlighting a different aspect of this sacred path: Kay Gillard, Carolyn Hillyer, Rebecca Wright, Jo Gray, Sarah Gregg and Melonie Syrett. Their wisdom, mentorship and inspiration shaped both my practice and my spirit.

I also want to express gratitude to the women who taught me the closing of the bones ritual, which has become beautifully interwoven with my drumming practice: Stacia Smales Hill, Rocio Alarcon, Francoise Freedman, Virginie Mandin, Gena Kirby and Naoli Vinaver.

To all the other women of the drum who shared their wisdom and enriched this book: Hollie Hope, Jane Hardwicke Collings, Rachael Crow and Barbara Gail.

To all the amazing women and people who shared their stories for this book. Stories are powerful medicine – they help us find ourselves in others' journeys. As Brené Brown says, "Stories are data with a soul." Thank you for giving this book more soul.

REFERENCES

Arns, M., Conners, C. K., & Kraemer, H. C., "A decade of EEG theta/beta ratio research in ADHD: A meta-analysis." Journal of Attention Disorders, 17(5), 374-383, 2013.

Ascenso S., Perkins R., Atkins L., Fancourt D., Williamon A., "Promoting well-being through group drumming with mental health service users and their carers." International Journal of Qualitative Studies on Health and Well-being. 13(1):1484219, 2018.

Avenga, L., "ADHD and drumming". 2024. gomadmusic.com/adhd-drumming

Baghat, R., Drums No Guns. 2020. rambhagat.com/drums-no-guns

Barkley, R. A., *Executive Functions: What they are, how they work and why they evolved.* Guilford Press, 2012.

Bellato, A., Arora, I., Hollis, C., & Groom, M. J., "Is autonomic nervous system function atypical in attention deficit hyperactivity disorder (ADHD)? A systematic review of the evidence." Neuroscience &Biobehavioral Reviews, 108, 182-206, 2020.

Bittman, B., Berk, L., Felten, D., Westengard, J., Simonton, O., Pappas, J., Ninehouser, M., "Composite effects of group drumming music therapy on modulation of neuroendocrine-immune parameters in normal subjects." Alternative Therapies in Health and Medicine. 7(1): 38-47, 2001.

Brandy C., "Global Movement of Women Playing Drums". 2008. womendrummers.org/wdi-events-and-activities/wdi-global-movement-of-women-playing-drums/

Bruchhage, M. M. K., Amad, A., Draper, S. B., Seidman, J., Lacerda, L., Laguna, P. L., Lowry, R. G., Wheeler, J., Robertson, A., Dell'Acqua, F., Smith, M. S., & Williams, S. C. R., "Drum training induces long-term plasticity in the cerebellum and connected cortical thickness." Scientific Reports, 10(1), 10116, 2020.

Cohen, JR., "This Drum I Play: Women and Square Frame Drums in Portugal and Spain." Ethnomusicology Forum. 17(1): 95-124, 2008.

Cortese, S., "The neurobiology and genetics of Attention-Deficit/Hyperactivity Disorder (ADHD): what every clinician should know." European Journal of Paediatric Neurology, 16(5), 422-433, 2012.

Cox, D. "What Western medicine can learn from the ancient history of psychedelics." 2024. bbc.com/future/article/20240910-the-ancient-history-behind-healing-trauma-with-psychedelics

Croxford, K., "DRUMBEAT Program Provides a Safe Space for Rhythmic Reflection". 2013. jjie.org/2013/10/07/drumbeat-program-provides-a-safe-space-for-rhythmic-reflection/

Ehrenreich, B., *Dancing in the Streets: A History of Collective Joy*. 2007

Eliade, M. *Shamanism: Archaic Techniques of Ecstasy.* Princeton Classics. Princeton: Princeton University Press, 2020.

Dellapiazza, F., Michelon, C., Vernhet, C., et al., "Sensory processing related to attention in children with ASD, ADHD, or typical development: Results from the ELENA cohort." European Child & Adolescent Psychiatry, 29(12), 1693-1704, 2020.

Deyo, L.J., "Cognitive Functioning of Drumming and Rhythm Therapy for Neurological Disorders" [undergraduate thesis]. Knoxville (TN): University of Tennessee; 2016.

Dunbar, R.I.M., Kaskatis K., MacDonald I., Barra V., "Performance of Music Elevates Pain Threshold and Positive Affect: Implications for the Evolutionary Function of Music." Evolutionary Psychology. 10(4):688-702, 2012 Oct 22

Fadiman, J., & Korb, S. "Might Microdosing Psychedelics Be Safe and Beneficial? An Initial Exploration." Journal of Psychoactive Drugs, 51(2), 118-122, 2019.

Fancourt, D., Perkins R., Ascenso S., Carvalho LA., Steptoe A., Williamon A., "Effects of Group Drumming Interventions on Anxiety, Depression, Social Resilience and Inflammatory Immune Response among Mental Health Service Users." PLoS One. 14;11(3), 2016.

Faulkner, S.C., "Drumming, rhythm and regulation through a polyvagal lens." Journal of Creative Art Therapies. 18 (1) 2023

Ferguson, M. J., *The Drummer and the Great Mountain: A guidebook to transforming adult ADD/ADHD*. Luminaia, 2014.

Flor-Henry, P. et al., "Brain changes during a shamanic trance: Altered modes of consciousness, hemispheric laterality and systemic psychobiology." Cogent Psychology. 2017.

Friedman, R.L., *The Healing Power of the Drum.* White Cliffs, 2000.

Friedman, R.L., *The Healing Power of the Drum* (Book 2). Pathway Book Service, 2011.

Friedman, Z. L., Ochoa, J., Prisco, D., & Seruya, F., "Connected Rhythm: A Scoping Review of Therapeutic Drumming as an Intervention for Autistic Individuals." American Journal of Occupational Therapy, 78(2), 2024.

Gingras, B., Pohler, G., & Fitch, W. T. "Exploring shamanic journeying: repetitive drumming with shamanic instructions induces specific subjective experiences but no larger cortisol decrease than instrumental meditation music." PLoS One, 9(7), 2014.

Golden, T.L, Magsamen, S., Sandu, CC., Lin, S., Roebuck, G.M., Shi, K.M., Barrett F.S., "Effects of Setting on Psychedelic Experiences, Therapies and Outcomes: An Exploratory Foray into the Nebulous Realm of Environmental Influences." Current Topics in Behavioural Neurosciences. 56:35-70, 2022.

Haidt, J. *The Anxious Generation: How the Great Rewiring of Childhood is Causing an Epidemic of Mental Illness*. New York, NY: Penguin Random House. 2024

Hamme, N., "Drum Journeying and Neuroplasticity: A Healing Breakthrough?" Final paper, Globe Institute of Sound Recording, 2017. soundhealingresearchfoundation.org/drum-journeying-and-neuroplasticity-a-healing-breakthrough/

Hardwicke Collings, J., "Drumming During Pregnancy and Labour," 2011, janehardwickecollings.com/drumming-during-pregnancy-labour/

Hart, M., and Gazzaley A., "Mickey Hart and Dr. Adam Gazzaley make history – visualising and sonifying brain activity in real time for live audience." mickeyhart.net/news/mickey-hart-and-dr-adam-gazzaley-make-history-visualising-and-sonifying-brain-activity-in-real-time-for-live-audience-420/

Hart, M., *Drumming at the Edge of Magic*. Harper San Francisco. 1990.

Henrich, J., Heine, S.J., Norenzayan, A., "The weirdest people in the world?" Behavioural and Brain Sciences, 2010.

Hope, H. "The sacred healing drum, divine healing wisdoms of the feminine, sound and the earth. "The Beauty of Perspective, 2024.

Huels, E.R., Kim, H., Lee, U., Bel-Bahar, T., Colmenero, A.V., Nelson, A., Blain-Moraes, S., Mashour, G.A., Harris, R.E., "Neural Correlates of the Shamanic State of Consciousness." Frontiers in Human Neuroscience. 15: 610466, 2021.

Jarvinen, J., Kaucher, B., "Drums from the North – a tale of a Shamanic Drum Maker". 2022. youtu.be/1UJdY7ZQiBI

Nicholas A. Kerna, Sudeep Chawla, Victor Carsrud, Hilary M. Holets, Stephen M. Brown, John V. Flores, Kevin D. Pruitt, Uzoamaka Nwokorie, Joseph Anderson II, Rashad Roberson, and Oghenetega Esther Ayisire. "Sound Therapy: Vibratory Frequencies of Cells in Healthy and Disease States." EC Clinical and Medical Case Reports. 2022.

Konopacki, M. & Madison, G., "EEG Responses to Shamanic Drumming. Does the Suggestion of Trance State Moderate the Strength of Frequency Components?" Journal of Sleep and Disorder Research, 2017.

Leach, A., "Exporting trauma: can the talking cure do more harm than good?" theguardian.com/global-development-professionals-network/2015/feb/05/mental-health-aid-Western-talking-cure-harm-good-humanitarian-anthropologist

Levine, P.A., "Healing Trauma: A pioneering program for restoring the wisdom of your body." Sounds True, 2008.

Litchke, L. G. & Bracken, M. M., "A qualitative study on the social-emotional benefits of Drumtastic Ability Beats® for children with autism spectrum disorder." American Journal of Recreation Therapy, 17(3), 37-47. 2018

Martin K.E. & Wood L.J., "Drumming to a New Beat: A Group Therapeutic Drumming and Talking Intervention to Improve Mental Health and Behaviour of Disadvantaged Adolescent Boys." Children Australia. 42(4):268-276, 2017

Maté, G., *The Myth of Normal: illness health and healing in a toxic culture*. Vermillion, 2024.

Maxfield, M., "Effects of rhythmic drumming on EEG and subjective experience", 1990, Thesis.

McKenna, T. *Food Of The Gods: A Radical History of Plants, Psychedelics and Human Evolution*. Rider, 1999.

Messager, S., *Why Postnatal Recovery Matters*. Pinter and Martin, 2020.

Messager,S "Forbidden trance: why medicine hijacks altered consciousness during birth," 2024.
sophiemessager.com/forbidden-trance-why-medicine-hijacks-altered-consciousness-during-birth/

Mungas, R. & Silverman, MJ., "Immediate Effects of Group-Based Wellness Drumming on Affective States in University Students." The Arts in Psychotherapy. 41(3):287-292, 2014.

Neff, A., "The window of tolerance", 2024 neurodivergentinsights.com/blog/window-of-tolerance

Neher, A., "Auditory driving observed with scalp electrodes in normal subjects." Electroencephalography and Clinical Neurophysiology,13: 449451, 1961.

Newson, L., "ADHD and the perimenopause and menopause", 2022. adhdfoundation.org.uk/wp-content/uploads/2022/08/ADHD-and-the-perimenopause-FINAL.pdf

Perry, B. D., & Dobson, C. L.Theneurosequential model of therapeutics. In J. D. Ford & C. A. Courtois (Eds.), "Treating complex traumatic stress disorders in children and adolescents: Scientific foundations and therapeutic models." 2013. The Guilford Press.

Polito, V., & Stevenson, R. J., "A systematic study of microdosing psychedelics." PLoS ONE, 14(2), 2019.

Porges, S. W. et al., "Respiratory sinus arrhythmia and auditory processing in autism: Modifiable deficits of an integrated social engagement system?" International Journal of Psychophysiology, 88(3), 261-270, 2013.

Porges, S. W., *The Polyvagal Theory: Neurophysiological Foundations of Emotions, Attachment, Communication and Self-regulation.* W. W. Norton & Company, 2011.

Ramos, F. I. O., Martins, K. G. T. F., Bachur, T. P. R., & Fonteles, M. M. F. "Correlations between stereotypes in ASD and neurotransmitters: a systematic review." Research in Autism Spectrum Disorders, 103, 102088, 2023.

Redmond, L., *When the Drummers were Women: a Spiritual History of Rhythm.* Crown Publications, 1997.

Reed, R., *Reclaiming Childbirth as a Rite of Passage: Weaving Ancient Wisdom with Modern Knowledge.* Word Witch, 2021.

Rojiani, R., Zhang, X., Noah and Hirsch, J., "Communication of emotion via drumming: dual-brain imaging with functional near-infrared spectroscopy." Social Cognitive and Affective Neuroscience. 1047 – 1057, 2018.

Saarman, E. “Feeling the Beat: Symposium Explores the Therapeutic Effects of Rhythmic Music.” Stanford University, 31 May 2006

Schrei, J., “Give the Drummer Some: Trance, Danger and Rapture in the Oldest Instrument of All”, The Emerald Podcast, online, 2021open.spotify.com/episode/2o5t6aKSs4PhNZiHF7T3Bj

Schrei, J., “How Trance Shapes the World”, The Emerald Podcast, online, 2024 open.spotify.com/episode/6SEdghh4v5kyQnvyhBfW2L

Schrei, J., “The Revolution Will Not Be Psychologised”, The Emerald Podcast, online, 2024 open.spotify.com/episode/3e5bkfY8mCsdhb9H39dHmy

Seliga, R. Indigenous Europe and Re-Membering History. 2024. innatetraditions.com/blog/Indigenous-europe-and-re-membering-history

Sheldrake, R., “The Science Delusion”. 2013. blog.ted.com/the-debate-about-rupert-sheldrakes-talk

Smith, A., *Women Drummers: A History from Rock and Jazz to Blues and Country*. Rowman & Littlefield, 2014.

Smith C., Viljoen J.T., McGeachie L., “African drumming: a holistic approach to reducing stress and improving health?” Journal of Cardiovascular Medicine. 15(6):441-446, 2014 June.

Sombrun, C., *Les Esprits de la Steppe: avec les derniers chamanes de Mongolie*. Albin Michel, 2012.

Stamets, P., “Low frequency Soundwaves dramatically encouraged mycelium to grow”. youtube.com/watch?v=fa5EBP3_1jg. 2022.

Strong, J., “REI Rhythms Beat Ritalin for Adult with Attention Deficit Disorder”. 2024. stronginstitute.com/resources/rei-rhythms-beat-ritalin-for-adult-with-attention-deficit-disorder/

Strong J., *Different Drummer. One Man's Music and its Impact on ADD, Anxiety and Autism*. Strong Institute, 2015.

Suh, E.S., “The use of group drumming-based music therapy with male adolescents in a school violence prevention program in Korea: A pilot study.” Psychology of Music. 51(3):606-625, 2023.

Sullivan, J., “Talking drums”, 2019, oxfordamerican.org/magazine/issue-107/talking-drums

Tedlock, B. *The Woman in the Shaman's Body: Reclaiming the Feminine in Religion and Medicine*. New York, NY: Bantam Books. 2005

Tekçe J., “Erbane drum, the voice of women”. 2022. anfenglishmobile.com/features/erbane-drum-the-voice-of-women-58177

Tyrell, I. & Griffin, J., “What are the ‘human givens’?” (no date) hgi.org.uk/human-givens/introduction/what-are-human-givens

Two Feather, W., 2004. Quoted in "Drums Alive®: A Research-Based, Multi-Disciplinary Drumming Fitness Approach to Brain and Body Health and Wellness." drums-alive.com/wp-content/uploads/2019/01/Palaestra-2018-Vol.-32.No_.-4.pdf

Visual Capitalist, The History of Psychedelics, 2021.
visualcapitalist.com/sp/the-history-of-psychedelics-part-1-of-2/ and visualcapitalist.com/sp/the-history-of-psychedelics-part-2-of-2/

Whitherhall, C. Beyond the Beat: 14 Extraordinary Health Benefits of Drumming, 2024. drumspy.com/is-drumming-a-workout/

Winkelman, M., "Complementary Therapy for Addiction: 'Drumming Out Drugs'". American Journal of Public Health, 93(4), 647-651, 2003.

Winkelman, M., *Shamanism: The Neural Ecology of Consciousness and Healing.* Bergin and Gavey, 2000.

Yap, A., Kwan & Y.S., Ang, B., "A systematic review on the effects of active participation in rhythm-centred music making on different aspects of health". European Journal of Integrative Medicine, 2017.

Yuhi, T., Kyuta, H., Mori, H., Murakami, C., Furuhara, K., Okuno, M., Takahashi, M., Fuji, D., Higashida, H., "Salivary Oxytocin Concentration Changes during a Group Drumming Intervention for Maltreated School Children." Brain Science. 16;7(11):152, 2017 Nov.

ABOUT THE AUTHOR

Sophie Messager bridges worlds that rarely meet. A former reproductive physiologist with a PhD, she traded her microscope for a medicine drum after experiencing the transformative power of an empowered birth. Her decade-long journey as a doula, birth educator, and author of *Why Postnatal Recovery Matters* deepened her exploration of the rhythms surrounding women's transitions.

Now a holistic life transition mentor, Sophie guides women through significant life thresholds – from birth to perimenopause and beyond. Her unique combination of scientific expertise and spiritual insight allows her to serve as a compassionate space holder for those seeking to harmonise their analytical and intuitive selves.

ABOUT WOMANCRAFT

Womancraft Publishing was founded on the revolutionary vision that women and words can change the world. We act as midwife to transformational women's words that have the power to challenge, inspire, heal and speak to the silenced aspects of ourselves.

We believe that:

- books are a fabulous way of transmitting powerful transformation,
- values should be juicy actions, lived out,
- ethical business is a key way to contribute to conscious change.

At the heart of our Womancraft philosophy is fairness and integrity. Creatives and women have always been underpaid. Not on our watch! We split royalties 50:50 with our authors. We work on a full circle model of giving and receiving: reaching backwards, supporting TreeSisters' reforestation projects, and forwards via Worldreader, providing books at no cost to education projects for girls and women.

We are proud that Womancraft is walking its talk and engaging so many women each year via our books and online. Join the revolution! Sign up to the mailing list at womancraftpublishing.com and find us on social media for exclusive offers:

womancraftpublishing

womancraft_publishing

womancraftpublishing.com/books

USE OF WOMANCRAFT WORK

Often women contact us asking if and how they may use our work. We love seeing our work out in the world. We love you sharing our words further. And we ask that you respect our hard work by acknowledging the source of the words.

We are delighted for short quotes from our books – up to 200 words – to be shared as memes or in your own articles or books, provided they are clearly accompanied by the author's name and the book's title.

We are also very happy for the materials in our books to be shared amongst women's communities: to be studied by book groups, discussed in classes, read from in ceremony, quoted on social media...with the following provisos:

- If content from the book is shared in written or spoken form, the book's author and title must be referenced clearly.
- The only person fully qualified to teach the material from any of our titles is the author of the book itself. There are no accredited teachers of this work. Please do not make claims of this sort.
- If you are creating a course devoted to the content of one of our books, its title and author must be clearly acknowledged on all promotional material (posters, websites, social media posts).
- The book's cover may be used in promotional materials or social media posts. The cover art is copyright of the artist and has been licensed exclusively for this book. Any element of the book's cover or font may not be used in branding your own marketing materials when teaching the content of the book, or content very similar to the original book.
- No more than two double page spreads, or four single pages of any book may be photocopied as teaching materials.

We are delighted to offer a 20% discount of over five copies going to one address. You can order these on our webshop, or email us. If you require further clarification, email us at: info@womancraftpublishing.com

ALSO FROM WOMANCRAFT

Creatrix

Lucy H. Pearce

Creatrix is more than just a fancy name for a female artist. She is artist plus… artist plus priestess, artist plus healer, artist plus activist: her work has both sacred and worldly dimensions. She is an energy worker first and foremost, weaving energy into form, colour, words and sound, in order to transform herself and those her creations touch.

What does it mean to live a life in service to your creativity, and in direct connection to the creative source? In this, her ninth book, Lucy H. Pearce, award-winning author of *Burning Woman, Medicine Woman* and *The Rainbow Way* shares…

- Powerful practical insight into all parts of The Creative Way.
- The unique challenges for women artists and writers.
- How to align with your authentic voice and The Work that calls you.
- Techniques for harnessing your powerful creative energy and dealing with fear, anxiety, creative blocks.
- How to earn your living creatively: building a social media platform, working sustainably, creating multiple income streams, networking when socially anxious…
- How our creativity can be our most potent transformational medicine.

With Creative Inquiries and Practices, this interactive book is written for all those that must create in order to live: for the Highly Creative, the Highly Sensitive, the multi-passionate, for those that shake when they share…

Soulful, serious-minded, irreverent and authentic, let Creatrix take you on a journey to the heart of your creative soul.

Walking with Persephone: A Journey of Midlife Descent and Renewal

Molly Remer

Midlife can be a time of great change – inner and outer: a time of letting go of the old, burnout and disillusionment. But how do we journey through this? And what can we learn in the process? Molly Remer is our personal guide to the unraveling and reweaving required in midlife. She invites you to take a walk with the goddess Persephone, whose story of descent into the underworld has much to teach us.

Walking with Persephone is a story of devotion and renewal that weaves together personal experiences, insights, observations, and reflections with experiences in practical priestessing, family life, and explorations of the natural world. It advocates opening our eyes to the wonder around us, encouraging the reader to both look within themselves for truths about living, but also to the earth, the air, the sky, the animals, and plants.

Crow Moon

Lucy H. Pearce

Three-time Nautilus award-winning author Lucy H. Pearce's previous best-selling book *Burning Woman* was an initiation of fire, *She of the Sea* an initiation of water and *Crow Moon* is an initiation of earth and air, a way back to the heart of ourselves through wild revelation.

Strikingly illustrated by the author, with contributions from over thirty women – artists, healers, authors – midlife women who have also been called by the strange magic of crows at decisive moments in their lives.